Technology, Culture and Competitiveness

The course of history has demonstrated the importance of technological change in the military, political and economic arenas. Perhaps more fundamentally, the ongoing and controversial evolution of a global culture and society also reflects the significant influence of technology. Not all of these developments can be attributed merely to technology, and its influence, while profound, is far from inevitable. Nevertheless, it plays a highly significant role in the international political economy – one that has been consistently overlooked and undervalued.

In attempting to give technology a central place in international political economy, this book is arranged into three sections. The first raises the basic issue of how to think about the subject. Four chapters question our ontological and epistemological assumptions and identify two broad and complementary approaches: the instrumental, where technology serves as a tool of power and as an object of policy; and the transcendental, where technology affects our view of the world, our way of understanding, interpreting and constituting 'reality'. The second part brings together chapters that examine a key question of cor ary policy debate: in what sense is technology a fundamental comp international competitive advantage and, consequently, what should tional, national, local and corporate policy be in the light of this? ' section provides case studies within the areas of finance, aviation ɛ mobiles.

The central focus of this volume is the importance of technology in int political economy. Within this overall approach, culture, competitiv globalisation provide three unifying themes that form a crucial p authors' work. This is a challenging and exciting new book for those st as well as for policy makers and the business community.

Michael Talalay was Senior Research Fellow at Nottingham Trent Un is now Principal Consultant in IT with the Butler Group. **Chris** Principal Lecturer in International Relations at the Nottingham Tren **Roger Tooze** is Professor of International Relations at the Universi Aberystwyth.

Technology and the Global Political Economy

Edited by Michael Talalay
Principal Consultant, Butler Group

Chris Farrands
Principal Lecturer, Nottingham Trent University, Nottingham

Despite its evident importance in our daily lives, technology has too often been ignored as a critical factor in international affairs and in national and corporate policy-making. This series places technology at the centre of explanation in theories of international relations and international political economy, aiming both to alter the way in which scholars and students think about these disciplines and to provide guidelines for policy-makers in the face of ever-increasing technological change. *Technology, Culture and Competitiveness* is the first book in this series.

Technology, Culture and Competitiveness

Change and the World Political Economy

Edited by Michael Talalay,
Chris Farrands and Roger Tooze

London and New York

First published 1997
by Routledge
11 New Fetter Lane, London EC4P 4EE

Simultaneously published in the USA and Canada
by Routledge
29 West 35th Street, New York, NY 10001

Typeset in Times by Routledge

Printed and bound in Great Britain by T. J. International Ltd, Padstow,
Cornwall

British Library Cataloguing in Publication Data
A catalogue record for this book is available from the British Library

Library of Congress Cataloguing in Publication Data
Technology, culture and competitiveness: change and the world
political economy/edited by Michael Talalay, Chris Farrands, and
Roger Tooze.
Includes bibliographical references and index.
1. Technological innovations - Economic aspects. 2. Competition,
International. 3. International economic relations. I. Talalay, Michael,
1947- . II. Farrands, Chris III. Tooze, Roger.
HC79. T4T4398 1997   96-43248
338'.064-dc20   CIP

ISBN 0-415-14254-7 (hbk)
ISBN 0-415-14255-5 (pbk)

Contents

Illustrations

Contributors

Philip Cerny is Professor of International Political Economy at the University of Leeds.

Chris Farrands is Principal Lecturer in International Relations at The Nottingham Trent University.

Vicki Golich is Associate Professor of International Relations at California State University, San Marcos.

Keith Hayward is Professor of International Relations at Staffordshire University.

Sally Hayward is EU Research Fellow in the Graduate School of Business, University College, Dublin.

John Howells is Lecturer in the management of technology and innovation at Brunel University.

Gerd Junne is Professor of International Relations at the University of Amsterdam.

Ronen Palan is Lecturer in International Relations in the School of Social Sciences at the University of Sussex.

Alan Russell is Senior Lecturer in International Relations at Staffordshire University.

Margaret Sharp is Senior Fellow at the Science Policy Research Unit (SPRU) at the University of Sussex.

Claire Shearman is a freelance researcher and consultant who has previously worked for the European Commission DG$\overline{V}$ and as a university academic in the UK.

Michael Talalay was Senior Research Fellow in International Political Economy at The Nottingham Trent University and is now Principal Consultant in IT with the Butler Group.

Roger Tooze is Professor of International Relations at the University of Wales, Aberystwyth.

Geoffrey Underhill is Lecturer in International Political Economy at the University of Warwick.

Gillian Youngs is an independent researcher and consultant dividing her time between the UK and Hong Kong.

Preface

This is the first in a series of books on technology in the global political economy, the aim of which is to mark out new ground in thinking about international relations. Each volume in the series will explore the idea that technology is a powerful force for change, disruption and restructuring in world affairs. Each, while drawing on different perspectives and experiences, will examine the assumption that 'technology' is more than just an artefact or a piece of kit, that it is closely interwoven with the culture, social organisation and practices, and political and economic power structures of society. Each, while analysing the particularities of its subject, will also investigate how technological change is a pervasive element in the processes of globalisation and the re-ordering of what is sometimes called the 'advanced capitalist' and sometimes the 'post-industrial' world. The series aims above all to put technology at the heart of contemporary debates about international relations (IR) in all of its possible meanings, where so much academic literature, while recognising that technology has some place in world politics, tends to relegate it to a secondary role.

To fulfil these ambitious goals, we aim to publish two or three volumes a year. This introductory book raises many of the key themes and debates which the series will explore. It is particularly concerned to bring together, on the one hand, specialists in IR and global political economy as a whole, and on the other, contributors who have extensive expertise in particular sectors or technologies. It also creates a dialogue between authors with a primarily academic or theoretical background and those who have more practical interests or experience. These discussions began with two residential workshops held first at Barnsdale Lodge by Rutland Water in May 1994 and then in Nottingham in September 1994. These produced a lively debate and led to a great deal of re-thinking – and re-drafting – in all of the papers. We would like to thank the contributors for all their very hard work. We believe that they found the process as stimulating an experience as we did, and we hope that the sense of innovative exploration of the issues is reflected to the reader in the quality of the book as a whole.

Michael Talalay and Chris Farrands
Series Editors

Acknowledgements

This book is one of the results of a research project on 'Technology and the Global Political Economy' funded by the Polytechnics and Colleges Funding Council (PCFC) as part of their research initiative from 1992 to 1995. The editors would like to acknowledge with gratitude support from the PCFC and from the Nottingham Trent University Humanities Faculty Research Fund. We would also like to thank Ms Clare Harrison and Ms Sybille Cheetham for research assistance and Ms Joy Knowles for secretarial support. We have enjoyed and benefited from conversations on the themes and ideas in this book with many colleagues and friends, including the contributors with whom we met in two residential workshops. To all of these individuals, as well as to our families, we express our sincere thanks. The responsibility for the contents remains, of course, with the authors individually.

We gratefully acknowledge the following premissions to reprint material:

- Chapter 11 by Philip Cerny first appeared as 'The dynamics of financial globalisation: technology, market structure and policy response' in *Policy Sciences* 27:319–342, 1994. © 1994 Kluwer Academic Publishers. Printed in the Netherlands. Reprinted by permission of Kluwer Academic Publishers.
- Chapter 12 by John Howells first appeared as 'Technology and globalisation - the European payments system as a case of non-globalisation' in *Technology Analysis & Strategic Management,* 8, 4:455–66, published by Carfax Publishing Company, PO Box 25, Abingdon, Oxfordshire OX14 3UE, United Kingdom (and Cambridge, Massachusetts). Reprinted by permission of Carfax Publishing Company.
- Figure 13.2, 'The aircraft industry production pyramid' (by G.W. Bernstein), in Chapter 13 by Vicki Golich, is taken from Thomas E. Pinelli, Rebecca O. Barclay, John M. Kennedy and Ann P. Bishop (forthcoming 1997) *Knowledge Diffusion in the US Aircraft Industry: Perspectives, Findings, and Strategies for Improvement*, Norwood, NJ: Ablex Press. Reprinted by permission of Ablex Press.

Michael Talalay, Chris Farrands and Roger Tooze

1 Technology, culture and competitiveness

Change and the world political economy

Michael Talalay, Roger Tooze and Chris Farrands

Technology has often played a decisive role in world affairs. The Roman roads held together the imperial domains. The longbow led to the English victory at Agincourt. The atomic bomb brought to an immediate end the war in the Pacific that might otherwise have dragged on for many months with far higher casualties. The combination of computers and telecommunications has revolutionised the structure of international finance and led to the seemingly dramatic erosion of national sovereignty. The manufacturing processes known as 'lean production' led to fundamental and far-reaching changes in the automotive industry (Womack *et al.* 1990) and certainly contributed to the success of the Japanese economy. The high cost of modern weaponry (notably SDI) was one of the factors that drove the Soviet Union into bankruptcy, bringing about the collapse of communism and the end of the post-1945 global structure. The industrial revolution heightened global inequality and increased by several orders of magnitude national and regional disparities of wealth and living standards (Kennedy 1993).

Indeed, the very fabric of society – the ideas, values and language that constitute it – all now reflect technological change. The printing press and movable type fundamentally altered the course of European civilisation and set it firmly on the road to secularisation. The automobile created a pattern of development responsible for the suburbanisation and strip development of the United States. Ultimately, technological change can destroy one lifestyle and create another. The Luddites tried to stop this process, but they failed; and where attempts to halt or reverse technological innovation have succeeded – as in China with the destruction of the foundries and the navy – the result has often been less than satisfactory in terms of both global power and local welfare.

Today, technology is enabling the creation of a global society. Modern developments in communications and transportation lead to 'one world', where local differences continue to exist but within the context of an ever-spreading global culture. Based on the English language, on Anglo-American pop culture, and on the Enlightenment concept of rationality, this global culture may not be to everyone's taste. Its desirability may be debatable. Its existence is undeniable.

All of these developments stem from technological change. Of course, while ubiquitous, technology is not the sole causal factor of any of them. Nor are its effects inevitable. The stirrup, for example, did not mechanistically cause feudalism. However, its appearance in Western Europe in the eighth century and its adoption by the Franks under Charles Martel did lead to a number of choices being made that turned what Lynn White (1962) has called a 'protofeudal' situation into a fully fledged feudal system. The development of feudalism cannot be adequately explained without acknowledging the vital role of the stirrup. The same logic applies to technology in general. It clearly is not the only factor involved in explaining change. It is however a potent one. Moreover – and herein lies the rationale for this book – it is a factor that has too often been ignored or defined away by those who seek to explain International Relations (IR) and International Political Economy (IPE).

Indeed, it was our growing sense that the burgeoning literatures on 'technology' and 'international political economy' were *not* adequately informing each other that provided the impetus for this investigation. Although studies of specific technologies and the IPE analysis of 'high technology' are clearly of great and increasing importance (e.g. Tyson 1992), it is equally clear that mainstream IR/IPE does not have at present what we regard as an appropriate and articulated framework which acknowledges the key role of technology itself as an integral part of the theory and practice of the world political economy. This is not to say that IR/IPE has ignored 'technology'. Indeed, as Ronen Palan demonstrates in the second chapter of this volume, the core of IR theory has been constructed around a series of (generally implicit) technological metaphors, and hence technology *per se* has been and is fundamental to theorising IR/IPE. But we would say that technology, where it has been thought important, has generally been explicitly analysed in a specific and narrow way. Technology has been defined by the discourses of IR/IPE as a particular and limited material phenomenon, largely to be treated as an exogenous and given factor – and hence all too often 'black boxed' (Rosenberg 1982) – and at the same time largely to be viewed as instrumental – as a tool or as an object of policy. Our unease is shared by others in IPE, notably Susan Strange who has consistently argued for a greater focus on technology and who recently observed that any real understanding of markets 'requires some sensitivity to the implications of rapidly changing technology – an aspect of political economy that social scientists... persistently overlook' (Strange 1994b: viii).

Of course, some branches of IR/IPE have almost fetishised certain technologies – particularly the technology of war, weapons and military power – with the associated danger of arriving at explanations/analyses from an implicit technological determinism. While the understanding of the technology of war and military systems is undoubtedly of crucial importance to our continued physical survival, all too often such an understanding has been developed in isolation from broader conceptions of security, welfare, and production (for an excellent attempt to broaden the basis of security studies see Buzan 1991). Other branches of IR/IPE have relied upon the structural changes produced and enabled by technological forces, but have not explicitly analysed these as integral to the international system – particularly the studies of transnational relations and interdependence in which technology is seen as a key part of the changed environment which produces interdependence (see for example Keohane and Nye 1977). For the most part, and with important exceptions to be discussed later, IR/IPE has not considered 'technology' as an endogenous and constitutive factor which forms a necessary part of our explanation and understanding of the totality of the world political economy.

A brief illustration will support this contention. Mainstream IPE consistently alludes to the importance of technology while equally consistently refusing to acknowledge this importance in the analytical frameworks utilised. Both Spero (1993) and Gilpin (1987) – two texts widely regarded as setting out the basis of IPE and very extensively used – chose not to include technology as a major factor of their analyses, and the otherwise comprehensive reader edited by Frieden and Lake (1991b) similarly ignores technology and its role, along with innovation, as a key driver of change. Exceptionally, Walters and Blake (1992) do consider technology as a core element of IPE and important enough to merit one chapter devoted specifically to it, of the nine in their book. This discussion is very welcome and, among other things, serves to demonstrate the problems of omitting such a consideration in the analysis of IPE. However, they focus almost entirely on technology as 'an objective of foreign policy, a means to achieve military, political, and economic goals, and an instrument to carry out foreign policy' (*ibid.*: 165). In other words, technology matters to IR/IPE because it alters state power and adds to the agenda and instruments of state policy – not the least because it changes the competitiveness of nationally based sectors of economic activity. This, for us, while a necessary element of the analysis of technology (see Part II of this volume), is not a sufficient conceptualisation of the relationship between technology and world political economy.

In case this argument is seen only as a comment on the orthodoxy of IR/ IPE, it is just as clear that most of the challengers to the orthodoxy have also not put technology in a central analytical position. Among those who *have* included technology, Susan Strange, who continues to develop the argument that technology has to be incorporated into our understanding of IPE (Strange 1994a), Richard Ashley, whose work includes a reconstructed political economy in which technology constitutes the very language of our experience (see particularly Ashley 1981) and Robert Cox are particularly noteworthy. Cox (1987) has developed a materialist analysis of production in which technology is a fundamental element of the structure of global politics. We would agree with Cox that 'it is more realistic to see technology as being shaped by social forces at least as much as it shapes these forces' (*ibid.*: 21), and that 'technology itself is a product of society and society's power relations' (*ibid.*: 313), yet we would wish to take the focus on technology further than Cox – if only to redress its lack of attention in the mainstream. For, despite the efficacy of the analyses presented by the above, and notwithstanding the contribution of the two authors discussed below, mainstream IR/IPE has been woefully slow to develop a technologically inclusive approach or to recognise the importance of technology in providing language and metaphors of theorising.

There are two recent and important exceptions to the general lack of attention given to technology in IR/IPE. Perhaps the most comprehensive attempt to elucidate the 'subtle and fascinating relationship between international affairs and science and technology' is that by Eugene Skolnikoff (1993: ix). This analysis offers very real gains in our understanding of the relationships and structures involved and of the complex interplay of science, technology, economy, society and polity at the international level. It is, however, constructed on the basis that 'the fundamentals of the nation-state system have not been altered as much as most rhetoric would lead us to believe' (*ibid.*: 7). That is, it is a state-centric analysis. For our purposes this framework and conclusion are limiting – we would wish to posit structural changes that *do* alter the 'fundamentals', but in ways that make it very difficult to recognise and conceptualise using the framework of conventional, state-based political analysis. What, however, is of the greatest significance is that Skolnikoff treats technology, not as an external given, but as a dynamic, integral and *constitutive* element of the international, and concludes, not surprisingly, that 'theorists must more adequately recognise the dynamic and subtle nature of the interaction of science and technology with international affairs' (*ibid.*: 246).

A second significant contribution to the understanding and role of technology from within IR/IPE is James Rosenau's iconoclastic and innovative study of systemic change and world order, *Turbulence in World Politics* (1990). Rosenau argues that technology has been one of the principal forces bringing about a fundamental transformation of world politics – in direct contrast to Skolnikoff's claim of evolution rather than structural transformation. For Rosenau, technology is the major factor of explanation in his evolution of the notion of the 'Two Worlds of World Politics' – the 'State Centric World' and the 'Multicentric World'. In terms of the sources of change driving turbulence, he argues for multiple causes, but 'all of them are seen as being initially responses to the technological upheavals that underlay the ever-growing interdependence of economic, political, and social life' (*ibid.*: 15). He identifies three dynamics as exogenous sources of global turbulence, but technology is the most powerful. 'It is technology... that has fostered an interdependence of local, national, and international communities that is far greater than any previously experienced' (*ibid.*: 17). We support Rosenau's arguments of the centrality of technology in explaining global change, but we differ in our emphasis that technology is *not* an exogenous force and has to be incorporated as endogenous to political economy. And where Rosenau often tends to treat technology as a given, we return to Cox's notion of technology as social product, only understandable within the context of particular structures of political economy, in other words endogenous and not exogenous.

There is, then, a clear and important theoretical and ontological lacuna in IR/IPE which has been exacerbated by the contemporary social construction of knowledge into science/non-science and its continued reflection and reproduction within and by academia. This tends to reinforce the notion of technology as artefact, or machine, and the production of this artefact as an autonomous phenomenon, driven by the logic of scientific and technological possibility, rather than the more persuasive view (we would claim) of technology as a social phenomenon, only understandable within the broad context of the patterns and structures of political economy, and particularly its liberal-democratic, capitalist forms in the late twentieth century.

Nor is the lack of analysis and theory helped by recourse (in classic IR fashion) to borrowing from the discipline that one might expect to have developed the most extensive and integrated analysis of technology and its generation/impact – economics. The field of economics has shared with IR/IPE a marked reluctance to engage with the nature of technology and related social processes. The profession of formal economics has by and large restricted analysis of technology to its impact on the production function, and has conceived of technology itself in a very limited sense:

> Economists have long treated technological phenomena as events tran-spiring inside a black box. They have of course recognised that these events have significant economic consequences, and they have in fact devoted considerable effort and ingenuity to tracing, and even measuring, some of these consequences. Nevertheless, the economics profession has adhered rather strictly to a self-imposed ordinance not to enquire too seriously into what transpires inside that box.
>
> (Rosenberg 1982: vii)

Consequently, it is not possible or indeed desirable to turn to orthodox economics for insight; nor, it seems, can we gain improved understanding from texts on international economics, which generally reinforce the conventional restricted economic view:

> An improvement in technology means that a larger output can be produced with given inputs of the factors of production. If the supply of these factors remains unchanged, such a technological change means that the production-possibility curve shifts outward to the right.
>
> (Ingram and Dunn 1993: 105–6)

While this may be true, it hardly exhausts the range of important questions that need addressing on technology!

To find greater emphasis on the role of technology, we need to turn to other broad social sciences – to political economy, to Schumpeter and the long wave theorists, to the literature on business studies (very broadly defined) and to a small but significant number of recent studies that bring together economics and technology (for example Dosi *et al.* 1990). However, as useful and important as these literatures are, none fully reflects and addresses the agendas and concerns of IR/IPE.

ELEMENTS OF A TECHNOLOGICALLY INCLUSIVE IPE

Rather than work towards a highly specified theoretical model of IPE, which carries greater risks of conceptual exclusion, our view is that it is more profitable to establish certain elements of an ontology of a technologically inclusive political economy. Here, we use ontology in the sense meant by Robert Cox when he writes:

> Ontology lies at the beginning of any enquiry. We cannot define a problem in global politics without presupposing a certain basic structure consisting of the significant kinds of entities involved and the form of significant relationships among them.... There is always an ontological starting point.
>
> (Cox 1992: 132)

A technologically inclusive ontology could (and should) form the starting point for the analysis of world political economy. We suggest that such an ontology should have, at least, the following elements.

The first element should identify what is included/excluded by the term 'technology'. As with any word, meaning changes with time, space and culture, and the values, preferences and language structure historically embedded into the word 'technology' are of fundamental importance. It is therefore not appropriate to seek a universal definition, as any such definition would be arbitrary. We should rather identify the broad contours of meaning and practice within specific and concrete historical structures. Skolnikoff provides a good starting point for contemporary usage when he uses the work of Harvey Brooks (1980: 66, quoted in Skolnikoff 1993: 13) to define technology as 'knowledge of how to fulfil certain human purposes in a specifiable and reproducible way' and hence, elaborating on this definition, that 'technology... does not consist of artifacts but of the... knowledge that underlies the artifacts and the way they can be used in society'.

This point is important for IR/IPE – technology is a form of knowledge, and consequently, from this conception of technology, the generation, ownership, use and control of such knowledge lies at the core of IPE (see, particularly, Strange 1994a). Further, a wide range of knowledges constitute 'technology', not just knowledge concerning material production: 'What might be termed "social" technologies, such as codified systems of management or computer software, are therefore appropriately considered technologies along with those that are physical in nature' (Skolnikoff 1993: 14). So the social structures of production and services – specifiable and reproducible organisational forms and behaviour patterns – are equally included in 'technology'. In this sense 'technology' should also include the notion of tacit social knowledge transmitted through informal social processes, interactions and culture. Much of our failure to properly understand the processes of economic transformation (for example in Eastern Europe) stems from an underestimation of the importance of informal knowledge as a constituent of technology. Margaret Sharp specifically argues the importance of a broad and non-formal notion of technology in this volume:

> technology is often complex, multi-dimensional, expensive to implement and specific to a particular firm . . . a large part of it is tacit knowledge (i.e. passed on by word of mouth and not written down) and derives from trial, error and learning, rather than from the systematic application of science.
> (Sharp, this volume, p. 93)

The second element should be an acknowledgement of the intersubjective nature of technology, necessary for both understanding and explanation. This intersubjective element acts as an unarticulated ontology, and '[T]he ontologies that people work with derive from their historical experience and in turn become embedded in the world they construct. What is subjective in understanding becomes objective through action' (Cox 1992: 133). Technology has both constructed and informed our experiences and language throughout history. It has shaped our perception of the world, the language we use and how we act in the world. To deny this is unwisely to relegate technology to a purely instrumental role within IR/IPE. And, although that instrumental aspect may be important and may deserve much further analysis (cf. Tyson 1992) it must be considered *within* a historical context and structure itself based on technological change.

Third, we should *explicitly* place technology in a central *practical role* in world political economy, and *explicitly* consider technology as an integral part of the *conceptual study* of political economy. It is endogenous to the problems and issues of IR/IPE rather than merely part of the context or simply an exogenous dynamic for change. As a product of social forces it must be theorised within the historical structures of world political economy. Part of this integral treatment of technology within IR/IPE would be the effort to work towards an explanation of technological change itself. Although such an explanation may not be the key focus of IR/IPE, we do need an adequate conceptualisation of this phenomenon, at the very least to avoid returning technology to its 'black box' but also in order to help formulate practical policy guidelines.

Fourth, a technologically inclusive ontology should treat politics and economics as indissolubly mixed and should regard the boundaries of each as questionable, defined by political practice and interests, rather than having absolute identities. Moreover, it should treat the boundaries and definitions of 'the international' and 'the domestic' in a similar way, as socially produced. Opening up these categories is not easy and is often difficult to sustain in the face of the power of existing ontologies, but is clearly necessary for our purpose here.

The final element is an emphatic rejection of exclusive state-centricity. The state is not an appropriate unit for understanding technology. Organisations – particularly the commercial firm – drive technology. However, equally, the state is in no sense unimportant. Technology needs to be understood within a multi-level, multi-actor historical context, with the state as one among a range of actors constitutive of the international/transnational system.

We would argue that an ontology of world political economy that included the elements adumbrated above provides a more satisfactory ontology of political economy than existing approaches. Each of the chapters of this volume incorporates one or a number of these elements – they all share the view that technology is necessarily a central part of any understanding and explanation of IR/IPE.

THE STRUCTURE OF THE BOOK

The book is constructed on three interlinked sets of questions. These questions were arrived at as part of the intellectual process of working through some of the analytical problems with the group of people we brought together to discuss technology and IPE. The first set of questions is primarily about ontology and concepts, relating to how we view the world. The second is policy oriented. The third is more focused on sectors, looking at how specific technologies have changed the nature of the world political economy. Each set of questions relates to the others and draws upon them, but each also provides a valid 'way in' to the multi-level issues and complex relationships that characterise technology. In this sense, the book can be read in any order – every chapter has to confront some of the underlying questions, but each uses a distinct empirical frame of reference.

The first set (Part I of the volume) addresses the basic question of how to think about the subject. Four very different chapters question our ontological and epistemological assumptions. They identify two broad categories, again closely linked: the instrumental, where technology serves as a tool of power and as an object of policy; and the transcendental, where technology affects our view of the world, our way of understanding, interpreting and constituting 'reality'.

Part II brings together a number of chapters which address a key question of contemporary policy debate: in what sense is technology a fundamental component of international competitive advantage, and consequently what ought international, national, local or corporate policy be in the light of this? Four chapters look at the 'positive' side of this issue while the fifth provides an interesting and highly instructive counter-example: it is a case study in failure.

The chapters in Part III focus on three core sectors of the world political economy – finance, aviation and automobiles – and ask how technological innovation in these areas has brought about change in the nature of the global political economy, in the structure of the international system, and in the distribution of power among the players in that system. Four of the chapters deal with existing, widely-exploited technologies. The fifth is an exercise in futurology – it addresses a technology with potentially significant consequences but still only in its infancy.

Though the three parts are clearly distinct, a number of common themes and concerns tie them together. One is the concern with the *centrality of technology* if we are to develop adequate notions of change in the world political economy. Second is the issue of *globalisation*. The prevalence of IT and telecommunications as enabling technologies ensures that 'globalisation' will be a major issue in any volume such as this. What, however, does it actually mean? And how does it relate to what appear to be the equally prevalent trends towards tribalisation and localisation? A third common theme revolves around the importance of *culture*. This area has often been, as one of the contributors notes, a 'missing dimension' in the field of international studies. Not so in these essays. While their conception of culture may vary, almost all of our contributors discuss its significance with respect to technology in general and more specifically to the influence of technology on international political economy. On the one hand, to what extent do cultural factors influence the shaping of technology? And on the other, how much does technology influence cultural patterns and homogeneity? What makes this particularly interesting are the very different conceptions of what culture is and how its influence makes itself felt. A fourth major theme is *competitiveness*. As IR/IPE increasingly becomes a matter of the 'low politics' of trade and commerce rather than the 'high politics' of war and diplomacy, the issue of competitiveness grows in importance. Whether on a national, a regional, a local or a corporate level, more and more the question of how can 'we' successfully compete is being asked. One of the key answers that emerges from the chapters that follow is that competitiveness depends very much not merely on access to technology but – critically – on the ability to absorb it. This is partly a matter, as some of the chapters make clear, of organisational and institutional structures, but it is also a matter of training and – especially – education. Moreover, there is a close link – again as a number of our contributors point out – between competitiveness and culture. Not only is culture a key element of competitiveness, but also there is a competitiveness among cultures. The transcendental and the instrumental meet in deciding which culture(s) will become the global standard. Here we see the inter-relatedness of our themes – culture, competitiveness and globalisation all mutually affect each other. And all are related to our final theme. This indeed reflects and contains the other concerns – it centres on the core problem of the nature, the locus and the focus of *power*. In what ways has technology altered the nature of power, how it is used, and who has it? In the classic terms of political economy, 'Who benefits?'

Part I

Thinking about technology and international relations

2 Technological metaphors and theories of international relations[1]

Ronen Palan

Our era has become cognisant of the powers of technology. Accelerating rates of technological innovation and rising capital costs are producing an increasingly technology-driven world economy. Technology has become one of the key factors in the new international competitive game (Strange 1988). In the future, we are told, knowledge and technology will divide the 'haves' from the 'have-nots' (Reich 1991).

The implication for International Relations theory (as well as for other social sciences) seems clear. Either face up to the tremendous challenge posed by technology and technological change, or else face oblivion. But placing technology at the centre of IR theory, laudable as it may be, may turn out far more difficult and challenging than we have bargained for. Besides the obvious difficulties which are caused by trying to add additional 'variables' onto existing theoretical frameworks, there are other, more subtle problems.

To begin with, recent discussions of technology tend to overlook the fact that technology is as old as human history. Technology may appear to have been largely excluded from current IR theories. But is this truly the case? Any would-be theorist must first of all grapple therefore with the question of whether existing theories are truly and profoundly free of technological undertones.

Second, and related, as Heidegger (1962), Mumford (1964), Foucault (1972), Bohm (1983) and Prigogine and Stengers (1984), to name a few, have demonstrated, technological advances are founded in broader epistemological and ontological 'breakthroughs'. Technology may present itself therefore as an *object* of enquiry, a means for attaining identifiable goals, but it also informs our epistemology in a way that only a 'constructivist' methodology begins to make sense.

The annals of the social sciences display clearly this dichotomy. Technology is addressed on two separate planes, the one privileging what may be described as *instrumental* thinking, the other privileging *transcendental* thinking. The one is concerned with technology as an instrument, a tool of human advance. Instrumentalist literature tends to treat technology as an undifferentiated but important intellectual ingredient which contributes to national competitive policies. Technology does not have to be always physical in character. Classical antiquity certainly recognised the elements that make up machines and produced as a result superb war machines and hydraulic pumps, but it developed, crucially, aspects of technology that were non-physical in nature: coinage, alphabetisation, stenography and geometry (Mokyr 1990). In recent literature, the emphasis is on the accumulative nature of human knowledge, and the enormous societal resources that need to be devoted for such an undertaking (see for instance Sally Hayward and Sharp in this volume).

Instrumental thinking can be contrasted with *transcendental reflection*, which is a form of inquiry into the relationship between technology, as a manifestation of human knowledge, and cognition. The latter presents technology not simply as an instrument or a tool, but as a social and hence symbolic activity by which humanity has learned to express itself. Durkheim has argued, in the traditional Kantian line, that all higher organisms possess a biological necessity to create a semblance of continuity and stability (1976). In its quest for making sense of a complicated world, the human mind employs whatever means, metaphors and analogies within its grasp that help it 'understand' its surroundings. So it may be argued that the various strands of human 'understanding', including 'scientific thought', are ultimately far more concerned with psychological security than with cognitive assurance.

Thus we find that historically, physical objects shaped to some extent philosophical reflections about order and change in society. Technological artefacts, in fact, often served as analogies and metaphors by which philosophers sought to explain their surroundings. Explanation and reflection, however, are not neutral. They help shape and transform the very 'reality' which they seek to explain. In this sense the transcendental nature of technology can be never be fully dissociated from instrumental thinking.

Technology therefore is an 'awkward' concept because it is debated contemporaneously on two separate and yet interdependent levels. On the one hand, the debate is on the theoretical status of technology-as-object. The ultimate aim of this exercise is to find a way of slotting the concept within an existing epistemological and theoretical framework. And yet this epistemological ground itself is shifting: questions are immediately raised not only about the object of enquiry, 'technology', but also about the disciplinary framework in which this object is supposed to lie: 'International Relations', 'state', 'policy' and so on. Consequently, as technology changes, so our conceptions of humanity, nature and society change as well. Furthermore, as our perception of technology changes, so our conceptions of the 'international' change with it.

I would like to argue in this chapter that technology has played therefore an important if largely unnoticed role in the development of International Relations theory. For the sake of simplification, I will present the thesis as a sequence of discrete logical derivations in which:

1 technological advances take the form of diverse interpretations of what technology is all about;
2 these interpretations help shape a broader conception of what the social setting is all about;
3 the resulting conception of society then serves as the basis upon which theories of international affairs evolve;
4 theories of international affairs then have concrete implications on the conduct of international affairs;
5 the resulting theories of international affairs then represent technology in a particular light. The latter defines our instrumental thinking.

This sequence leads me to the conclusion that the so-called third industrial revolution may be at the root of the most profound transformation that International Relations theory has experienced since the end of the Second World War. We are witnessing an inversion in our conceptions of the very problematic of International Relations! Traditional IR theory was implicitly premised on the assumption that the unities, the states, were given and knowable, but the relationships between them were unstable. Now, an inversion seems to be taking place and relationships are perceived to be empirically ascertainable. The problem however is that the unities, the states, are alterable. *Relations of hierarchy and competition are taken to be the essence of the international* (or the global). The focus is therefore no longer so much on what may be gained in the international sphere – how the state/society complex can obtain values – but how identities can be sustained in a 'turbulent' world.

Concretely, I will try to establish a correlation between technological advances and three stages in International Relations theory (and practice): the human body and political realism; the systems approach and the rise of interdependence schools; information technology and the growing interest in national competitive strategies.

THE MECHANICS OF REALISM

It is a delightful irony that 'political realism', which prides itself for its anti-idealism, offers such a rich source for a 'transcendental' critique of International Relations theory. As I have argued elsewhere, realism is rooted in a hi-tech theory of an age gone by (Palan and Blair 1993).

'Hi-tech' machines like organisms and mechanical clocks offered visible evidence of complicated processes that maintain unity in change.[2] They served as readily available analogies that helped shape human understanding of itself and its surroundings. As philosophers began to grasp the incredible complexity of nature, they sought to obtain comparable symmetry and harmony in human society by closely imitating the work of nature. In addition, the experience of an intricate machine like the human body served to underlie the intimate relationships that unite parts with the whole. Nature served as a metaphor for human society. 'The state has a natural priority over the household and over any individuals among us', concluded Aristotle, '... [because] separate hand or foot from the whole body, and they will no longer be hand or foot except in name' (1981: 60–1). Cicero likened the head of the state to the spirit that rules the human body. Grotius and Puffendorf developed their theories of sovereignty on the conception of the state as an organism or moral person (Gettell 1924: 399) Such metaphorical associations are still discerned in the concept of the 'body politic' and its modern biological derivative, the 'social *structure*'.[3]

From the fourteenth century, machines and automata became the prevailing analogy for intelligent life in Europe.[4] Newtonian mechanics inspired a generation of Baroque thinkers whose views of society were grounded in their understanding of mechanical devices. A number of important and influential treatises from la Mettrie's *L'Homme Machine* (1748) to Herbert Spencer's *The Man Versus the State* (1884) debated the finer details of the analogy. The concept of 'circulation', for instance, originated in the sixteenth century in the discipline of hydraulic engineering to describe the flow of water. William Harvey viewed blood in similar terms and adopted the metaphor for medicine. Hobbes, following his famous visit to Italy, began to view money in similar terms as well (Gustatz 1983). Blood circulation, money circulation, financial liquidity, appear nowadays as impartial observations of purely descriptive value. But they are not. Money circulation carries undertones of a healthy body nourished by blood. Our understanding of the financial system is therefore closely tied to a conception of a world neatly divided into 'bodies politics'.

Such metaphorical associations had deeper impacts. The advent of liberalism with its emphasis on 'individual' sovereignty coincided with the emergence of the modern sovereign state possessing, it was held, a personality of its own. The homology was celebrated in common mechanical metaphors. Thus Hobbes inquires:

> Why may we not say, that all *automata* (Engines that move themselves by springs and wheeles as doth a watch) have an artificial life? For what is the *Heart*, but a *Spring*; and the *Nerves*, but so many *Strings*.... Art goes yet further, imitating the rationall and most excellent worke of Nature, Man. For by Art is created that great *Leviathan* called a *common-wealth*, or *State* which is but an artificial Man; though of greater stature and strength than the Naturall, for whose protection and defence it was intended; and in which, the *Sovereignty* is an Artificial soul, as giving life and motion to the whole body.
>
> (Hobbes 1951: 81)

Society was therefore conceived as a higher organism. Whether the organisms, humans and societies alike, were spiritual unities or mere mechanical articulation of parts, was at the core of a dispute between religious scholars and the secular movement. But the notion of a sovereign community, or the 'state', as a separate and internally differentiated functional social body, became well entrenched.

Persistent use of organic and mechanical metaphors perpetuated the perception of a world divided among well organised bounded communities. The 'reality' – although such terms appear alien in this context – was far from it (Hall 1986). But the conceptual interdependence between organisms and societies did not stop there. Just as humans were provided with critical faculties for rational thought, so the state was thought to possess its innate cause: the celebrated notion of the 'reason of state'. And just as individuals employed their faculties in pursuit of their 'desires', so the state sought to fulfil its distinct 'desires': the accumulation of power and prestige.

I have argued elsewhere (Palan and Blair 1993) that the theory of the personality of the state produced the first coherent realist theory of International Relations,[5] a point made so cogently by one of its early proponents, Henrich Treitschke:

> Treat the State as a person and the necessary and rational multiplicity of States follows. . . . Just as in individual life the ego implies the existence of the non-ego, so it does in the State. The State is power, precisely in order to assert itself as against other equally independent powers. War and the administration of justice are the chief tasks of even the most barbaric States.
>
> (Treitschke 1916: 19)

Indeed, one could extrapolate the opposite: cease to treat the state as a person, or as a coherent unity, and the entire realist edifice crumbles. The metaphor of social closure, borrowed from the high-tech artefacts of the day, served, in other words, as the underlying model for an emerging theory of International Relations.

Since the realist theory was assembled from, and was an expression of, an organic metaphor, theories of human nature inspired a core of 'realist' conceptual constructs. The Cartesian problematic of body and soul – the two elementary concepts of Baroque psychology – found expression in the unity of 'territoriality' and 'reason of state' (Botero 1956) – the two elementary tools of realist thought. Territory is viewed as a form of concretisation of the social body. The organic cohesion of the 'sacred land' had therefore to be defended *at all cost*. Defence of the land was tantamount to the survival of the 'individual-state'. 'Security' therefore was beyond questioning. We find echoes of such ideas in today's International Relations theory. States, maintains Waltz as if it was a matter of fact, are imbued with 'survival instincts' (1979). Never mind that the notion of a 'sacred land' was a pagan relic of days when the gods resided in the hills and in the valleys and in things. Days when 'each tribe rejoiced in its peculiar deities, looking on the natives of another country who worshipped other deities as gentiles, natural foes, unclean beings' (Bryce 1968 [1864]: 90). Nationalist ideologies embrace them all. At the same time this higher body of state-person was infused with higher goals and desires, the so-called 'reason of state'. International Relations theorists like Morgenthau (1967) or Northedge (1976) made their pitch on the ground that individuals who occupy responsible posts 'in the state' are capable of distinguishing between their interests and the interests of the higher body. They are 'servants' of the state, and hence the abstraction called state, and not the social forces that make it up, is the 'unit of analysis' of International Relations.

The metaphorical linkages produced additional 'insights': just as human society is ultimately an agglomeration of individuals, so 'international society' is believed to consist of a collection of states (Bull 1977). Like individuals, these state-persons conduct their affairs verbally and affectively – i.e. through diplomacy and the threat of war. They may exchange goods and ideas. But such exchanges are ultimately sanctioned and regulated by the state.

The realist theory of International Relations is therefore rooted in specific metaphors which derive from the 'high-tech' machines of ages gone by. That is not to say that organic metaphors are the sole foundations of realist thinking. Clearly, the critical impulse owes much to the secular movement, and furthermore, can be traced to the rise of the world market, to the capitalist mode of production and to the rise of nationalism. But the realist theory presents an understanding of the world shaped by its metaphorical implications. In this view, the state-person employs all its powers, physical, spiritual and cultural, to advance its 'national interests'. It produces a view of the state as an *end* and technology as one of the many tools. Technology is viewed therefore merely as a set of techniques to be used or not as the case may be by the state to advance its goals. The dominant theory of International Relations, therefore, has only passing interest in technology (Talalay and Farrands 1993).

'LIBERAL' SYSTEMS

But 'classical' realism (another misnomer) underwent significant modifications, not least, I would like to submit, because of the accelerating pace of technological change. The advent of the giant firms, enterprises which spanned entire continents, whose success was credited to their organisational and logistical aptitude, alerted contemporaries to the powers and strength of rational thought. A perceptible transformation (a culmination of a long historical process, no doubt) in popular attitudes to technology had become evident. The Baroque fascination with goods and machines was suddenly replaced by a renewed interest in the principles that govern and give rise to such machines. 'Technology' began to be associated more and more with the application of 'scientific principles' to manufacturing, to production and to bureaucracies, as well as to the broader conception of social life.

The preoccupation with the functional principles that linked parts with the whole helped to shape a new perception of society. Functionalist theories

(Benedict 1935; Radcliffe-Brown 1952) were soon supplemented by broader systemic theories (Parsons 1937). Sorokin, for instance, maintained that society was a system 'characterised by the existence of a tangible causal or functional interdependence of its parts upon one another, of the whole upon its parts, and of the parts upon the whole' (Sorokin 1941: 4). The concept of society was soon replaced by the 'social system' (Parsons 1937), and politics by the 'political system' (Easton 1953).

Like the organic and mechanical metaphors before, the systems approach 'represents an attempt to elaborate a method of synthesising knowledge using a uniform language which allows for the integration of the theories of the various scientific disciplines' (Landry 1987: 17). And just like previous metaphors, the systems approach never achieved the objective formal status it aspired to, but ended up producing new 'knowledge' about the subjects it was supposed to help understand. In this new perception, societies were deemed no longer 'natural' communities, but rather artificial entities, shaped by reason and will. By the early twentieth century bureaucrats in the United States and the British government began to adopt such scientific principles in the running of the state.[6] In Britain, the Haldane Committee proposed in 1918 to restructure the British government on functionalist lines, citing 'the establishment of the formal structure of authority through which work subdivisions are arranged, defined and coordinated for defined objectives' (Thomas 1978: 80) as their ultimate aim. The American government adopted these new principles under the acronym POSDCORB.[7] State bureaucracies worldwide were subsequently reorganised along functionalist principles as well.

The systems approach shored up the impression that communities were not outward expressions of the bonding of the 'people', but essentially agglomerations of individuals, held together by artificial means, a chore performed by the 'political system' or the state, the law and the police. The systems approach also implied that the closure of the system, i.e. territoriality, was critical to (and yet never a guarantee of) the smooth running of society. The lack of interference from outside was deemed an absolute prerequisite for the internal functioning of the system. The idea of *system autonomy* found expression in the rising fortunes of the concept of 'national self-determination' (as opposed the more aggressive and isolationist previous conception that placed the stress on the defence of the 'sacred land'). Sovereignty and sovereign equality were the obverse side of this systemic conception. As Hedley Bull (1977) taught, sovereignty must be guaranteed both 'internally' as well as 'externally'. The emphasis may have shifted in the post-war era from 'national' to self-determination, but as much as the concept lost spiritual connotations, it gained in practical value. National self-determination was deemed essential for the proper functioning of the 'social system'.

The social system had to be internally efficient, and externally adaptable. Robert Dahl (1976) and David Easton (1953) proposed that democratic principles of open government and pluralism were superior instruments of social order. Consequently, the belligerent face of the 'realist' states, who faced each other like 'gladiators in the ring' as Hobbes saw it, has undergone subtle changes. No longer oblivious of their surroundings, state-systems now form a partnership with their environment: they are 'interdependent'. The state-system is no longer aggressively acquisitive, but far more concerned to limit perturbations, to achieve balance and homeostasis. Keohane and Nye (1977) explained varying degrees of perturbations, holding that some states are 'vulnerable' while others are merely 'sensitive' to their surroundings. But as much as they try to adapt to their environment, states now strive to shape and affect the environment to suit their internal conditions (Stopford and Strange 1991). The state-system is therefore also a learning system. It adapts to its environment by continually restructuring itself. It identifies goals and pursues them to the best of its knowledge.

So how did technology come to be seen during this phase? Since 'technology' lies at the intersection of practice and cognition, it did not fit very well. The focus on the relationships between parts and the whole could not accommodate cognitive manipulation and symbolic transmissions. 'Technology' simply did not behave as 'parts' or 'wholes'. It did not share the discrete properties. It lacked the boundaries which are so indispensable for systems-approach manipulation.

Technology, however, could not be avoided. It was categorised therefore as an environmental factor, an idea which was introduced into International Relations by Keohane and Nye. In this context it is worth paying close attention to the way they chose to formulate their problematic. The opening statement in *Power and Interdependence* reads as follows:

> Interdependence affects world politics and the behaviour of states; but governmental actions also influence patterns of interdependence.
>
> (Keohane and Nye 1977: 5)

Soon enough it becomes clear that 'world politics' stands for the way the realists describe world politics. At the same time, Keohane and Nye suggest that 'world politics' was undergoing profound changes under the impact of an external force they label 'interdependence', which under close scrutiny turns out to be an umbrella term which includes technological advances in communication and transportation that are integrating the world and hence affecting the behaviour of the state as well as 'world politics'. 'Interdependence', therefore, stands for technological change. Technology, however, is externalised and presented as a secular external force.

Keohane and Nye therefore brought technology in by *externalising* it: placing it at the centre of their notion of an environmental change. Technology is viewed as an external force, to which states are now increasingly required to adapt. This is still the favoured theoretical solution to the problem posed by technology and technological change in International Relations.

IN THE KINGDOM OF SIGNS

Our era is defined by communication. From the first computerised war simulated 'in reality', to the post-industrial society, the impending death of paper money and the electronic superhighway, technology is increasingly associated with knowledge and communication. Information technologies are producing not only wonderful high-value-added products, they also confuse our deepest ontological and epistemological beliefs (Vattimo 1992). The advent of the third industrial revolution is coinciding with post-structuralism, deconstruction and post-modernity syndromes. As a result our conception of society is undergoing profound changes. As I will try to demonstrate, International Relations theory is changing as well.

Daniel Bougnoux says that we live in the 'kingdom of signs' (*l'empire des signes*). In his words:

> Man ... inhabits a world not made of things, but a 'forest of symbols' in which representations (not only verbal representations) constitute the familiar order ... this empire of signs, which doubles our natural world like a semisphere.

> (Bougnoux 1993: 93, my translation)

This is a crucial distinction. In the traditional world of social science, 'reality' contrasts with imagination and myth. The sciences are characterised by a quest for an objective truth. An appropriate methodology and factual evidence distinguishes the scholar from the propagandist. But as Debray (1981) points out, it is immaterial whether Jesus, Muhammad or Marx was right or wrong, or whether God, the Nation or the Working Classes *really* exist. Enough people modified their behaviour because of these prophets and their categories so that the imagined unity of the people in the nation or the 'myth' of the working classes became therefore a *reality*. But what happened to the 'real' reality meanwhile? Can we say that it had an independent existence separated from myth? Hardly. Jacques Lacan therefore expanded the limited concept of 'reality' of positivist thought[8] to include the three categories: the Real, the Imagined and the Symbolic (Hall 1972). According to Bougnoux, the semisphere, or the constructivist world which combined the Real, the Imagined and the Symbolic, represents better the milieu which we call the 'social world'. So while traditional Social Science theory 'imagines' that we exist in the atmosphere, the 'reality' is that we inhabit the *semisphere*.

The semisphere does not recognise societal closure in the traditional sense because it is not a world purely made of 'things', but a realm of relationship between things and cognition. Or put differently, societal closure is essentially an imagined closure, or as Anderson (1983) called it, an 'imagined community'. The alleged 'units of analysis' of International Relations therefore possess no physical reality in themselves. Or more to the point, physical evidence of closure – border fences, customs offices, etc. – must be interpreted in conjunction with the holistic imaginary conception of closure (Poulantzas

1979). The perception of closure of this imagined community is obtained through the spontaneous (although not exclusively so) articulation of discursive, symbolic and legal means. The traditional metaphors derive from analogies of the human body, machines and so on, and thus in traditional sociology social closure is perceived as real-concrete (this, in my view, is the underlying cause of the bifurcation between holism and nominalism). In contrast, the post-structuralist perspective views social closure essentially as imaginary closure. The unities that make up International Relations are therefore only 'relative' unities.

Exchange as well is increasingly seen in a different light. Cognisant of the semispheric milieu, technology takes on a new pertinence and meaning. 'Goods' that are exchanged are no longer viewed purely for their exchange value. In fact, our perception of economic exchange has been stretched in opposing directions, ending up depleting the very concreteness of the goods that are being shuffled around. International exchanges are viewed essentially as *informational flows*, connecting, as Marx notes, 'individuals who remain indifferent to one another' (McLellan 1980: 66). International exchanges are therefore not (primarily) about fulfilling needs and supplying demand, but increasingly viewed as structured avenues for dissemination of specific bits of information. Goods are the letters and words in a new *structural* language of international exchange.

An example which is not strictly 'technological' (although I can easily cite 'technological' examples) derives from a discussion which I stumbled upon by M. Fortes on the dynamics of cultural contact in the old Northern Territories of the Gold Coast. Fortes concerned himself with the diffusion of cultural traits in the Northern Territories and more specifically with the socio-economic effects of the missionary service. He quotes approvingly Livingstone's aphorism that 'wherever a missionary lives, traders are sure to come, they are mutually dependent and each aids the other'(1936: 31), and examines the mechanism of such interdependence. I will quote extensively to demonstrate the precise moment when a seemingly benign 'cultural contact' becomes a decisive element in the transformation of society.

The missionary, an agent of an alien culture, inserts himself into the existing pattern of behaviour.

> A missionary in Africa is seldom merely 'a man going about with a Bible under his arm'. . . . He generally offers essential and much desired services to the community, a school, or a hospital, or even so apparently trivial a thing as a football at the disposal of the idle youth. Such service creates links of dependence and a context of prestige which ensure a tolerant hearing for his specifically Christian teaching. The polyvalency of functions is a well-established attribute of primitive institutions.
>
> (Fortes 1936: 31–2)

Once accepted, the missionary acts like any general endowed with Clauswitzian logic. He sees a gap and seizes upon it:

In the patrilineal and patripotestal communities of the Northern Territories, young men generally seem to respond most rapidly to mission teaching. It is not merely a question of youth. The ancestor cult is the dominant religious institution there. Now young men, though always participating freely in rites and ceremonies and often as fully conversant with details of ritual as their fathers, seldom have direct ritual responsibility.... In such communities where religion is more a matter of doing than of thinking, a young man often has no religious obligations to renounce by conversion.

(Fortes 1936: 32–3)

The conversion is smooth. For a while the two 'religions' coexist side by side, but this state of affairs cannot remain forever. The missionary essentially is attacking a strategic point of that society:

The cult of common ancestor is one of the main sanctions of patrilineal family and clan cohesion, and, on the other hand, the foundation of a solidarity between matrilineal kindred which breaks down the exclusiveness of the patrilineal group.

(Fortes 1936: 35)

Once the fundamental beliefs of that society are undermined, the effects are devastating: the existing social order virtually melts away.

The point is that the exchange of goods and hence of knowledge is not seen any more purely as transaction between two bodies that are profoundly impervious to the exchange. The 'exchangers' undergo a metamorphosis as a result of the exchange: we may say that exchange, interaction, defines the exchangers. This notion is at the core of the changing character of International Relations theory.

INTERNATIONAL RELATIONS IN THE SEMISPHERE

The sort of questions that Lacan raises about the relationship between the Real, the Imaginary and the Symbolic impinges upon our conception of International Relations. While conventional International Relations is increasingly concerned with the fragmentation of international politics (allegedly caused by the decline of the USA), at issue is in fact the breakdown of one of the governing assumptions in International Relations, the assumption of the uni-dimensionality of reality. And if *reality* is in danger of fragmentation, and social closure is seriously questioned, then how should we understand this notion of 'inter-national relations': relations between whom? What do we mean by 'relations'? What precisely is the status of the geographical diffusion of technical knowledge when it leaps, so to speak, from one society to another?

What is then International Relations (or International Political Economy for that matter) when its constitutional 'units of analysis' are questionable?

One of the proposed answers is that 'really' there is only one global spatial context. But this solution is of interest only to the extent that it points to space as a serious factor to be considered. Beyond this, the problem is not spatial but contextual. The more profound response, which we are witnessing now in International Relations, is the progressive if subtle inversion in the relationship between unities and interactions. Traditional International Relations proposed that the unities, states, were given, yet the relationships between them were unstable. International Relations as a discipline was concerned therefore with 'relationships between' known entities. Now, relationships are static, and unities are variable. As a consequence the focus of the discipline is shifting subtly but steadily away from the study of relations between these entities to an enquiry into the nature of the entities themselves in the international and global context.

Is there any evidence of such a shift? I think so. If only because a decade or so ago the list of the ten most influential International Relations texts was dominated by abstract theorisation of the 'international system' (Vasquez 1983), whereas today the focus has shifted firmly to societies and social practices. A sample of recently influential manuscripts might include Cox's *Production, Power, and World Order: Social Forces in the Making of History* (1987), Krasner's *Structural Conflict: The Third World Against Global Liberalism* (1985), Rosecrance's *The Rise of the Trading State* (1986) and Strange's *States and Markets* (1988). One may cite other causes for the shift in interest in International Relations. The end of the Cold War is one popular explanation. But the above-mentioned texts were all published, let alone conceived, long before the collapse of the Soviet Union. The growth of the Japanese economy is another plausible explanation. But then the increasingly competitive international environment cannot explain this odd, belated and hopelessly uninformed discovery of the so-called action-structure problematic in International Relations.

There are in addition suggestive developments in the 'practice' of International Relations – although clearly as the process still takes place we can only begin to grasp its significance. As stated above, in the new perception of social relations the state is no longer conceived as a container, or an autopoetic system, let alone a 'body politic' – indeed, the very notion of a discrete, independent 'body politic' brings on a smile. In the rising fortune of the neo-Weberian 'statist' interpretation, state and politics are viewed as forms of interchange that impinge on the life of the population in a given area: politics is another market, another form of exchange. In their influential book Auster and Silver (1979: 16) have argued that societies are 'distinct but often interrelated markets for the provision of punishment and protection'. This new perception of the state had been adopted wholeheartedly by neo-realists. The underlying theme, however, has concrete practical implications. The concept of sovereignty, which was understood to be the legal expression of the autonomy of the 'political body', has undergone subtle change because there was no organic political body, nor indeed a 'real' system out there, of which it could be an expression. In other words, sovereignty is no longer conceived as an expression of some deeper unity among the people, but is viewed now as the central defining matrix of the nation. The discreteness of the nation-state does not define itself in the concept of sovereignty but the other way around, sovereignty defines the unity of the people, which otherwise, as 'multi-cultural societies', have little else to unite them.

As the 'mystical' body of the nation is being questioned, so sovereignty is increasingly viewed as a form of power relationship. Sovereignty is deemed to offer control over circuits of exchange. Sovereignty therefore can be apportioned, divided, bargained for, and aggregated according to needs. One can transfer bits of one's sovereignty, i.e. control, to a higher hybrid like the EU or NAFTA. One can negotiate one's sovereignty away. The 'markets' may become sovereign. In the modern world of the third industrial revolution it becomes increasingly acceptable that the very essence of our social life, society, is simply another negotiable reality.

CONCLUSIONS

This chapter has proposed that there is a complex if hidden history to technology in International Relations theory. The correlation between the changing perception of technology and the evolution of theory and practices of International Relations are as suggestive as they are difficult to prove, no doubt. Nonetheless, the common assumption that 'technology' has played a marginal role in International Relations must be questioned.

NOTES

1 I would to thank Brook Blair, James Babb, Chris Farrands and in particular Mike Talalay for their helpful comments on earlier drafts of this paper.
2 Nowadays, we tend to make a distinction between natural or organic entities and artificial artefacts. The latter are assumed to be ordered by the mechanical principle of organisation. In fact, the concept of 'organisation' derives from organism. Thus natural and artificial orders were thought to derive ultimately from the same sort of principles.
3 The notion of social 'structure' evolved in the works of the early functionalists like Benedict (1935) and Radcliffe-Brown (1952) who drew inspiration from biology.
4 'Broadly speaking the Greeks viewed the world as an organic system. The renaissance changed the analogy to the machine. The new picture of the clock-work "watch-world" displayed both the religious convictions in a created world order for the world and the desire to find a Creator playing the role of the watch-maker' (Barrow and Tipler 1986: 20).
5 Although many realist ideas originated earlier, in liberal critiques of dynastic politics.
6 Administrative rationalisation has its roots much earlier, in the eighteenth century. But explicit use of 'scientific principles' dates from the early twentieth.
7 P   Planning

O   Organisation

S   Staffing

D   Directing

C   Coordinating

O   –

R   Reporting

B   Budgeting

8 'Positivism', says Piaget (1965: 16), 'is a certain form of epistemology which neglects or underestimates the activity of the subject in favour of verification or the generalisation of the verified laws'.

3 Culture and the technological imperative
Missing dimensions[1]

Gillian Youngs

In a global age the relationship between culture and technology is central to any complex analysis of power. A developed perspective on the global political economy reveals inter-related cultural and technological factors as key transnational characteristics.[2] Whether we think in terms of the global threats of nuclear technology and environmental pollution (Beck 1992), the sophisticated strategic surveillance systems representing military and commercial interests (Kato 1993), or the multimedia global marketing of consumer capitalism, we confront such factors. They signal that technological developments are as important for the meanings which they sustain or introduce into global existence as for the practices which they define (see the previous chapter in this volume by Palan). This chapter contends that we have yet to realise sufficiently the challenge which this situation presents for analysis of global power relations. Indeed we are inhibited by a significant tendency to assume a particular relationship between culture and technology. This approach penetrates both spatial and temporal interpretations of global relations and makes universal claims in both these contexts. Thus it contributes directly to understandings of how these relations are mapped within or across territories, and the ways in which they change over time. The approach intrinsically identifies culture as the servant of technology.

CULTURE AS THE SERVANT OF TECHNOLOGY

The so-called post-Cold War context has boosted the tendency to identify culture as the servant of technology. With the breakdown of the ideological struggle between East and West, the political, economic and cultural space has been left for a unifying principle in global relations. This principle is increasingly being identified as technology. Whether one looks to Eugene Skolnikoff's (1993) depiction of science and technology as key 'evolutionary' influences in international affairs, Paul Kennedy's (1993) technologically driven view of how to prepare for the next century, or Francis Fukuyama's (1992) notion of technological progress as a future form of 'global culture', there is one fundamental message. Technological advances determine to a large degree who has power, how much and for how long. They overshadow the influence of contesting cultural factors and even offer the possibility of subsuming them altogether. Technology has transnational force. It is identified as a key dynamic in the changing nature of global relations. Culture in contrast is generally synonymous with national culture. It is viewed in a bounded, i.e. state, context, and thus has a static quality. It only comes into the picture to the extent that it is judged as supporting or inhibiting technology.

In broad terms the distribution of global power is understood on the basis of the technological 'haves' and 'have-nots' (Kennedy 1993: 194). The depiction of cultural factors as influential in determining on which side of this power divide a country is placed is especially clear in Paul Kennedy's analysis. It identifies demography as central to understanding who are 'the winners and losers in the developing world' (*ibid.*: 193). Associated with the problem of Africa's 'demographic explosion', Kennedy explains, are poverty and limited healthcare and educational provision (*ibid.*: 193–227). One reason why the tide of 'demographic boom' cannot be easily turned 'is traditional African belief systems concerning fecundity, children, ancestors, and the role of women' (*ibid.*: 213). The attack on cultures which stand against technologically driven 'global forces for change' is forthright:

> Far from preparing for the twenty-first century, much of the Arab and Muslim world appears to have difficulty in coming to terms with the nineteenth century, with its composite legacy of secularization, democracy, laissez-faire economics, transnational industrial and commercial linkages, social change and intellectual questioning. If one needed an example of the importance of cultural attitudes in explaining a society's response to change, contemporary Islam provides it.
>
> (Kennedy 1993: 208)[3]

Kennedy's conclusions make it clear that the developed economies have asserted the technological principles guiding the global market, and winning or losing for less developed countries is determined by the degree to which they can accommodate them (*ibid.*: 225). Such a perspective on global relations embraces traditional notions of development and modernisation. It does so in a way that places technology in an overtly hierarchical relation to culture: technology dictates its requirements and culture is there to serve them. The closer cultures can come to meeting the needs of technology, such as high levels of education and training, the more positively they are viewed. Kennedy's arguments are presented as a detailed description of the rules of the global power struggle as we move towards the next century. Certainly it cannot be denied that technological capabilities contribute significantly to defining the terms of that struggle (Strange 1994a; see also the chapters by Russell and Farrands in this volume). But an important question needs to be raised. Does the relationship between technology and culture posited by this kind of approach enable us to investigate fully the interplay between technological and cultural factors in forming and transforming global power relations? The descriptive format of Kennedy's analysis of global relations does not encourage us to pose such a question at all. One is left with a sense of *that's just the way it is.*

Francis Fukuyama's (1992) 'end of history' thesis adopts a similar hierarchical attitude to the relationship between technology and culture but overtly idealises it in a way that does open up the possibility of the question. Fukuyama's argument is distinctive in the way that it sets out at great length the particularities of its claims as well as the grounds for their supposed universal relevance. The Fukuyama thesis is explicit about its global intentions in describing the conditions of existing relations and the bases on which they have changed and will continue to change. Technology is identified as a key motor of that change, an essential support for the argument that we have reached 'the end of history'. Technology helps to extend the global embrace of 'liberal democracy' and 'economic liberalism' which have combined, according to Fukuyama, to form a destiny towards which all of humanity is inevitably moving. Clearly, technology is understood as a transnational force which separate national, regional or bloc cultures accept, nurture or resist in varying degrees and for a range of reasons (Fukuyama 1992: 31–51). Science and technology are depicted as 'irreversible' forces and thus crucial links between past, present and future (*ibid.*: 88– 108). They represent, from Fukuyama's perspective, a defining continuum in human history, driving social and economic developments associated with industrial and 'post-industrial' trends (*ibid.*: 89–97). The economic opportunities and political recognition offered by combined liberal economic and political principles are argued to provide the most supportive social setting for these developments (*ibid.*: 98–125).[4] This is the global message which, according to Fukuyama, is increasingly coming to be understood and acted upon:

> The enormously productive and dynamic economic world created by advancing technology and the rational organization of labor has a tremendous homogenizing power. It is capable of linking different societies around the world to one another physically through the creation of global markets, and of creating parallel economic aspirations and practices in a host of diverse societies. The attractive power of this world creates a very strong *predisposition* for all human societies to participate in it, while success in this participation requires the adoption of the principles of economic liberalism.
>
> (Fukuyama 1992: 108)

The global technological imperative is understood as being fuelled by the aggressive competitiveness of states, the 'universal' aim of economic growth, and technology's own momentum (*ibid.*: 73–85). Adherence to the power of 'technical rationality' (Ashley 1980) and its associated social supports is depicted as one of the rules of the 'liberal' club whose global membership is viewed as inevitably growing. From Fukuyama's standpoint, technology provides not only a vital part of the explanation for why we have reached the end of history but also a justification for the claimed 'universal' relevance of this situation. Interestingly, he overtly associates technology directly with the creation of a new form of 'global culture':

> It is not the mark of provincialism but of cosmopolitanism to recognize that there has emerged in the last few centuries something like a true global culture, centering around technologically driven economic growth and the capitalist social relations necessary to produce and sustain it.
>
> (Fukuyama 1992: 126)

TECHNOLOGY AS CULTURE/THE TECHNOLOGICAL IMPERATIVE AS HISTORY

The discussion so far has highlighted the tendency to establish a hierarchical relationship between technology and culture in the analysis of global relations. This hierarchy asserts technology as the dominant dynamic influence, the transnational force; and culture, in general, as the static bounded notion of national or state culture. The Fukuyama thesis extends this fundamental approach to the point of identifying it as a defining characteristic of the 'end of history' and its 'universal' nature. The distinction between technology and culture disappears and technology takes over *as* culture. In order to be clear about the implications of such a conclusion we need to probe further the meaning of establishing a hierarchical approach to the relationship between technology and culture in the investigation of global political economy. This hierarchy locates technology as the subject and culture as the object; technology as the realm of effective influence and action, and culture as the receiving domain of that influence and action. Culture may influence the degree to which technological goals may be successful or otherwise, but the technological imperative establishes the rules of the game. In order to express the global power of technological developments, such an approach abstracts technology and culture from one another and opposes them in a way that fixes the power relationship between them. Just as other familiar oppositional frameworks such as man/woman or science/nature assert a subject/object power relationship, so does this approach to technology/culture.[5]

Critical recognition of the need to explore exactly how technology and culture are being related to one another in any form of analysis disrupts any idea that such analysis can be regarded merely as description of what is being claimed as the real conditions of global existence. The term 'merely' is the key one here. While the analyst may argue that the power of technology as a global force justifies such a hierarchical framework, that still does not tell us everything we may need to know about the effects of its adoption. In fixing the supremacy of the power of technology over culture, this hierarchy also inhibits any open consideration of possible interaction between cultural and technological factors. Interest in culture is strictly delimited in line with its position as the object of technological influence. This interest then focuses on the degree to which cultural factors favour or disfavour technological developments. These, broadly speaking, become the parameters of interest in culture. And culture, in the context examined here, tends to be assumed as state-bounded culture, or cultures, to be more precise.

The problem is compounded by the utilisation of this hierarchical perspective on technology and culture in explanations of global history. While this is overt in the Fukuyama thesis it is clearly also a consideration with regard to the Kennedy and Skolnikoff investigations referred to above. Technology as a driving force in human history is a common thread here. History, in significant senses, is indeed *reduced* to developments associated with technological advance and the supporting characteristics of the global capitalist system. It is easy to see the importance of states within that system in Fukuyama's thesis, which places emphasis on politics as well as economics. A distinctive element of Fukuyama's explanation of global relations is the stress on the *combined* role of liberal economics and politics in meeting human needs, material and non-material. His claim that we can talk in terms of 'universal' history at all is highly dependent on his arguments concerning the attractions of a certain form of state organisation, i.e. liberal democracy, coupled with liberal economic principles. Fukuyama's position rests on idealised notions of liberal politics and economics. It views them very much as open frameworks offering seemingly endless opportunities for individual material gain and a social sense of self.[6] Thus the 'global culture' which results is a technologically driven liberal political economy (Fukuyama 1992: 126). This idea of a global culture signals the transnational triumph of the technological imperative. The implicit suggestion is that 'technical rationality' (Ashley 1980) as championed by the politics and economics of liberal capitalism *is* culture. The assertion erases the importance of any other understanding of culture.

The notion of 'global culture' in this context conveys a particularly powerful universalistic message.[7] It indicates a significant and broad acceptance of the technological imperative as steering a whole *global* way of life: it identifies technology as intrinsic to understanding what life is actually all about. Technology comes to concern meaning as much as practice. But this process happens implicitly rather than explicitly, in ways which militate against, rather than encourage, a critical engagement with it. In its depiction of a universal destiny defined in terms of a *West-centric* combination of scientific/technical rationality and 'liberal' politics and economics, the Fukuyama perspective is neo-colonial in turn, a kind of post-imperialist dream or vision of the ultimate triumph of the *West*. The establishment of technology as culture within this framework is presented as a given. The question of the relationship between technology and culture is sealed, as it were, and safe from consideration. If technology and culture are synonymous and the technological imperative supported by liberal political economy the sum of human history, and we are said to have arrived at 'the end of history', then the foundations of the future as well as the past and present are settled. According to Fukuyama, we know what we need to know about where we are going and the main difference exists between those who have arrived and those who have yet to do so. Or, as he defines it, the main global division of interest is between the 'post-historical' part of the world and 'a part that is still stuck in history', broadly speaking between the 'developed' and 'underdeveloped' worlds (Fukuyama 1992: 276, 385).

As already stressed, Fukuyama's thesis is notable for the overt nature of its 'universal' claims, but the earlier discussion of Kennedy's technologically driven perspective on how to prepare for the next century demonstrates implicit similarities in its approach to history and global power relations. Indeed his rather gloomy viewpoint elevates the impact of technological change to the status of a universal challenge with which even the most powerful have difficulty coping (Kennedy 1993: 333–5). However, it makes clear that economic growth and the technological developments associated with it are a crucial key to who will win and lose in the global power game, albeit with the recognition that there is a need to pay attention to the issue of sustainability (Fukuyama 1992: 346–7).

TECHNOLOGY, GLOBAL CULTURE, GLOBAL POWER RELATIONS

Analyses of global power relations which assert the primacy of technology over culture, to the point where technology becomes understood as a global and homogenising form of culture, do not provide the ultimate solution to the difficulties we face in interpreting the increasing complexity of the possession and operation of power in the global political economy. They effectively block the opportunity of opening up a consideration of how technological and cultural factors interact as dimensions of power. They do so in a range of ways. The first and most important is a reduction of technology to the technological imperative, i.e. the evolutionary under-standing of technological progress or advance. A brief consideration of the notion of technical rationality will assist our understanding of both the meaning and implications of this reductionism. This notion refers to a way of explaining and legitimising ideas of so-called progress. Technical rationality is a *particular* means of understanding human behaviour and choices, and social development.

Richard Ashley's (1980) assessment of 'technical-rational logic' empha-sises its dehumanising qualities. In continually pressing the principle of ever-expanding human control over the environment it leads to a situation where:

Human knowledge, skills and capacities to communicate are used, not self-reflectively, but as instrumentalities of problem-solving, control and domination.

(Ashley 1980: 251)

According to Ashley's analysis, 'technical-rational logic' confounds the fundamental 'interdependence' of humans with one another and with their environment: it objectifies and seeks to control via the application of 'knowledge and skills' and ensures that the *concepts of autonomy, knowledge and power are soldered into one* (*ibid.* 209–16). While his arguments assert that such logic is 'false' in its conflictual need-producing momentum, they also recognise that it is 'true' in its apparent relevance to the differentiated situations of humans in the present era (*ibid.*: 214–15). Ashley's alternative, 'rationality proper', while including problem-solving, retains critical awareness[8] of the problematic of human/human and human/environment 'interdependence' (*ibid.*: 215–16). In essence Ashley's position criticises the idealist and ahistorical tendencies of technical rationality in its adherence to a belief in the universal applicability of the principal of human control whatever the circumstances. Technical rationality represents an interpretation of human development over time through this guiding principal. It represents first and foremost a belief in, and a commitment to, the continued and universal relevance and possibility of that control. To reduce our understanding of technology to the technological imperative, or to technical rationality as described here, is to reduce it to that belief and that commitment. This is centrally an abstract approach to technology. It is a representation of technology as an ideology of *progress* (Tenbruck 1990). It constrains thinking about technology and human potential in a highly particular fashion:

> Technical rationality proclaims human freedom by denying the deterministic influences of historical processes, and in so doing, it is entrapped in complicity with the historical processes it is unable to imagine or criticize. Rationality proper commences the search for human freedom by allowing that human beings, in their thinking as in their choices, are distinctly unfree of historical-processual influences.

(Ashley 1980: 216)

The idea of the technological imperative as some kind of global homogenising culture actually draws our attention away from a substantive consideration of technology and power in the global political economy. It is an abstraction and as such is endowed with a timeless quality. If such an approach is dealing with the issue of power at all it is doing so only in terms of the power of the technological imperative as an ideology of *progress*. This is clearly important and should be addressed. As Ashley has explained, 'technical rationality is embedded, layer upon layer, in society's manifest structures and forms' (*ibid.*: 215). However the assertion of the technological imperative as global culture is just that, an assertion. It does not offer the potential for critical consideration of its meanings and implications. So we are left merely with an approach to technology which does no more than affirm the powerful role of technical rationality in determining human destiny. This certainly tells us something about the nature of power in the global political economy. It indicates the centrality of the technical-rational ideology of progress but it offers little assistance with the investigation of the ways in which that ideology is played out in global relations, or how it is linked directly to different forms of concrete human activity and experience such as production and consumption. In order to understand why this is the case we need to return to the opposition between technology and culture.

This opposition establishes a hierarchy in which technology is the dominant concept. The discussion of technology as technical rationality emphasises the degree to which this hierarchy's positioning of culture in an oppositional mode aligns it with irrationality. Culture can be regarded as the servant of technology, the object of technology, because technology is rational, and culture irrational. Technology is the dominant concept and therefore it follows that rationality rules or should rule, and can ultimately be expected to rationalise the irrational. This sense of technology as rational and culture as irrational is easily identified with Paul Kennedy's discussion of cultures in terms of those which support technological progress and those which counter it. The rational/irrational approach to technology/culture is also clear in Fukuyama's 'end of history' thesis. The 'end of history', the triumph of the technological imperative as global culture is, from his perspective, the ultimate victory of technical rationality. But this reduction of an understanding of technology to an ideology of global *progress* hinders rather than helps our endeavours to investigate detailed and substantive aspects of technology and power.

BEYOND AN UNDERSTANDING OF TECHNOLOGY AS IDEOLOGY OF PROGRESS

A focus on the relationship between culture and technology which does not collapse both concepts into a notion of technology as ideology of progress is necessary. Such an approach offers the possibility of developing a broader understanding of both technology in general and specific forms of technology. It prompts exploration of the cultural meanings implicit in and generated by particular applications of technology. Just as we need to think of technology in a wider sense than ideology of progress in order to do this, we also need to think of culture in a wider sense than national or state-bounded culture. The opposition between technology and culture outlined above, which posits technology as a dynamic transnational force in global relations and culture as a static and nationally-defined entity, is completely misleading. The nature of a global market and the technologies that facilitate its operations draw our attention towards the importance of the transnational qualities of cultural factors. In order to consider this further it is necessary to discuss how we can think differently about the relationship between technology and culture if we reject the oppositional framework. It is important to remember just how strongly such a framework militates against serious and open examination of the links between technology and culture. Its intention is to assert the primacy of technology over culture, and ultimately to efface the idea of culture except to the degree that it represents the idea of technology.

We can, in developing an alternative approach, think about technology and culture as referring to the domains of practice and meaning, but we must not do so in any oppositional sense. For it is quite clear that practice and meaning are interconnected in complex ways in human existence. Just as technology cannot be regarded as a value-free, purely practical domain, culture cannot be thought of as merely concerned with the realm of ideas. Technology is a direct expression of human interaction with the world and, as such, represents a link between thought and practice (Levinson 1986). Basically technology concerns the human capacity to put ideas into action and to develop and use tools and applications for assistance where necessary. But technology is not abstracted from socio-historical processes, it is embedded within them. It is both produced by and influential in those processes in an ongoing fashion. If we adopt a fairly broad approach to culture then it concerns the way in which we live our lives through the specific allocation of meanings to practice. Technology represents the practices we develop to enable us to express such meanings, whether through forms of organisation or production. If we treat culture as 'a whole way of life' (Williams 1990: xvii) then technology is a vital means of its achievement. But when technologies are introduced they become part of culture and thus contribute to the generation of cultural meanings. The key here is not to abstract technology and culture from one another but to recognise the degree to which, as realms of practice and meaning, they interact as part of human social dynamics.

The recognition of technology as an expression of human creativity in the widest sense of that term is of particular assistance in this context. It reminds us that technology is fundamentally a form of human interaction with the environment, an expression of the relationship of humans to the world. It puts the human element back into our consideration of technology. It is less abstract in this way than the reduction of technology to technical rationality – to an ideology of progress. It is more concrete in that it discourages us from assuming technology as a given, as the technological imperative, and encourages us to view it in a social context, to relate it to meaning and power and the forms of organisation, production and consumption, through which they are formed and transformed. The characteristics of the global market direct our attention in this respect to the transnational interaction between technological and cultural factors. It is this interaction which demonstrates the challenges we face in understanding the precise nature of social contexts and how power is exercised and experienced within and across them. Holding on firmly to the dual interest in technology and culture in the manner discussed here is an essential aid to the development of our understanding of the highly differentiated positions of the various participants in the global market. It helps to ensure that we do not take the term 'global' to mean uniform or universal. The collapsing of technology and culture into technology-as-culture does encourage us to adopt such a universal perspective. It leads us to think about 'the global' as a symbol of the triumph of technical rationality as expressed through technological progress and the supporting political and economic frameworks of the capitalist system. This approach to technology and culture in global political economy presents only a partial picture of power. It is undoubtedly important to consider the degree to which global capitalism does incorporate a triumph of technical rationality, but the participation in and experience of this is differentiated to the degree that perceiving it in a *universal* sense is of limited use.

THE TECHNOLOGICAL IMPERATIVE AND TIME/SPACE CONSIDERATIONS

Probing the time/space implications of the approach to technology and culture which presents technology *as* a form of global culture helps us to understand more deeply the nature of its universal claims. We need in this context to think about the ways in which the technological imperative presents interpretations of time and space and relates them to one another. The status of the imperative as an abstraction is fundamental. We must recognise that this abstraction relates to both time and space. This is signalled by the identification of the imperative as an ideology of progress. It is evident that such an ideology presents a particular understanding of time.

Time is measured principally on an evolutionary basis with regard to technological progress. Interest in socio-historical circumstances is reduced to those which relate directly to the perceived existence or lack of such progress. This situation is captured perfectly in Fukuyama's (1992: 276, 385) vision of a world 'divided between a post-historical part, and a part that is still stuck in history'. It is important to note the extent to which this approach to time or history is reductive. Despite its universal claims, it is a highly particular interpretation of time.[9] It allocates no priority to a broad consideration of the relationship of technology to socio-cultural processes over time in different geographical/spatial contexts. It introduces a kind of techno-determinism into our understanding of time and space (Smith 1990: 180). It presents a worldview which collapses understanding of space and time into the standard modernisation model of technological *progress*. This worldview delimits our spatial awareness of global relations within the terms of this *progress*. It seals our understanding of change across space and time into this specific framework. Importantly its understanding of power is reduced to this mode. Thus the only kind of analysis of power that can really be achieved is that of the differentiated position of various social entities, generally, in this case, states, along the evolutionary line of technological *progress*. While this assessment of power may have some use it hardly offers any comprehensive possibilities for a detailed examination of the varied forms and operation of global power relations. Furthermore, in its reductive approach to change it does little to sensitise us to the identification of the detail of transformative challenges to existing social relations.[10] Its focus on change is at the most general level: that of movements of societies from underdeveloped to less-developed to developed status. These definitions relate, of course, to the West-centric modernisation model. Their use in such a manner does not necessarily lead to any analysis of their meanings in contrasting contexts. Indeed the technology/culture oppositional framework fails to prompt any sense of the need for such analysis.

This is crucial because the impact of technological and cultural factors on time/space relationships is a vital dimension of the investigation of power in the global political economy. If we are seriously interested in understanding global power relations we must take account of the ways in which technologies facilitate and shape relations in and across societies around the world (see the chapter by Shearman in this volume). One of the major influences of technology this century has been its varied capabilities to disrupt previously established understandings of the links between time and space in association with practice (see Harvey 1990). This is one of the key ways in which technology can truly be said to have changed the meaning of the ways in which lives are lived at work and play. Communications, information and media technologies in particular emphasise cultural transmission as an influential dimension of global power relations. These technologies indicate the need to consider the ways in which information, whether of an overtly cultural kind or not, is presented and packaged. The computerised global stock market has its messages in this respect just as much as satellite television transmissions of American soap operas and CNN news bulletins. And, global networks, by their very nature, can tend to obscure the issue of origination, i.e. where and when, as well as for what specific purposes, material has been generated. They signal the need for a penetrating approach towards communication as well, underlining the importance of avoiding simplistic notions of *passive* audiences. Cultural contexts of production, transmission and reception are all relevant to our understanding of the power relations involved.[11] The global media may well reach different social groups in different parts of the world with the same message, but if we are interested in exploring the subtleties of global power relations then these facts provide an insufficient basis for our considerations.

We need to investigate the different meanings that are generated and transformed in such situations and this requires us to take account of the interplay of technological and cultural factors in the whole process of communication. Indeed taking the interaction of technology and culture seriously leads to the recognition of communication *as* a process. In other words we are persuaded to break down its component parts, to seek out the different technological and cultural factors at work throughout its many stages of development, operation and reception.

TECHNOLOGY, CULTURE AND POWER IN THE GLOBAL POLITICAL ECONOMY

The global market fuses technological and cultural dimensions through the production and distribution of commodities and services. It is principally concerned with the attachment of meanings to products. The intricate and varied parts played by technologies in contributing to the development of these meanings is a key characteristic of the global market. Notions of technology as the technological imperative are of limited assistance here. In this context technology is directly contributing to the need for a re-evaluation of what we understand by the term culture in relation to global political economy. This requires us to address the fact that production and consumption are 'more than simply material aspects of subsistence' (Friedman 1990: 327). Products and services are an important dimension of the way in which we experience the world and relate to it, socially and individually. This is the case through our involvement in processes of both production and consumption, which can be understood as part of 'the practice of identity' (*ibid.*).

The products of media-based entertainment systems such as film and television illustrate the complexities of the interaction of technological and cultural factors. These products not only employ advanced technologies as a means of communication but they integrate high-tech applications into their creative processes. The technique known as 'morphing' is an interesting and powerful example. Computer technology is used to transform images apparently seamlessly from one to another before your very eyes.[12] Technology and cultural representation are integrated in a highly complex fashion. We can see a fusing of applications of technology across a number of areas involving both practice and meaning in such a situation. Media such as video and film rely on advanced technology for their production, distribution, marketing and consumption, but they also utilise technology as an essential element of the creation of their cultural messages. In these circumstances the power of technology is being *celebrated* in a multidimensional manner across the realms of practice and meaning through different stages of the production and consumption process. Technology gains a kind of iconic status which goes beyond any simple notion of technical rationality. Capturing the pervasive complexities of technology in the global political economy thus requires the development of an awareness of its interaction with cultural factors.

Technology is intrinsic to questions about science, ecology, the military-industrial complex, the changing nature of production and the expanding global communications market. It is relevant to the widest range of human activities and concerns. Its *practical* import in such areas is clear, its interaction with cultural aspects less so. These need to be brought out, to be thought about deeply, if we want to further our understanding of power and technology. We need to break down the monolithic approach to technology as the technological imperative because this inhibits exploration of the detailed nature of the relationship between power and technology. Differentiated participation in and experience of global capitalism are significantly influenced by the interaction of technological and cultural factors. Investment, trading and communications networks link societies, firms, and governmental and non-governmental international and global institutions, but they do so in diverse ways. While there may be some homogenising dimensions to this networked experience, there are also important distinctions to be drawn in contrasting socio-historical circumstances. These distinctions cannot be addressed in an analytical model which reduces the technology/culture relationship to a state-centred comparison on the basis of points along the *development* scale. Participation in the global market and its communications systems does not fit neatly into this model. The range, applications and effects of technologies across different societies and sections of societies around the world cannot be captured by this model. We need a much more open approach to the relationship between culture and technology which both recognises them as transnational factors in global relations, and understands that their fixed points of origination, manipulation and experience are vital to an understanding of their influential role in global power relations.

This approach to technology and culture is an essential way to develop our analysis of power in the global political economy. It does so in a fundamental sense by encouraging us to ask a whole series of questions about the *nature* of the global political economy. It assists us in moving beyond the actors and statistics framework of definition. While clearly it remains essential to identify which participants have the most control over investment, research and development, production, and distribution, we need to know more about the demand as well as the supply side of the equation. We need to probe the many cultural dimensions of global capitalism. We need to recognise that the global marketplace is concerned with the exchange of meanings, significantly those attached directly to products and services.[13] These meanings cannot be accounted for, in anything but the most limited fashion, in an actors and statistics framework. They are missing dimensions. If we wish to include them in our considerations we must recognise that global political economy cannot be summed up by descriptions of its material characteristics. The key players in leading-edge weapons and production technologies must be of principal concern, but identifying them and the volumes of their various activities is, in some respects, only a beginning. The statistics hide a whole range of socio-cultural factors influencing political and commercial agendas. They tell us more about *what* is happening in the global political economy than *how* it is happening. They fail to signal the importance of the complex interaction of different agendas in different contexts. They fail to stress the political, economic and cultural *processes* which have produced them over time. If we are interested in how technologies are generated, transformed and applied in contrasting settings we need to investigate these processes. If we hold on to an interactive notion of the relationship between technology and culture we can achieve this. If we settle for the oppositional stance towards technology and culture the chances are that we cannot.

NOTES

1 I would like to thank other contributors to this volume for their helpful comments during the preparation of this chapter. Detailed suggestions from editors Michael Talalay and Roger Tooze were of particular assistance. I am grateful also to Margaret Law for research assistance with this project.
2 There is an extensive literature on 'transnational relations'. See for example Keohane and Nye (1970). The term transnational is used in a general sense here to indicate operation across rather than within national boundaries.
3 Kennedy's analysis does stress the need to differentiate between the circumstances and capabilities of different Islamic states.
4 A substantial part of Fukuyama's thesis is devoted to this area. For a further discussion see Youngs (1996).
5 See Richard Ashley's (1989) explanation of 'logocentric discourse'.
6 I have argued elsewhere that this approach to the liberal paradigm avoids critical discussion of the causes of persistent inequalities and a detailed interest in the location, exercise, and effects of economic and political power (Youngs 1996).
7 For a broader critical discussion of the universalistic nature of the Fukuyama thesis see Youngs (1996).
8 See also Cox (1981).
9 For a discussion of the universal and the particular see Ashley (1984: 268–9).
10 On the question of social change see Scholte (1993).
11 Work on cultural imperialism has opened up these kinds of issues. See Tomlinson (1991). See also Smith (1990).
12 See Derry (1992). See also Jackson (1993).
13 Writings on the nature of postmodernity in particular have explored this issue. See, for example, Jameson (1991) and Bauman (1992). See also Ulrich Beck (1992) on the 'risk society'.

4   Technology as knowledge

Generic technology and change in the global political economy

Alan Russell

Scholars of international affairs are becoming increasingly interested in the relationship between technology and change in the global political economy. The importance of the subject is matched only by the difficulty in knowing how to approach it. Not only is there a lack of satisfactory intellectual frameworks, but – equally off-putting – the pervasiveness of technology creates a very practical problem of where to begin. The objective of this chapter is to make a start at addressing both of these issues. It suggests a theoretical framework based on the idea that technology is an aspect of 'knowledge' and thus can be approached by using Susan Strange's concept of the 'knowledge structure' – and the importance she places on it in her analysis of power in international political economy. On the practical level, this chapter tries to make the case for using the concept of generic technology as a satisfactory compromise between the vague generalities of 'technology' writ large and the very narrow detail of any specific technology. Moreover, because generic technology is important to the fields of economics and business studies (Dicken 1992), it facilitates our posing new questions and seeking new answers from an interdisciplinary base. Recent calls for more such interdisciplinary awareness should not go unheeded (Strange 1991; Dunning 1993).

The chapter is organised in the following way. It begins with a brief discussion of the nature of knowledge – not in an attempt to precisely define this concept but rather in order to indicate that viewing technology as 'knowledge' is a fruitful way of getting a handle on it. This is followed by a summary of Strange's approach to IPE, showing why her emphasis on the knowledge structure is both appropriate and useful as a framework for exploring the influence of technology in IR/IPE. The next two sections will focus respectively on the growing interest in issues of technology and knowledge in the fields of economics and business studies. Insights from these fields need only be taken a little further to prise open cultural, political and ideological issues central to IPE. The exploration of generic technology that then follows, reinforces a conclusion that IPE *must* increasingly address technology as knowledge. Overall, it will be shown that Strange's framework is appropriate for locating the instrumental and transcendental dimensions of knowledge and technology (see Palan in Chapter 2 above), while drawing attention to their impact in terms of structural power. Beyond this, however, generic technology asks questions which straddle the concerns of economics, business studies and IPE, and suggests our answers require some integration of their respective viewpoints.

KNOWLEDGE AND TECHNOLOGY

The concept of knowledge is open to a variety of different interpretations. Most straightforwardly, it is often conceived in terms of 'knowing things' about something. We tend to recognise the knowledge of experts in areas as diverse as financial markets, scientific research, and the medical and legal professions. Past generations would have similarly recognised and appreciated the skills of craftsmen, equally the product of long apprenticeships to their trades. Such images of knowledge – as the result of learning, involving the acquisition of information and specialist understanding – are well established. At the level of philosophical and epistemological discourse, comparable longstanding traditions focus attention on the nature of knowledge (Russell 1946). The logic of understanding, the methodology of knowledge generation, the utility of knowledge and the nature of reason, all have long taxed the human mind (Kuhn 1962; Ryan 1973; Chalmers 1982). Other academic disciplines such as economics, sociology, business studies and, belatedly, international relations (Haas 1992; Skolnikoff 1993), have all addressed 'knowledge' and, in association, 'information'. Market knowledge, knowledge as power, knowledge contained within firms, and knowledge-based 'epistemic' communities (Haas 1992) represent examples from these fields.

A search for definitions must also take account of historical context and changes in the conventional wisdom of what constitutes knowledge. Drucker traces changes in definitions of knowledge resulting sequentially from the industrial, the productivity and the managerial revolutions, culminating in what he articulates as a post-capitalist 'knowledge society'. He observes that : 'What we now mean by knowledge is information effective in action, information focused on results' (1993: 42). He goes on to suggest that there are multiple *knowledges* in contemporary society and economy, each of which he calls a discipline:

> A discipline converts a 'craft' into a methodology – such as engineering, the scientific method, the quantitative method or the physician's differential diagnosis. Each of these methodologies converts *ad hoc* experience into system. Each converts anecdote into information. Each converts skill into something that can be taught or learned.
>
> (Drucker 1993: 42)

This image of multiple sets of instrumental knowledge is not at odds with most observers' intuitive understanding. Drucker neatly encapsulates a

contemporary and general understanding of the term. He usefully emphasises the 'disciplinary' basis of knowledge, with its wide range of specialisms
and inherent compartmentalisation.

This conception of knowledge also fits technology rather well. What is the
latter if not a 'discipline' or 'information effective in action'? Other
definitions support this idea. Technology has generally been described as
industrially useful knowledge; the processes of acquiring such knowledge; in
turn encapsulated in invention, innovation, and dissemination; protection of
knowledge; economic production; know-how; continuities and discontinuities in knowledge generation and its spread, including imitation, openness or
embeddedness; and so on (Rosenberg 1976; Roy 1978; Johnston and
Gummett 1979; Skolnikoff 1993).

Technology intuitively meshes with our idea of knowledge as 'know-how'.
In this sense, both technology and knowledge have an instrumental
dimension – to use the terminology set out by Palan in Chapter 2 of this
volume – or a 'practical or operational level' in Strange's words (1991: 37).
Knowledge, however, also has what Palan refers to as a transcendental
element – or what Strange calls the realm of 'ideas' (*ibid.*). In this sense, it is
related to 'belief systems and their associated value preferences that inhibit or
validate some kinds of actions rather than others' (*ibid.*). Strange clearly
illustrates this in reference to medieval Christendom, where the beliefs taught
and preserved by the Church had far-reaching influence. Thus, the Church
had authority over 'rulers of states, merchants and craftsmen in the market'
and claimed 'a monopoly of moral and spiritual knowledge' (Strange 1988:
119–20). Today we can include the predominance in western society of a
materialist set of values, reinforcing the instrumental application of knowledge in the market to achieve Drucker's notion of knowledge, proving itself
in action. Beyond that, there is the manipulation of beliefs, ideas and culture,
through the use of knowledge and information, to open markets for
products. The examples of film entertainment, notably from Hollywood,
and the often cited Coca-Cola culture can suffice here, both encapsulated
within the widespread use of global marketing strategies (Gill and Law 1988:
61; Frieden and Lake 1991b: 143).

This distinction between instrumental and transcendental images of
technology and knowledge is not as clear as might be supposed. Founts of
economic wisdom, such as the IMF and the World Bank, through *instrumental* applications of currently fashionable economic insight have sought to
transform many developing economies. Their 'advice' and application of
conditionality in respect to loans are intended to enhance economic
efficiency and to establish 'appropriate' growth strategies (for example via
export-led activity and following domestic economic restructuring) (M.
Williams 1994). A partial consequence has been *transcendental* changes in
the value systems and culture of the societies concerned (Cox 1987: 357–68;
Ofuatey-Kodjoe 1991: 174). Social structures and patterns of political
influence can shift, and a general westernisation is seen to follow increasing

exposure to transnational economic interactions. One of the underlying themes of this chapter is that while we can on conceptual grounds appropriately distinguish the instrumental view of knowledge and technology from a view embedded in culture and beliefs, we cannot separate them in terms of their collective impact on the global political economy. The cultural dimension (Youngs, this volume) and the instrumental are themselves highly *interdependent*. For example, as Strange points out (1991: 37), 'when systems of accumulating, storing, or communicating information change, the change is apt to have a direct and sometimes quite a substantial effect on the bargaining power of actors as well as on the prioritised values of the system'.

This particular example is especially appropriate for the purposes of this chapter because it is an instance of a *generic* technology. Generic technology can be taken to refer to a technological innovation or set of innovations with a shared *genus*, observed to affect large portions of the economy. Dicken (1992) follows Freeman (1987a) in identifying five generic technologies that have brought changes in technology systems, which not only affect many parts of the economy but also create totally new industries. These comprise: information technology, biotechnology, materials technology, energy technology, and space technology (Dicken 1992: 98).[1] Because of their pervasiveness, generic technologies provide an attractive case to examine in relation to the global political economy. They are particularly suited to addressing the linkages between the instrumental, the transcendental and power. This, and the fact that generic technology is important to the fields of economics and business studies, facilitates our posing new questions and seeking new answers from an *inter*disciplinary base. Thus there are enabling characteristics involved, while the path to widespread industrial impact is itself a major focus of interest. In other words, some technological innovations themselves may filter through many economic or industrial activities, previously displaying weaker connections. Pervasiveness, shifts in technological paradigms (as discussed below) and cultural impacts all raise questions of *power* in international political economy. There are issues of who controls technological knowledge and who gains from it, including who is empowered by it. Generic technologies may have characteristics that reflect particular elements of knowledge and its place in the global political economy. That 'place' has been very interestingly theorised by Strange in her analysis of the knowledge structure.

THE KNOWLEDGE STRUCTURE

Strange has outlined an analytic framework for studying international political economy; defined as the relationship between states and markets – or the 'study of those international and global phenomena that have an inherently economic, political, and social dimension' (Stiles and Akaha 1991: xi). Four mutually supporting primary *structures* are identified, within which various categories of actor interact. The primary structures of security, production, finance and knowledge are defined and conceptualised as mutually supporting. Within these, the relative power of actors represents a key explanatory variable. Important as this is, Strange argues that even more significant is the application of *structural* power, defined as 'the power to decide how things shall be done, the power to shape frameworks within which states relate to each other, relate to people, or relate to corporate enterprises' (Strange 1988: 25). For Strange, the four primary sources of structural power in the global political economy are therefore: 'control over security; control over production; control over credit; and control over knowledge, beliefs and ideas' (*ibid.*: 26). In her framework this categorisation of power is preferred to a more common separation of economic and political power. The importance of this should be stressed. Strange offers a means to place power at the heart of IPE without reducing the concept to one of merely instrumental activity *vis-à-vis* one agent to another. While acknowledging the relevance of actors attempting to influence each other through capabilities in their control, her framework, in addition, encompasses the disposition of power within structures and the possibilities of 'nonintentional' power, where the appropriate view is from the 'receiving side' (Guzzini 1993: 461). This latter dimension of power is of great significance. When actors, be they states, firms or individuals, are affected by the actions or position of others, regardless of the others' intentions, then there is a structural phenomenon at play. As Guzzini points out, structural power may also be impersonal, 'because the origin of the produced effect is not located at the level of actors' (*ibid.*: 461– 2). This distinction between structural power and relational power, combined with the deliberate avoidance of artificial distinctions between economic and political dimensions, offers great scope for understanding the place of knowledge in IPE.

It is the knowledge structure that is most relevant to the concerns here. The knowledge structure 'determines what knowledge is discovered, how it is stored, and who communicates it by what means to whom and on what terms' (Strange 1988: 117). Consequently, power and authority are conferred on 'those occupying key decision-making positions in the knowledge structure' (*ibid.*). This embraces those who are entrusted by society with the storage of knowledge and the generation of more knowledge, and those who control 'in any way the channels by which knowledge, or information, is communicated' (*ibid.*).

Strange notes that technological changes have influenced the knowledge structure and in turn the production structure, resulting in the centralisation of power with the big transnational corporations (TNCs). Similarly, technological changes have altered the finance structure, something all too obvious in the last decade or so, and the security structure (*ibid.*: 129). Thus structural power is exercised *transnationally* over the global economy. In this respect, the analyses provided by Strange and Drucker each contribute uniquely to the writing on the 'globalisation' of the international political economy (Drucker 1993; Jones 1995: 11–13). In 1988, Strange concluded that three broad developments were occurring: competition between states was increasingly becoming 'a competition for leadership in the knowledge structure' or a place at the leading edge of advanced technology; there was an increasing asymmetry between states, as political authorities, in the acquisition of knowledge and in access to it; and change in the knowledge structure was 'bringing about new distributions of power, social status and influence within societies and across state borders'. As she succinctly put it: 'Power is passing to the "information-rich" instead of the "capital-rich" ' (Strange 1988: 132–3).

Strange offers an excellent lead for the field of IPE, in providing both a framework of analysis and a rationale to study knowledge and technology in an interdisciplinary fashion. Knowledge becomes an *object* of relevant study. In turn, the knowledge structure affects the operation of the global political economy, including other structures identified by Strange, making it an *explanatory variable*. Embedding technology within the knowledge structure allows it to be conceived as an endogenous influence. It does not exist 'out there' in a 'black box'; rather it is, as noted above, both object and agent – at one and the same time. Strange's approach leads one to view technology as being transcendental as well as instrumental and also to focus on the relationship between technology and political and economic power. In sum, Strange provides a very useful and intellectually satisfying theoretical framework for integrating technology and change into an overall approach to IPE.

THE ECONOMICS OF TECHNOLOGICAL INNOVATION

Economists are also increasingly taking this broad view of technology. They are becoming more prone to look within the 'black box' of technology (Rosenberg 1982) and to treat technological progress in endogenous terms (Dosi 1988a; Foray and Freeman 1993).[2] Among others, Giovanni Dosi has contributed much in a growing investigation of technology, within economic activity and growth. He has also, from time to time, offered summaries and comments on the major trends. For Dosi there are problems with excessive reliance on either market-pull (demand side) theories of technological innovation or technology-push (supply side) theories (Dosi 1984: 7–85). Rosenberg (1976) has used a dual focus on both demand- and supply-side forces in attempting to integrate technological knowledge. Although there appears to be no escaping the pull of the market, identified as consumers' needs or a 'common category of human wants', he introduces supply-side factors such as the state of scientific knowledge, the prevailing level of technological skills, and the specific characteristics of raw material inputs.

One of the more useful departures by economists to approach the diverse aspects of technological knowledge and its diffusion – and one particularly significant for an IPE perspective – is the concept of a *technological paradigm*.

By modifying this established concept, some operational and cultural aspects of the knowledge structure can be accommodated, including power. Dosi's work in this area has been of much significance and derives from the conceptualisation of scientific progress articulated by Lakatos (1974) and Kuhn (1962). The following definition is instructive both in terms of what it includes and what it omits:

> Both scientific and technological paradigms embody an *outlook*, a definition of the relevant problems, a pattern of enquiry. A 'technological paradigm' defines contextually the needs that are meant to be fulfilled, the scientific principles utilized for the task, the material technology to be used. In other words, a technological paradigm can be defined as a 'pattern' of solution of selected technoeconomic problems based on highly selected principles derived from the natural sciences, jointly with specific rules aimed to acquire new knowledge and safeguard it, whenever possible, against rapid diffusion to the competitors.
>
> (Dosi 1988: 1127)

Dosi gives us examples of the combustion engine, oil-based synthetic chemistry and semiconductors. He suggests that the technological paradigm is both an *exemplar*, or artefact, that is to be developed and improved (such as a car or an integrated circuit) and a *set of heuristics* ('e.g. Where do we go from here? Where should we search? What sort of knowledge should we draw on?'). Linked to this is the notion of a *technological trajectory*, which is the 'activity of technological process along the economic and technological trade-offs defined by a paradigm' (*ibid.*: 1128). Continuous change reflects progress along a technological trajectory, while discontinuities are 'associated with the emergence of a new paradigm' (Dosi 1984: 78). This conceptualisation has considerable merit. It facilitates an historical perspective of continuous and discontinuous change, and it opens up the Kuhnian image of puzzle-solving as an element of progress within the accepted framework of the paradigm. This view of technology also differs from much of traditional mainstream economics which, in black-boxing technology, saw it as information generally applicable and easy to reproduce and reuse (Dosi 1988: 1130). It certainly makes technology endogenous and interdependent with other economic processes.

Despite these strengths, the concept of a technological paradigm is underdeveloped. Kuhn had something more in mind, in his application of the term paradigm to scientific progress. He also referred to paradigms in a sociological context as representing a 'community' of the practitioners of a scientific speciality pursuing shared goals, reflecting common educational experience and professional initiations (Kuhn 1962: 176–7). While Dosi qualifies his image, by acknowledging 'tacitness' evident within technological paradigms and the 'looser' application of the concept *vis-à-vis* technology, there is scope to include shared belief and community elements of paradigms as applied to technology. In effect a technological paradigm reflects a *politically and/or sociologically* sensitive dimension whereby those who advocate technological development, within a particular technological paradigm or trajectory, both share beliefs and tend to export their beliefs and ideals beyond their own community. We could perhaps go as far as describing a process of socialisation for the 'technologist', akin to the way a scientist is socialised into a scientific community defined by the theories it accepts and the prevalent paradigm (Ryan 1970: 142). This involves more than the operation of firms and markets, to include, coming closer to Drucker and Strange, the processes by which technological education takes place within society, the relationships of power in this process and the relationship with culture. Interesting examples include: the culture and beliefs shared within the nuclear energy industry (Pringle and Spigelman 1981), often seen to be at odds with other sectors of society; the striving for consensus within ethically problematic areas of innovation, such as reproductive technologies (Warnock 1985); and the cultural consequences of the development of information superhighways (see the chapter by Shearman below). [3]

Dosi's concept of technological paradigm is complemented by further associated concepts. The term 'technological system' also pervades much of the literature on the economics of innovation, with the emphasis being on the *linkage* of sectors, or 'several branches of the economy' (Freeman and Perez 1988: 46). Technological systems are thus '*networks* of agents interacting in a specific economic/industrial area under a particular *institutional infrastructure* or set of infrastructures and involved in the *generation, diffusion, and utilization of technology*'. The networks form around 'knowledge' or 'competence' flows rather than the flows of ordinary goods and services (Carlsson and Jacobsson 1993: 77–8). Changes in technological systems are ultimately far-reaching and derive from 'a combination of radical and incremental innovations, together with *organisational* and *managerial* innovations affecting more than one or a few firms' (Freeman and Perez 1988: 46). Consequently, the transformation of technological systems can be associated with changes in significant technological paradigms or the appearance of radically new ones. As will be seen below, the knowledge structure can subsume the individual technological paradigm and its individual social, cultural and political context.

Other writers have suggested that considerably more profound transformations should be described in term of changes in 'techno-economic paradigms' (Perez 1983). These reflect 'changes in technology systems which are so far-reaching in their effects that they have a major influence on the behaviour of the entire economy' (Freeman and Perez 1988: 47). It is hard to conceptualise such transformations without a political and social dimension – evident in the observation of Freeman and Perez that associated with successions of techno-economic paradigms come 'painful' processes of structural change. The focus is more akin to the longer-term Schumpeterian waves or Kondratieff cycles, whereby changes in techno-economic paradigm:

have such widespread consequences for all sectors of the economy that their diffusion is accompanied by a major structural crisis of adjustment, in which social and institutional changes are necessary to bring about a better 'match' between the new technology and the system of social management of the economy.

(Freeman and Perez 1988: 38)

Transformations are so radical, with the diffusion of the new technology being so pervasive, as to apply in almost any industry. The examples of oil technology and microelectronics are proffered by Freeman and Perez. Interesting as such long-wave analysis is, it has less immediacy to it than Dosi's concept of technological paradigm. Our IPE focus must include long-wave analysis (Freeman 1984) and fundamental dislocations to the global economy following far-reaching and radical innovation, but the concern here is more with technological paradigms as potential building blocks within the knowledge structure.

Dosi presents an image of novel technological paradigms (or broad technological approaches) competing with each other and older established technological paradigms. This image can be enhanced by invoking structural power (in instrumental and cultural contexts) in the explanation of processes of selection. It is here that Dosi's ideas of change and continuity in paradigms and trajectories meets with Strange's ideas of structural power, to answer the two critical questions of how paradigms change and whose paradigm succeeds.

There is, however, at least one further complication. The economist examining technological progress may have to choose between a focus on aggregate markets and aggregate supply-side factors, and behavioural (and sociological) theories of the individual firm (Chiaromonte and Dosi 1993). Alternatively he may attempt industry-specific or sectoral studies, applying both macro- and micro-economic insights. Dosi – along with other economists such as Pavitt (1984) and Freeman (1982, 1984, 1990) – is, however, pushing the frontiers of the economics profession outwards. Perhaps it is inevitable when it comes to looking at technology and innovation, that they must explore the relationship with knowledge and information in terms of the public/private interface as well as firms, markets and sectors. In taking this direction they begin to embrace the concerns of IPE. The application of frameworks such as Strange's can build upon the above, drawing together the demand- and supply-side issues, internalising the policy and political processes (Castells 1993), applying various concepts of power while being sensitive to the instrumental and the cultural, and all in a more truly global context.

An important actor within this approach is the firm. Business corporations are at the heart of the process of technology dissemination, and are prime movers in innovation. IPE cannot and does not ignore the firm. Given the progress being made in the field of business studies, exploring the place of knowledge and technology in the affairs of corporations, there is good reason to add some of their insights to those of the economists. In any case, Strange calls on IPE to explicitly embrace the concerns of the field of international business studies, something evident in her own recent work.

FIRMS AND KNOWLEDGE

In criticising the business studies field, Strange argues that its theories of the firm are essentially inward-looking. Firms are thus perceived as hierarchies that pursue objectives in their own interest. Very little attention is given to relations with other hierarchies, including other firms, political parties, governments, or international organisations. International history, international relations and IPE all have something to offer for business and management studies (Strange 1991: 46–7). Much as Rosenberg provided a timely critique of his economic colleagues, Badaracco (1991) provides a challenge to his business studies colleagues, with overtones of Strange's criticisms.

In particular, Badaracco provides an excellent study of the erosion of the boundaries of companies. In common with other writers (often in different fields) he examines the inter-firm alliances that have sprung up in recent years. He also notes that the erosion of company borders extends beyond the links with other companies. He goes further than economists, such as Dosi and Pavitt, in exploring the firm-based location of innovatory knowledge (often proprietary). What makes his contribution of particular interest here is his explanatory focus for this growing phenomenon. The blurring of the boundaries of US companies he sees as being in response to 'the powerful knowledge-driven forces reshaping their economic environment' (Badaracco 1991: xii; on related points see Junne in this volume). Knowledge, in a variety of forms, thus represents a new 'engine of wealth' at work. In particular, he distinguishes between embedded knowledge and migratory knowledge as 'ideal types', and between commercialised and commercialisable knowledge. The idea of embedded knowledge compares well with the firm-specific view of knowledge considered above, and refers to the specialised capabilities developed within firms, leading to competitive battles over capabilities as well as products. In contrast, migratory knowledge disseminates quickly, often in several directions at once, contained in designs, in machines and in individual minds. From this he proceeds to analyse the processes by which knowledge diffuses between firms, involving complementary capabilities that are usually specific rather than generic, and limitations on transfer, such as barriers and the embedded nature of knowledge contained within some organisations.

Badaracco observes a reversal of key aspects of the product cycle perspective (Vernon 1971). Firms, he concludes, are developing new pathways along which knowledge can migrate, involving, for example, collaboration among researchers from overseas facilities and increasingly initial applications of new technology occurring in overseas operations (Badaracco 1991: 43). This, not least, gives governments more leverage to play foreign direct investors off against each other over issues such as technology transfer. Of most significance is Badaracco's view that it is becoming harder to identify where the boundaries of individual large firms lie, a factor that potentially hinders government efforts to restrict the outflow of scientific knowledge deemed politically sensitive or strategic. The issue of identifying the borders of firms is taken up by Kogut and Zander, in arguing that their domestic and international growth is a product of technology transfer. In other words, firms grow by their 'ability to create new knowledge and to replicate this knowledge so as to expand their market' (Kogut and Zander 1993: 639). The transfer of knowledge to subsidiary firms is dependent on the efficiency by which a firm can transfer knowledge compared with its competitors. This follows from the degree of tacitness of the knowledge and the experience required to assimilate it. In other words, they challenge the idea that knowledge is a public good with zero marginal cost in its transfer. Strange similarly challenges this idea, noting that, unlike the control of production or credit, knowledge can have strong characteristics of a public good, but it is not 'truly a public good in the sense that the term is used by economists, for the value of the supply to those already holding the knowledge may well be diminished when it is communicated to others' (Strange 1988: 118). Thus Kogut and Zander (1993: 629–30) see the migration of knowledge as involving costs accruing from 'codifying and teaching complex knowledge to recipients', and this leads to a situation of firms specialising in the transfer of tacit and idiosyncratic knowledge. The view that knowledge is not a public good can also lead to the logical conclusion that trading in knowledge within an industry, especially in the form of know-how, is a significant phenomenon (von Hippel 1991; Alic 1993). This general conclusion is supported by Dunning who observes that, at least within the industrialised world, 'the amount of intra-industry trade in knowledge and information has risen sharply', with no one nation having a 'technological hegemony' (Dunning 1993: 11).

All this makes establishing sources of power difficult. The erosion of the borders of both firms and states (see Palan, this volume) may make it difficult to discern discrete 'actors' of relative influence. In terms of the knowledge structure, this reinforces a structural image of a transnational network with 'diffused sources and agents that contribute to the global political economy' (Guzzini 1993: 456–7). It may of course be possible to identify hubs within such networks from where intentional and non-intentional power derives. On a larger canvas this is part of a range of broad and interrelated changes taking place in the primary structures of the global political economy. The process of globalisation (Jones 1995) reflects rapid transformation in the structures of production, finance and knowledge (Cox 1987; Stopford and Strange 1991: 32–64). The erosion of the borders of states and firms adds to the general complexity in establishing the distribution of power in bargaining situations

(Stopford and Strange 1991: 214–18), and in determining the characteristics of structures as they evolve – a dimension of structural power.

If the study of IPE is to progress, in addressing technological change in the global political economy, it must take on board (international) business studies contributions (Stopford and Strange 1991) as well as developments in economics. Although not introduced here, the same should be said of sociological discussions and historical study of technology and science. However, interdisciplinarity is not without costs. IPE is already a broad house as it is. This expansion of interests will be at some expense. As no study can cover everything we become more focused on issue areas, sectors, or phenomena like technology in this instance. Nevertheless, it is possible to illustrate how combining the literatures from the economics of innovation, international business studies and IPE can be lucrative. Generic technologies are of interest to all of these areas because of their pervasiveness in the global economy. The following section will examine generic technologies within the context of global technological changes and innovation processes. The exposition of the importance of generic technology is enhanced by applying an interdisciplinary focus.

GENERIC TECHNOLOGY

It is the breadth of their impact or *potential* impact that make generic technologies, 'which are capable of being put to multiple uses' (Dunning 1993: 5), of particular interest. Technologies of the same genus, that are seen to influence a wide range of industrial activities and which may even create new industries, are almost by definition founded upon migratory knowledge. Radical breakthroughs may of course initially depend on researchers' embedded expertise (such as the skills of publicly funded microbiologists in the early 1970s prior to the development of genetic engineering). Subsequent dissemination of the knowledge may continue through public networks, inter- and intra-firm activities. Thus in biotechnology we have seen numerous alliances between firms, often across national borders, and often involving hesitant established firms and adventurous new start-ups. Yet at some stage the generic technology must become migratory despite frictional difficulties. This affects the operations of firms as Dunning notes:

> As recently as 20 years ago, only a rudimentary knowledge of a limited range of technologies was required. Not so today, when an understanding of the interaction between a variety of generic technologies and the materials on which they are based may be key ingredients to success.
>
> (Dunning 1993: 13)

Competition in markets becomes centred on ways to apply the generic development for specific concerns or 'consumer needs'. Generic industries can display elements of both continuity and discontinuity in their impact on global economic processes. Both information technology and biotechnology have depended on specific technological breakthroughs (micro-chips and gene splicing for example) but have subsequently displayed characteristics of continuous improvement and impact. Generic innovations can have an early impact in some industrial activities, while there are notable lags in the impact elsewhere. Who would have supposed the laser would come to be at the heart of a system for playing recorded music? (BBC 1994). More speculatively, if Schumpeterian or Kondratieff long waves are considered, generic technologies may be factors in the clustering of technological developments that go beyond new technological paradigms, triggering new growth cycles, new techno-economic paradigms or indeed leading to Foray's (1993: 3) 'dazzling contribution to the wealth of nations'. Information technology is possibly this significant (Carnoy *et al.* 1993). A report produced for the OECD in 1989 endorsed the view of biotechnology representing a new technological paradigm and provides a speculative analysis of its potential to usher in a new technological system or techno-economic paradigm. Nevertheless, it injects caution in making long-term predictions of the ultimate impact of biotechnology, noting the difficulties in identifying trends in the pervasiveness through different sectors (OECD 1989: 44–55).

Using the concept of technological system, however, does suggest *interrelatedness* between technological components such that 'the features and the behaviour of each component of the system influence the features and the behaviour of the other components with strong qualitative effects that are not fully reflected by price signals' (Antonelli 1993: 194). Antonelli, for example, analyses information and communication technologies in terms of interdependent diffusion, externalities and complementarities within a broader technological system, which affect products, processes and uses. Technological systems can be described in relation to technologies of considerable complementarity or, more broadly, in terms of the interrelatedness of industrial sectors (Dosi 1984). Further, the impacts are not confined to the 'present' system but diffuse through 'generations' of technology leading to potentially new technological paradigms and new technological systems. The study of technology within the field of economics may have looked at particular innovations with respect to issues of *causality*, highlighting paths of technological development and the place of technology in terms of markets (extensively surveyed by Dosi 1988). In contrast, a focus on generic technologies and technological systems requires explicit acknowledgement of *interdependence*. Such a focus also encompasses discontinuities in technological advance and diffusion (Farrands, this volume). Assuming a situation of interrelatedness between sectors, Dosi suggests far-reaching implications:

> The emergence and establishment of new technological paradigms is likely to be correlated with a substantial body of untraded knowledge and experience.... Much of this knowledge, although untraded, might, however, be appropriable.

> (Dosi 1984: 288)

Untraded technological advantages might be thus an asset to a state; oligopoly may represent efforts to internalise untraded elements of technological change; and, in line with Badaracco, technological interdependencies might be a driving force behind the diversification of companies. His next conclusion is of great significance to the conceptualisation of the knowledge structure:

> Even if intra-firm international diffusion is rapid, as long as country-specific advantages reproduce themselves through time, the country of origin is likely to maintain a relatively favourable trade position.
>
> (Dosi 1984: 290)

In other words there is great incentive to acknowledge the importance of competing for a place at the 'leading edge' of advanced technologies (Carnoy *et al.* 1993), many of which have generic characteristics – with multiple uses derived from the same basic technological development. This directly links to the relative power of national groups within the knowledge structure and for some states their position may be such that they have structural power, whether intentional or non-intentional. Consequently, there are grounds to suggest that it is possible to identify hubs in the transnational knowledge network from which industrially articulated generic knowledge diffuses. Biotechnology is a case in point. The origins of much success in the new biotechnology, since the early 1970s, lies with US publicly funded research in conjunction with start-up firms. Many larger firms, from around the world (including Europe and Japan), slower to embrace the new innovations, forged transnational relationships with US start-up firms and publicly funded research institutions (Daly 1985). A nation with a population sympathetic to a technological infrastructure is, therefore, more likely to host technologically oriented firms and to embrace the social transformations driven by pervasive technologies.

The path to technological pervasiveness is, however, influenced by more than just the economics and technical characteristics of the technology. For example, there are often complex issues involving 'technology transfer' from the public sector to the private sector as well as transfer from one country to another. National prowess in the technology concerned becomes of significance to governments, sometimes invoking their intervention to distort markets by various means and to speed the industrial take-up of innovations (Milner and Yoffie 1989). A politicised agenda of concerns may surround the social and cultural impacts of the new technology, where the relational and structural power of participants may be as relevant as the science and economics of the developments. Issues of social acceptability have dogged genetic engineering; information and communication networks may radically transform traditional work patterns; while already electronics and information technology change the way our children play and the way we are entertained (Youngs, this volume). There may also be social costs following economic restructuring as traditional industries become compelled to adjust to new technology or, more fundamentally, are replaced by new industries founded upon the advances.

Generic technologies are undoubtedly significant from the perspectives within economics and business studies that focus on technology and knowledge. Major inventions are involved, as well as lags in innovation and diffusion. In this, the diffusion process is particularly of interest because of the pervasiveness of impact. Should a generic technology, in isolation or in conjunction with other innovations, herald a new technological system or more immediately a new technological paradigm, then the structural power and shared orientation of those championing the new paradigm may be very significant in setting the societal and international ground rules. New technology clearly brings national and international policy issues (Skolnikoff 1993), but it is not clear who sets the running in issues of technological standards and other policy constraints. Biotechnology firms lobbied the Bush administration over the Biodiversity Convention to the effect that it was not adopted by the US until the arrival of the Clinton administration. Even then it was accepted with the intention of pressing for a retrospective interpretation of the Convention, favourable to US industrial concerns (Miller 1993). Such is the entangled nature of the international communications industry today (with the involvement of established telecommunications firms, new information network suppliers, software providers and governments), that it is difficult to even define a shared paradigm, never mind establish the global hub of structural power. Complex as all this may be, it is, nevertheless, of tremendous significance for the study of IPE. The field has for too long marginalised the place of technology and knowledge. There is enough of importance in generic technologies as a specific category to establish the case for further IPE attention, and Strange's framework offers a way forward.

THE IPE OF GENERIC TECHNOLOGY DIFFUSION AND IMPACT

Conclusions from this study are partial because it opens up a research agenda. The direction of this research must be to include a greater effort in IPE to incorporate the work of colleagues in other disciplines. IPE has always done this with the issue areas it has pursued in the past. However, an explicit focus on knowledge and technology is only beginning in the field, and the interdisciplinary search must also begin anew. The work of economists, examining technological dynamism, and business studies contributors, exploring the effects of technology and knowledge on the firm, must be noted. It is significant that colleagues in those fields are increasingly coming up against the concerns of IPE. Technological paradigms and the progression of technology can be located within the knowledge structure, with emphasis on the cultural and operational aspects of both relational and structural power. Of course as Strange reminds us, the knowledge structure is interdependent with the other structures of production, security and finance – all obviously influenced by technology.

This brief study also leads to the conclusion that the linkage between technology and globalisation is extremely important, but also subtle and complex. IPE takes a global orientation. Much of the field acknowledges the transnational aspects of the global political economy, albeit with quite different explanatory focus (Keohane and Nye 1977; Cox 1987). The structural framework of Strange is also sensitive to this. Structural power can be seen in relation to a global network coalescing around key positions. Thus Strange sees the US as centrally placed in the respective structures. The work of international business studies offers a new challenge to our conceptualisation. Many writers in recent years have challenged the traditional realist, or neo-realist, emphasis on the state as a political unit. State borders have undoubtedly eroded with globalisation. What must be added is a corresponding acknowledgement of a trend towards the erosion of the borders of large *firms*. However, it is all too easy to see the globalisation process as the extension of a westernised liberal market phenomenon. Much of the non-IPE literature addressed above is biased in this respect, which has added a distortion to the integrative effort, that subsequently must be able to cater with North–South issues amongst others.

Generic technology provides an excellent category of technology in raising IPE concerns because of the global pervasiveness of many of the examples. Its instrumental and cultural significance have been demonstrated although the impacts of these are not separable. Being in 'at the birth' of a new generic technology may reflect power of one sort or another. Being consistently in at the birth of new generic technologies represents structural power, assuming the ability to exploit this position. However, given our image of a diffused and permeated global political economy, the diffusion and diversity of generic technologies may be difficult to disentangle from the general processes of globalisation, including the instrumental and transcendental features. At best we might try to map the hubs of the transnational networks involved. Thus the competitive place of the US, Japan and Europe may be identified, not as states or regions, but as highly significant network hubs that display structural power. This power is not necessarily within the control of states or firms, but because of the effects *on other parts* of the transnational global system, is sometimes 'non-intentional' structural power.

NOTES

1   This listing is not without its problems. Space technology for example represents 'big' technology, dependent to some large measure on government for sponsorship and direction, while biotechnology has in contrast been described as 'high intensity' science (Ravetz 1979), where activity takes place at many levels and in many diverse public and private locations. Information technology (and biotechnology to an extent) cover many earlier-generation activities and represent their own clusters of technologies in some measure.

2 Nearly all of this effort falls within a methodological stance rooted in positivism. Their debates, while highly relevant to our concerns, are nevertheless not greatly at odds with the general concerns of the professional economist. Unfortunately, a positivist methodology limits the scope for introducing political, social and cultural insights because values and culture within social groups, the effects of which are empirically observable at one level from the outside, include an intersubjective dimension, inaccessible by a positivist methodology (Kratochwil and Ruggie 1986; Murphy and Tooze 1991a; Gill 1993). This is not to denigrate such contributions but to locate them within a positivist tradition which, despite limitations, still has much to offer.

3 Parts of the above discussion of Dosi's concept of technological paradigm, its modification and potential linkage with the knowledge structure, have been expanded elsewhere (see Russell 1995).

5 The end of the dinosaurs?

Do new technologies lead to the decline of multinationals?

Gerd Junne

With the implosion of communism, post-war history has come to an end. The introduction of new technologies and the acceleration of technological development since the 1970s have certainly contributed to the collapse of communist regimes. Many observers hailed the collapse as the final victory of capitalism over socialism. Capitalist corporate economies seemed to be the undisputed winner. But this may be a misperception of what actually happened. Much more might have crumbled than just centrally planned economies. What is in crisis are large bureaucratic structures in general, which have difficulties in adapting to the rapid change which the world has been undergoing since the 1970s. Giant multinational corporations, rather than being the big winners after the demise of communism, might just be next for the chop. They may be too similar to the large combines into which many of the socialist economies were organised. As a result, they may not be much more viable than corporate structures in socialist countries finally turned out to be.

In this contribution,[1] I shall argue, first, that the *introduction of new technologies within large corporations* has not only intensified control by central management over the different parts of a corporation, it has also contributed to a trend towards decentralisation: it has empowered individual units within corporations. Second, the *introduction of new technologies into the environment of large corporations* has very much fostered this trend towards decentralisation, because rapid and unpredictable change necessitates fast reactions, which are only possible with short decision-making procedures which are inhibited by elaborate corporate hierarchies. Third, I describe the *proliferation of small companies* which may go much further than our official statistics reveal, if we take into account that business units within large corporations have increasingly to act as if they were rather independent. They may in the future more resemble small independent companies for which the fact that they form part of larger corporate structures may matter less and less. Finally, I shall discuss some of the *economic and political consequences of these changes* at the national and at the global level.

APPLICATIONS OF NEW TECHNOLOGIES IN MULTINATIONAL CORPORATIONS

New technologies that were introduced on a large scale in the 1970s were all related to electronics, especially information technology. It is still first and foremost this cluster of technologies which has widespread social and economic consequences; other new technologies have not yet reached the stage in which their application has a far-reaching impact on society.

New technologies were first introduced in manufacturing and used to automate the production process in a new (flexible) way. This had considerable consequences for the international division of labour, since it helped to reduce the share of labour costs in total production costs and thus slowed down the shift of industrial production to low-wage countries, especially in South-East Asia.

More important for the structure and future of multinational corporations (or large corporations in general), however, were the somewhat later applications in *streamlining the flows of information* within the corporation.[2] This gave top management a more direct access to much information compiled within the company, especially at the cost of the many layers of middle management which became redundant in this process. It seemed, therefore, that the new possibilities to centralise information would help top management to centralise control, and to some extent this happened in many companies.

However, the information which can be centralised in this way is only a small part of the information which is necessary for successful decision making. It is comparatively easy to centralise information flows on financial assets, on orders, sales, production, stocks, and capacity utilisation, etc. This kind of up-to-date information can provide central management with the *illusion of control*. They have the kind of information which is supplied to the participants of management simulation games. They know what *is* in their company, but they do not know what *could be*.

In a situation characterised by continuous rapid change, managers need another type of information, which cannot easily be computerised but necessitates face-to-face contact with staff at the operational level. They need information on future market opportunities, new production possibilities, technological changes, adaptiveness of staff and hardware to new products and production processes. Without this information, they can take decisions on their computer screens, but often these decisions will not be implemented.

This type of 'soft' information is often available at the operational level. But in most organisations, it does not reach the top, because the structures and forms of communication impede the flow of this type of information (see Roobeek 1993).

In order to take adequate decisions, both types of information have to be combined. An increasing number of corporations has come to the conclusion that it is easier to combine this information at the operational level rather than at the top of a company. With access to the type of data that until now was only available to top management, lower echelons can bring the 'hard' and the 'soft' information together and react rapidly and in a flexible way to changing circumstances. These organisations tend to be much more successful than those that try to centralise all flows of information, but thereby create an overload which inhibits fast decision making.

It is for this reason that the concrete use of information technology in large corporations finally tends to empower decentralised units, rather than decentralising operations while centralising control.[3]

This trend contributes to the trend towards a 'horizontal corporation'. This is a corporation in which traditional hierarchies have by and large been replaced by self-managing teams which are organised around specific processes rather than rigid tasks (Byrne 1993b).

THE NEED TO ADAPT TO RAPID TECHNOLOGICAL CHANGE

It is not only the *internal* use of new technologies that has a strong impact on corporate structures. Companies have to adapt to technological (and other) changes in their *external* environment, and this implies changes in corporate structures as well.

The introduction of new technologies has increased the volatility of many aspects of the external environment. Productivity increases were large throughout the post-war period. However, in the 1950s and 1960s, changes had been more continuous, in the same direction, so that they were easier to predict. Now, many changes are discontinuous and less predictable.

Part of this is related to a fundamental change that has taken place in basic economic mechanisms. Most economic processes are characterised by declining returns to factor inputs. The more input, the more the output per unit of input (capital, labour, etc.) will decline. Declining returns lead to equilibrium situations. But actually some parts of the economy, especially the high-technology sector, do not experience diminishing returns any more that would lead to an equilibrium. Instead, 'high technology is subject to increasing returns' (Arthur 1993: 6). The company which is able to bring a specific new product to the market first may reap large benefits. Prices for the new product are still high. If a company invests large amounts of capital, it can even determine the industry's standards. The higher the investment, the larger the scale of production, the lower the price can be for the individual product, and the better will be the competitive position. Japanese electronic companies have in many instances invested strongly in targeted markets, acquiring dominance in many sectors of the industry in this way. For the latecomer, on the contrary, it may be difficult to earn the original investment back. Prices will have fallen, markets are more saturated, foreign standards are established, and competitors will have advanced a long way along the learning curve, making it difficult to catch up.

Processes in which increasing returns play a role are often highly unstable. This invites state intervention, which makes developments even less predictable. To cope with these uncertainties, companies merge or conclude strategic alliances, which can alter the ballgame in any given market from one day to the next and introduce yet another element of unpredictability.

Headquarters managers in large corporations are not only out of touch with what really happens on the workfloor of their own working companies, they are also mostly unaware of the specific ins and outs of the changes in the particular environment for a concrete product group. Bureaucracies in large companies are out of touch with the consumer, and too unwieldy to coordinate change.[4] Therefore it is necessary that they restrict themselves to the broad lines of strategic orientations, but leave more detailed decisions to those responsible for specific fields of operation.

THE PROLIFERATION OF SMALL COMPANIES OR RELATIVELY INDEPENDENT BUSINESS UNITS

The old assumption about the permanence of corporations is no longer valid. Especially during the last two decades, many bluechip companies disappeared. Some were devoured by others in friendly or unfriendly mergers, and many were broken up during the 1980s in a predatory series of raids, in which companies or even individuals, backed by enormous credits from banks, 'aimed to break up their victims and sell off their limbs, rather than join them to others' (Sampson 1989: 42).

We can see that the average size of industrial firms in industrialised countries, as measured by the number of employees per establishment, increased up to about 1970, but then *declined* again. There are differences from country to country and from sector to sector, but all in all, an identifiable trend exists. In an analysis of firm-size in the United States (based on measures of employment), there was no noticeable shift in the size distribution of firms between 1976 and 1986. However, within the manufacturing sector a pronounced shift in economic activity away from large firms and towards small enterprises has taken place (Acs and Audretsch 1991). In the engineering sector, the mean firm and plant size has dramatically fallen, and there has been a marked increase in the share of sales accounted for by small firms.[5]

There are, of course, many forms of indirect control of one company by another (see Ruigrok and Van Tulder 1993), and if these manifold lines of control are taken into account, the trend may be somewhat less pronounced. But still it does exist, because it may be less and less in the interest of the larger company to exercise full control. And, on the other hand, large companies (which, after all, continue to exist) have to behave more and more as if they were composed of smaller companies.[6]

Unilever, for example, recently had to move its headquarters to new premises. In spite of the fact that Unilever continues to grow at a breathtaking speed (the company swallows about two other companies *every week*), premises for headquarters had become *too big*. Unilever had encouraged its subsidiaries to no longer fall back on central services, but to see whether they could get such services at a lower price elsewhere.

As a counter-tendency to the wave of mega-mergers and acquisitions which has characterised the last ten years, many companies, on the contrary, started to break up voluntarily. Often the split into rather independent divisions is a step on the way to the break-up of the group.[7] There are different motives for doing so in any individual case, e.g. regulatory reasons (as in the case of the split-up of AT&T and the creation of the seven 'Baby-Bells'), the incompatibility of different research traditions (as in the cases of ICI and Eastman Kodak), a move to keep part of the company unaffected by negative publicity of another (as in the case of the American tobacco industry,[8] where the tobacco branch becomes isolated from other company activities), or efforts to get rid of legal obligations (as in the case of the German steel concern Krupp, which could avoid the strong worker participation in decision making, mandatory for large firms in the German coal and steel industry, by splitting up into components, none of which reaches the critical threshold). But mostly, another rationale is stressed, as in the case of the recent reorganisation of the German airline Lufthansa, which turned its divisions into subsidiary companies.[9] Many companies claim that they split their operations in order to achieve greater market orientation, shorter lines of decision making, increased flexibility, and more rapid reactions to external change.

It is this change *within* corporate structures which makes it difficult to come up with statistical evidence on the trend proclaimed. While there are statistics about the number (and size) of nominally independent companies, this does not say anything about the degree of dependence on other companies. They may be fully controlled subsidiaries of large companies without any leeway for independent decision making. Individual divisions or business units of large corporations on the other hand, while not being independent legal units, nevertheless may enjoy a larger freedom than legally independent companies. Therefore we can only illustrate our argument with examples, but not provide conclusive statistical evidence that would 'prove' the trend.

If we look at the actual discussion in the management literature, we can see that most of the current buzz words refer to or imply *smaller size*, whether this is

1 time-based competition;
2 unit management;
3 core competence;
4 learning organisation;
5 network organisation;
6 flat organisation;
7 integration of functions, or the like (cf. Witteveen 1994).

One of the latest approaches is the trend towards the 'virtual corporation' (Davidow and Malone 1993; Byrne 1993a).[10] This is a temporary network of independent companies, linked by information technology to share resources in carrying out specific projects. Companies would use information technology to join in temporary partnerships with others in order to grasp specific market opportunities.[11] If it becomes widespread, the virtual model could become the most important organisational innovation since the 1920s (Byrne 1993a). It would enable small specialised companies to join forces with others, spread the risks of costly operations, and compensate for the specific deficiencies that they have. The 'model' for such networks can be found in the present-day film industry, where a producer for every new film will contract a director, hire a camera team, rent a studio and bring together the actors necessary for a specific cast. Once the film is made, the team dissolves again.

Taking this trend to its limits, one could speculate that 'we are approaching an *economy of one-person organisations*' of specialists who combine in ever new permutations with others to carry out specific tasks (*Fortune*, 4 April 1994).[12]

Whenever we think that we can identify trends, we should try to be explicit about the limits of these trends – in time, space, and sector-wise. The trend towards smaller companies may hold true in fields where 'economies of scope' become more important than 'economies of scale', but not in those areas where large numbers of more or less identical products continue to be produced (to some extent we find it even here, because the end product – for example a car – may more and more consist of modules produced by independent suppliers). In manufacturing, the material flow of products through an assembly line keeps different parts of the production process together. But with a decreasing share of manufacturing proper in total added value and an increasing share of all kinds of 'services' even in 'manufacturing' companies, it becomes easier to break up the total into activities carried out by different companies (or divisions). The trend towards a 'service economy' thus may bring the trends described in this contribution more to the fore.

But will the trend continue forever? The argument is largely based on a quick pace of continuous technological innovation. This is typical for the first phases of a 'long cycle', when the introduction of new basic technologies sparks off a whole series of innovations throughout the economy. This cycle, however, may come to an end, and ripening technologies and saturated markets may lead to a long recession. While small companies have a number of advantages in good times, large companies are relatively better off in bad times. Consequently, in a period when the introduction of new technologies slows down, the trend indicated here might be reversed.

It is an open question, however, whether we shall see a repetition of the historical 'long cycles' in the future. It might well be that the development and introduction of new basic technologies now begins long before the impact of the last basic innovations tapers off. This would imply that the different S-shaped curves of innovative activity due to new sets of basic technologies follow each other at shorter intervals, and that new developments are well under way when the stimulating effects of former basic innovations start to be felt less. The most successful companies actually tend to be those companies that do not wait until other companies outcompete their products, but replace their own products by better ones while they are still market leaders. As long as the accelerated pace of technological development continues, the trend towards smaller companies (or more independent business units) which are better able to jump on new opportunities is likely to continue. Only a major recession which would make it difficult for smaller companies to get access to capital would probably interrupt this trend.

MACRO-ECONOMIC AND POLITICAL CONSEQUENCES

The proliferation of relatively independent business units – either independent companies, or subsidiaries of larger companies which themselves take strategic decisions – has very far-reaching macro-economic and political consequences, both at national and international level. If, for example, a large number of companies simultaneously embarks on a 'lean and mean' strategy, it is obvious that large-scale unemployment will result.

In this section, four different kinds of impact will be discussed:

1 macro-economic consequences at national level;
2 macro-economic consequences at global level;
3 political consequences at national level;
4 political consequences at international level.

1 Macro-economic consequences at national level

A larger number of smaller companies makes me expect that there will be larger business-cycle fluctuations: small companies are more adaptive. They probably react in a more flexible way to market signals. That exactly is their advantage with regard to larger companies. The latter absorb some of the economic shocks. They are expected to carry many of their employees through a crisis. Some of them have an explicit policy not to lay off anybody. Smaller companies often cannot afford such principles.

Less cushioned by the absorptive capacity of large corporations, the amplitudes of business cycles may become larger. The cycle length, however, may become shorter for the very same reason: since small companies can be expected to be better able than large companies to climb out of the crisis and to take new initiatives, their activities may help to overcome economic crises quicker than might have been the case otherwise. (Whether this really is the case, is an unanswered empirical question. One could also argue that smaller companies do not have the resources to practise a kind of countercyclical behaviour: if their income is low because of a recession, many of them will not be able to take initiatives which will help to get the economy out of the crisis.)

Amplitudes of business cycles will become larger, but the cycle length might become shorter. If, with decreasing size, barriers of entry become smaller, then competition will increase. Competition will increase even in oligopolistic markets, because even the competition *within* large corporations (between business units) is going to increase. Figures on overall market shares which do not take internal corporate structures into account, thus may not convey a true picture of the intensity of competition.

2 Macro-economic consequences at global level

Since many companies will be less tied to a kind of conglomerate, they will look for their supplies beyond the corporate borders and try to get them wherever they are cheapest. Very often this will be abroad. Thus the proliferation of small companies will lead to an intensification of international links between national economies.

It can also be argued that small companies, on the contrary, will be more inclined to look for local or regional suppliers, because they are less able to afford the transaction costs involved in international or even intercontinental transactions. However, this is probably less and less the case. With the expansion of electronic data banks, even small companies have good access to international information systems, and where the companies themselves lack the capacity to look for foreign partners, their banks (or chambers of commerce and other institutions) will help them. While international business connections used to be a privilege of size, they are increasingly open to a broad range of companies (UNCTAD 1993).

In order to survive, small companies will often have to specialise much more than larger companies. Being highly specialised, they will more often than not find their national home market too limited and will be forced to internationalise. For the same reason, they can internationalise successfully, because they probably have a competitive advantage in their field of specialisation and can create product niches (see Acs and Audretsch 1990: 150).

As a result, one might expect that small firms would, on the input as well as the output side, depend more on international markets than other firms, and thereby contribute to the further internationalisation of national economies.

However, they are not able to use the spread of their international activities in the same way as large integrated companies. Multinational corporations have often been accused of 'creative' transfer pricing practices in international intra-firm trade – to transfer profits, avoid taxation, or anticipate exchange rate changes (see Murray 1981; Eccles 1985). If, however, the units at both ends of the transaction have become independent profit centres, it becomes much more difficult to manipulate transfer pricing, because each unit will want to maximise its commercial benefits. Thus intra-company prices will resemble the arms-length prices of transactions between truly independent companies. Even if more independent business units do not insist on arms-length prices out of their own profit interests, company headquarters may order them to do so to set the price signals correctly which, especially in a quickly changing environment, may be important for the long-term survival of a corporation. As a result, internationalisation by a larger number of relatively independent firms (or business units) might lead to less destabilising results than the international expansion of large corporations.

Finally, the process of 'descaling' might open up new opportunities for developing countries. Insofar as necessary scale is a barrier of entry for many firms in developing countries, industrial activity might become more evenly spread internationally. Alcorta (1994) discusses this possibility. He comes to a negative conclusion, which may be correct, but for different reasons than those that he puts forward. He concludes that while 'optimal' product scales may be falling, this is not the case for plant and possibly also firm scales, which he sees increasing. This is contrary to the basic assumption of the present contribution. His sceptical conclusion with regard to the possibilities of developing countries, nevertheless, is probably correct – not for reasons of the necessary plant and firm size, but due to the fact that highly specialised small firms can only survive in an environment in which a host of other firms can provide the services and inputs that the specialised firm cannot produce itself. Developing countries often lack this 'tissue' of complementary economic activities in which specialised small firms can thrive. Another problem is that these firms would need a highly skilled and flexible labour force which is often not sufficiently available in developing countries.

3 Political consequences at national level

Smaller companies are much more dependent than larger companies on a smooth functioning of the social system of which they form part. They are much more dependent on the *external provision of inputs* of all sorts (supplies, educated labour, health services, social insurance, information and network contacts, social peace). They depend more than large companies on the state guaranteeing the social conditions of production.

We may therefore expect that there is going to be a *new demand for an active state*.[13] These pressures will not only result from the reduced ability of companies to create and maintain the social conditions of production, but also because of larger business cycle fluctuations (see sub-section 1 above) and a higher degree of internationalisation (see 2 above), which makes state intervention necessary to compensate those who are negatively affected by the more intensified international competition (see Figure 5.1).

However, the relationship between the different parts of a company will not necessarily be symmetrical. There will often remain a clear hierarchy in decision making. Although this hierarchy may play less of a role in day-to-

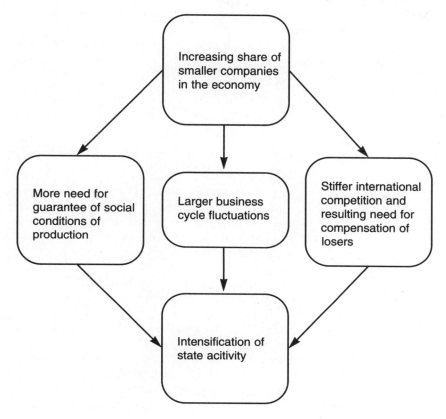

Figure 5.1 Political consequences of an increasing share of smaller companies in the economy

day management, the more strategic issues (including political influence on the company's environment) will mostly be decided at one centre.

Cox (1994) describes the change in corporate structures in the following way:

> The crisis of the post-war order accelerated the shift from Fordism to post-Fordism – from economies of scale to economies of flexibility. The large integrated plant employing large numbers of semi-skilled workers for the mass production of standardised goods became an obsolete model of organisation. The new model was based on a core-periphery structure of production, with a relatively small core of relatively permanent employees handling finance, research and development, technological organisation,

and innovation, and a periphery consisting of dependent components of the production process.

(Cox 1994: 46–7)

The more dependent the components remain, the clearer might be the political articulation of a company. Where the components get more independent, however, political articulation may become more diffuse as well.

4 Political consequences at global level

The pressure to intensify state activity will take different forms in different countries, given their divergent economic and political structures and different power constellations. As a result, state activities will differ from country to country in form and intensity, while becoming more intensive in general. More state-centric notions of the economy, however, will make it more difficult to continue the kind of 'managed multilateralism' which actually characterises the international economic system (Sandholtz *et al.* 1992: 176). The result might be 'managed rivalry' at best, or outright cut-throat rivalry and open hostility at worst, the concrete outcome depending on much more than changing corporate structures, of course.

However, this is not necessarily the case if increased state activity does not centre on central government, but if, instead, local and regional governments get more responsibilities. As a result, different communities, districts or regions within a country may compete with each other (and other regions in other countries), but there will be less pressure on central government to use protective instruments which would cause international tension and retaliation.

There are good reasons to believe that state functions, indeed, will increasingly be carried out by decentralised authorities rather than nation-wide central agencies. One of the reasons is that the same problems and trends that cause the break-up of large corporations also work in the public sector. Hoggett (1991 for example) has analysed the parallel developments in private business (the emergence of the 'flexible firm' with its different forms of decentralisation, teamworking and franchising) with decentralisation and quasi-market strategies by public agencies. The necessity to adapt quickly to fast-changing circumstances with different consequences for different regions has contributed to this shift in state activity. The more public tasks are shouldered by local authorities, the less they will cause international conflict between states.

The distribution of public tasks among different levels of authority, however, will not be the same in all countries. Different countries have different legacies in this regard and will show a different inclination to either centralise or decentralise responsibilities for public affairs (cf. Orrù 1994). These differences can lead to international as well as domestic conflicts in their own right. They can lead to international conflicts between the governments of countries with a centralised structure on the one hand and a decentralised structure on the other, when the regional and local authorities in the country organised according to federal principles do not apply agreements concluded at the international level. They can also lead to domestic conflicts within the less centralised country, when central and local authorities cannot agree on the applicability of clauses in international agreements.

The proliferation of small companies will thus intensify the trend away from 'managed multilateralism' to international relations characterised by more intensive international rivalry not only among states, but more generally among public bodies.

CONCLUSION

In this contribution, I have tried to show how the introduction of information technology within firms, together with the accelerated pace of technological development in the firms' environment, leads to a proliferation of small firms and more independent business units within larger firms. Such a change in corporate structures, in turn, has far-reaching consequences for the global political economy. It leads to larger business-cycle fluctuations with a shorter cycle length. That means that up- and down-turns of the economy will follow each other more quickly. Small companies will depend more than large companies on the public provisions of many inputs of production (venture capital, educated labour, raw materials, telecommunications and transport infrastructure, etc.). Their increasing importance, therefore, might lead to calls for a more active state (be it at a supranational, national or regional level). More active states, finally, may lead to increased rivalry among states and difficulties in managing the international economic system.

NOTES

1 I thank Annemieke Roobeek, Marianne Marchand, and the editors and contributors of the present volume for their comments on earlier versions of this manuscript.
2 The introduction of complex Management Information Systems (MIS), however, had also some counterproductive effects. Any MIS must resort to some 'subjective judgement in allocating overhead among the principal profit centres, in establishing transfer prices for products moving between divisions, in determining an internal cost for capital, and, in some instances, in allocating revenues from final sales' and in allocating overhead costs. Where the assessment of managers depends on indicators of success derived from such systems, it becomes rational for the individual manager to invest in negotiations on the system, because small changes may result in considerable improvements in gains and reputation – without any additional benefit to the company at large (see Ginzberg and Vojta 1985: 18).

3   The argument developed here does not contradict the contribution of Margaret
    Sharp in the present volume, where she shows that R&D efforts within large
    corporations are not spread to affiliated companies, but continue to be concen-
    trated in the home country. The partition of large companies into relatively
    independent units does not take place along *national* or *geographical* lines, but
    along *product lines*. This means that R&D continues to be done in the home
    country, but individual divisions may become more independent in deciding on
    the direction of R&D efforts.

4   See the example of the 'elephantine' bureaucracy at the world's largest retailing
    company, Sears (with more than 500,000 employees in the late 1980s), which
    created ample space for smaller, more efficient retailers (see Sellers 1988).

5   Acs and Audretsch (1990: 148). The 'size distribution of firms, and in particular
    the share of industry sales accounted for by small firms, varies across manufac-
    turing industries. The presence of small firms is found to be greater in industries
    where scale economies and capital intensity, as well as advertising and R&D, do
    not play an important role. There is, however, evidence that, by pursuing a
    strategy of innovation, small firms can at least somewhat offset their size-inherent
    cost disadvantages' (*ibid.*).

6   This is especially true in a sector like publishing, where the large publishing
    houses have to support the smaller publishers after takeovers, because they
    guarantee the best access to and maintenance of a good portfolio of authors.

7   An example is the recent reorganisation of the British car component manufac-
    turer and vehicle distributor BSG International into Britax International, which
    holds BSG's manufacturing operations, and Bristol Street Motors, which holds
    the group's vehicle distribution and servicing business (*Financial Times*, 27 May
    1994).

8   Many US tobacco manufacturers have been suffering downward pressure on
    their share prices because of increasingly intense opposition to smoking in the
    US, threats of anti-smoking legislation and lawsuits seeking damages for
    smoking-related diseases. Splitting off the tobacco operations from the non-
    tobacco part of the business is considered as an option for enhancing stock-
    value (*Financial Times*, 27 May 1994: 19).

9   Lufthansa has split its operations into Lufthansa Cargo, Lufthansa Technik and
    Lufthansa Systems (information technology), with EDS taking a share of 25 per
    cent in Lufthansa Systems Gmbh. The main company will only retain the finance
    department, the personnel department, and the two divisions of Passage and
    Operations.

10 The name is derived from the term 'virtual memory' which describes 'a way of
    making a computer act as if it had more storage capacity than it really possesses.
    The virtual corporation will seem to be a single entity with vast capabilities but
    will really be the result of numerous collaborations assembled only when they're
    needed' (Byrne 1993a).

11 A precondition is a national or even international telecommunication infra-
    structure linking computers and machine tools. This communications highway,
    together with common standards for swapping design, drawings and other work-
    in-progress, and informational data bases, would permit far-flung units of
    different companies to quickly locate suppliers, designers, and manufacturers
    through an information clearing-house. Once connected, they would sign
    'electronic contracts' to speed link-ups without legal headaches (Byrne 1993a).

12 With some time-lag, this trend follows the trend towards 'one-person households'
    in highly industrialised countries, as if there was some kind of entropy law
    functioning with regard to social organisations. Both trends have increased the
    development potential of capitalism by expanding demand. The trend towards
    one-person households has continuously expanded the demand for durable

consumer goods (TVs, refrigerators, washing machines, etc.), while the trend towards 'one-person business units' has expanded the demand for investment goods: small companies on average invest more per employee than large companies.

13 This does not yet say anything about the level at which state functions will be carried out: local, regional, national, supranational; or by which type of actors (public or semi-public institutions).

Part II

Technology as the foundation of international competitive advantage

6 Interpretations of the diffusion and absorption of technology
Change in the global political economy

Chris Farrands

The purpose of this chapter is to explore the argument that there are patterns of diffusion and absorption of innovations which shape the international political economy of technology change. The problem of how technologies are diffused, and how this shapes the flexibility, competitiveness and productivity of national economies, has been a central issue for at least a generation. As Reich (1992) among others has argued, it is increasingly seen that the basis of skills and expertise – human capital – across the global economy shapes the distribution of wealth and power. The process of technology diffusion, which means the diffusion of skills, licences, patents, know-how and techniques much more than the diffusion of machines, redistributes the capacity of firms and national economies to respond competitively to global change. The chapter falls into three main sections. The first is a review of the general idea of technology diffusion and its relevance to patterns of change in a global economy. Second are some specific cases of technology diffusion within firms and organisations, together with a discussion on diffusion processes in a particular sector, new materials; this empirical material is largely based on original work including interviews in the four organisations examined. The third part of the chapter is a consideration of some of the issues which these case studies seem to raise for IPE, where even those arguments familiar to students of technology policy are distinctive and relatively new.

Advanced technology industries are characterised by distinctive knowledge structures which explain their particular patterns of change and development. Strange (1988) has argued that knowledge structures are a main element which shapes relations in the global economy. Talalay and Farrands (1993) develop the idea that an understanding of knowledge structures is important in particular in looking at the relations between changes in the global political economy and technological changes. Other chapters in this collection look at the significance of Strange's argument from different perspectives (especially Russell). This chapter will explore the idea that the diffusion of innovations shapes the processes of change in the international political economy, strongly influencing but not determining the speed and direction of globalisation processes. Diffusion, it will be argued, can be seen primarily as a function of corporate activities, and the chapter will look in some detail at diffusion processes within major companies as a part of global change, although it is not claimed that all innovation diffusion can be reduced to intra-company relations.

In thinking about diffusion, we need to look at how knowledge is understood and received, how it is 'read' (cf. also Hall, 1993). But to understand the reception of innovations in the global economy will also demand a recognition that different organisations (firms, networks, public authorities) have varying capacities to absorb innovative knowledge. In some cases, the nature of the organisation itself may militate against or promote the reception of innovations: diffusion is thus a function of the capacity to absorb innovations. But in some cases the nature of the knowledge may be difficult to transfer because of factors in the collective understanding of the receptive culture, which block out innovative ideas. Successful innovative organisations may nonetheless suffer from a burden of having innovated too much or too recently to enable them to respond to further change, while other organisations may be in effect blind to innovations because of their investment cycle, or because of the priority of other business or financial demands. The ability to absorb innovations also depends on how innovative knowledge is structured, who has power over it and through what means, and what the pattern of competition and substitutability is for the innovative product or service. It depends equally on political and social constructions of what is acceptable or desirable, and on whose interests are threatened, as Underhill also shows in his contribution to this volume. The structure of competition is thus a shaping force in innovation, but, it will be argued, is in turn shaped in important respects by patterns of knowledge diffusion.

CONCEPTIONS OF DIFFUSION AND TECHNOLOGICAL CHANGE

Diffusion theories have an important place in the history of social science as a whole. They are significant not only as part of the history of the growth of understanding in the nineteenth and twentieth centuries, but also because they help us to draw back from the narrower focus of economics and technology to ask critical questions about the nature of diffusion as a whole and the underlying assumptions we make in academic research. There are a number of well-known 'diffusion problems'; their handling illuminates our thinking about links between cultural, economic and linguistic change (Benedict 1935). Thus one dilemma is the interpretation of the diffusion of a succession of techniques for metalworking associated with particular objects and levels of technical skill across the prehistoric Mediterranean. Chadwick (1958) shows how different assumptions about diffusion patterns led to different, and for a long time quite erroneous, theories about how to decipher Minoan Greek texts which held a key to the interpretation of much of the history of the end of the middle Bronze Age in the Mediterranean. An equally difficult and longstanding problem is the understanding of the

English settlement of Britain in the fifth and sixth centuries: how far did a set of 'English' communities replace Romano-British society by conquest? Or was the English settlement concurrent with a surviving Romano-British society at least in the countryside, a longer-term process of mutual absorption rather than a shorter and more violent confrontation? How were 'German' influences diffused through Britain? Martyn Whittock (1986) has shown how our understanding of the evidence for this has evolved as historians have moved away from a search for a unified theory to identify a much more diverse and varied pattern of occupation which mixed colonisation with occasional raids and with extensive trade and quite a lot of peaceful settlement. The answer to these questions depends partly on how far the analyst is prepared to accept messy and partial solutions rather than seeking to identify and then impose a uniform model which, given the available archaeological evidence, must link technology, artefacts, language and culture if it is to satisfy.

Nineteenth-century anthropology was deeply imbued with a set of assumptions about the relatively uniform growth of knowledge, with assumptions that with the 'right' techniques a whole mastery of the past is possible, and with a sense of ordered progress in the growth of knowledge. Benedict (1935) provides an early critical overview of these theories. These assumptions continued to influence understanding through the 'functionalist revolution' (which Palan also discusses in this volume). If, as Hall (1993) has argued, we have to review the way in which we think about our own conception of what constitutes and shapes 'knowledge' before we can make knowledge claims, this is nowhere more important than in discussions of interpretations of the diffusion of knowledge itself. This argument in effect echoes the views of Murphy and Tooze (1991a) and Stopford and Strange's (1991: 58) image of a 'bonfire of received ideas': we have to rethink ideas about technology diffusion if we are rethinking the relations between technology and the global economy, and in doing so we have perhaps to rethink what we hope we are looking for in theorising the subject.

IS DIFFUSION A PROBLEM AT ALL?

One view of the diffusion of innovation is that it hardly poses a problem at all, that innovations and the process of innovation move relatively easily around an economy, or would do so given reasonably efficient markets and the marketisation of knowledge, new products and new processes. Firms, in this view, do not have very long to exploit the characteristics of inventions unless they are able to build them into new products and processes through which they can achieve large first-entrant advantages in particular areas. But innovation as such does not create very great or very lasting advantages because it cannot, in this view, be protected. Even the existence of tighter intellectual property rules may not achieve the intended effect. This view of innovation assumes that any firms that want to adopt an innovation can do so relatively cost-free. It assumes that the opportunity costs of abandoning older existing technologies and knowledge, including the human skills which embody them, are relatively negligible. It also assumes that competition keeps firms relatively equally efficient in their use of capital, and ignores the distinctive role which human capital plays in innovation. The diffusion literature outlined in the next section has evolved out of a sense of the inadequacy of this orthodox neo-liberal view and the assumptions which it embodies. I would argue that firms do not in fact have an equal capacity to benefit from the innovations of others even if these are put on a plate in front of them. Firms and other institutions (networks, public bodies) have highly differentiated capacities to respond to innovation. Furthermore, in a global business environment, we should expect that differentiation to be that much greater, since knowledge is more imperfect, skills more varied, uncertainty higher, oligopoly more prevalent, and regulation more diverse.

The view of orthodox liberal economists – that innovation diffusion is relatively straightforward – also underestimates the importance of process engineering capacities in the management of change. And it underestimates the importance of people as holders of unique knowledge and understanding through their know-how. This creates in effect barriers to entry into new technologies, since firms or organisations which have innovated have not simply imported capital (machinery). Indeed, we have argued strongly that technological change is not simply or even primarily a function of machinery, and that technology is embedded in culture and in social practice, and that it can only be understood in this way (Talalay and Farrands 1993). An interpretation of technology-as-culture-and-organisation requires a distinctive view of technology change and the way in which diffusion may take place. It puts a much greater emphasis on possible barriers to diffusion, and implies that diffusion processes are processes of differentiation. In a global environment of technological change, this implies that globalisation itself is a process of differentiation, of the reconstitution of heterogeneity rather than one of convergence or homogenisation (Farrands and Talalay 1994). Innovation is therefore a real issue which requires serious study both as a management problem and as a cultural question, and forms an important element in our understanding of the place of technology change in the global political economy.

THE DIFFUSION OF INNOVATIONS

Freeman (1982, especially 214–18) provides a starting point for the discussion of diffusion, arguing within the framework of a Schumpeterian long-wave model that innovations are diffused in very particular patterns that derive from a complex of social, economic and organisational factors. He argues that technology diffusion is important in economic growth, unequally distributed over time and between companies and countries. It is promoted by market forces allied to elements of culture, belief systems, political power structures and the research base. The structure of economic growth and the pattern of recession and growth is crucial, but not in itself determining, of the pattern of the innovation system as a whole. At the time this work was published, this recognition of the importance of non-economic elements in innovative behaviour was relatively unique, but it has subsequently been developed in a wide range of studies. Stoneman (1982) developed a more orthodox economic explanation, but one which also recognises that there is a range of possible positions on how far strictly economic factors can explain diffusion patterns as opposed to behavioural models which seek to take account for a wider range of possible motives and goals between diffusing organisations and their environment. Parente and Prescott (1994) argue that we can understand knowledge diffusion as a function of the strength of barriers to the adoption of new technologies and techniques, and show that barriers impose costs which firms must overcome. In economies with larger barriers, firms innovate themselves or change more slowly; in systems which are more open and have lower barriers to diffusion, technology transfer rather than in-firm innovation or standing still is demonstrably more common.

Technology diffusion can take the form of knowledge transfer between regions or countries, and is in this form clearly an important issue in the promotion of economic development (Freeman 1982: 179–86; Reddy and Zhao 1990). Doval Adan (1992) explores the role of foreign direct investment in the growth of advanced technology industry in one of the most technically underdeveloped Spanish regions, Galicia. Stopford and Strange (1991) and Teece (1987) point to the importance of the growth of global oligopolies as forces shaping the spread of ideas and innovations in the world economy. Mansfield *et al.* (1977) and Sahal (1982) provide a body of argument over the nature of the transfer of knowledge from scientific research to industry and through industry from firm to firm and sector to sector. In general, the purpose of much of the literature has been to explore how far technology transfer and diffusion can be a factor in the growth and competitiveness (or failure to compete) of national economies (Porter 1990; Reich 1992; Cusumano and Elenkov 1994). Especially in Britain and the US, this has been an important question since the 1950s. But it is also a question which haunts important areas of the development debate in the Third World. There is a much larger literature on diffusion, but this summary at least starts to set the boundaries of an agenda for the purpose of this argument.

VARIED PATTERNS OF DIFFUSION WITHIN COMPANY STRUCTURES

Even in a short chapter, it is important to stress the variations of diffusion systems in the global economy. These variations owe something to cultural difference, but also depend on organisation and established patterns of business practice, ideas, entrepreneurship and firm strategy. Firms are clearly principal actors in this process, and we can illustrate the different ways in which firms are organised to manage innovation diffusion within their organisation. This section follows Dunning (1994) in exploring the diversity of firm behaviour in innovation as sectors become increasingly globalised.

Firms may not, of course, be the only agents of diffusion: other channels include inter-university exchanges, research contacts, and the system of publication and academic conferences. As Teece (1987) and Storper and Harrison (1991) have shown, the production system as a whole is a critical shaping force in the diffusion pattern. They also agree with Jovanovic and MacDonald (1994) that competitive structures in the market condition incentives to innovate, and show that those incentives vary in their impact not only inter-sectorally but also between different parts of large organisations and between firms in a given sector. More specifically, the system of patenting and licensing shapes important dimensions of diffusion processes, including the speed of diffusion and the relative costs of different kinds of innovation. However tightly firms try to protect their patents, new information and new techniques will be copied more or less quickly, and most patents probably have a 'real life' much shorter than their formal legal period as ideas and techniques are copied and as expertise leaks through the movement of key staff (Mansfield 1985). But among many contested claims about the globalisation of the world economy, it is clear that an increasing amount of activity is in the hands of global firms (which does not mean only very large firms). The pattern of global innovation is also shaped by relations within major innovating companies and research bodies, and amongst networks of firms where the particular structure of exchange and management of the network frames the distribution of costs and benefits amongst participants and hence the likely pattern of innovation within the network (Midgley *et al.* 1992). Particular cases suggest that there are very diverse patterns of innovation which depend on their organisation and management culture, on the way in which leading managers define their role, and on the structure of power relations within and between organisations.

These factors are not easily susceptible to economic modelling, and the more one looks at the detail of how diffusion processes work within companies, the more diverse they may seem. Four examples are considered here, although they certainly do not exhaust the possible ways of managing this problem. These examples are the Swedish-Swiss engineering firm Asea-Brown-Boveri (ABB), the transnational nuclear research organisation the Institute Laue-Langevin (ILL), the European groups of the computing firm Hewlett Packard, and BOC, a firm which was once a British Empire based industrial gases firm (British Oxygen), and which is now a genuinely global medical, pharmaceutical and chemical firm although it retains a base in high-value gas supply.

ABB was formed in 1988 out of the merger of two important firms which looked as if they were progressively losing their competitiveness, partly to compete more effectively in the European Community market, but also to maximise a worldwide potential (*Electrical Review*, 19 April 1989). Although organised around certain core technologies (transport, heavy machinery, defence electronics, electrical supply), the company is heterogeneous and faces serious problems in diffusing the results of its own research effectively from one part of the business to another. The company has evolved with a very distinctive 'flat' structure of organisation where there are no more than two layers of management between the top level and the main production units. Financial control is strict but innovation and experiment are encouraged. This requires a rapid and effective system of communication within the firm, and groups of researchers or managers with comparable interests who come from different parts of the structure are encouraged to meet. A system of financial and social incentives is designed to facilitate the movement of innovations around the group. But innovations are not 'traded' around the group as they are in many other firms.

In Hewlett Packard, the main pressure is also on promoting speed of innovation and of diffusion around the whole firm. HP have created an internal communications system (inevitably using their own hardware and software) to promote innovation exchange and debate. They also create a culture of continuous innovation through small research meetings in which all staff of all grades are encouraged to take part, with financial and other incentives for successful groups. Product divisions do not 'sell' innovations to others through an internal market within the company, but are given a kind of royalty on sales as an incentive. The first priority for HP is to innovate, and to have a culture of continuous change, but the whole structure and ethos ('the HP Way') is designed to enable not just individuals but also the firm as a whole to learn rapidly. Mistakes (at least within limits) are encouraged because they may teach lessons. If there is a 'key' to HP's ability to innovate rapidly it is the institutional learning capability which its organisational structure and culture creates rather than the absolute novelty of any particular innovation it has made, its marketing strength, or its ability to take technologies quickly from rivals and build them into its products.

The Institute Laue-Langevin is a joint European research institute in nuclear and fundamental physics based in Grenoble in France established by intergovernmental agreement. It provides a centre for British, French and German scientists to work together, although staff of other nationalities are admitted by invitation. ILL is intended first of all to be a centre of basic research, but it has assumed a major role as a centre for the diffusion of knowledge and, perhaps especially, of techniques, in nuclear research. In order to promote this diffusion, it has faced a series of conflicts between the culture and interests of the community of scientists involved and the concerns of government officials to exercise financial control and to ensure that important results with economic or security implications to not leak uncontrolled out of the institute. This creates a direct conflict of cultures and working methods which has led to repeated problems over staffing and management even though the centre has a deservedly prestigious record as a research centre. Insofar as the dominant culture is one of scientists who are anxious to work together and exchange results inside and outside the institute, and in so far as scientific research depends on the diffusion of results to other institutions in order for them to be replicated and checked or disproved, the ILL is a model of scientific and technological diffusion. But the conflicts this creates for the major stakeholders come down, very often, to the desk of the personnel managers, in what can be an acute form. This is very often expressed through threats of budget controls or cuts.

BOC has evolved from a national middle-ranking corporation to a large global player through concentration on technology clusters. It has sought to move from its traditional business – high-volume, relatively low-value gases for industries such as steel production – into the production of high-value gases for consumers in the medical and advanced technology industries. Through this growth it has shifted its technological emphasis to other healthcare products and medical equipment. Most of the growth occurred very quickly from the mid-1970s through acquisitions. The separate divisions were subject to a tight overall control by the now largely American management which promoted financial efficiency and often severe divestment strategies to get rid of activities which did not represent what were seen as core businesses. A key problem for the group has been to move ideas around where new innovations, especially cost-cutting process innovations, have been made in one part of the group. As BOC operations have become more worldwide in scope, this has become all the more difficult. But managers are primarily concerned with financial efficiency and believe that it does not matter very much whether innovations come from within the group or from outside, and the company has evolved what is in effect a full internal market for innovations: divisions and individual plant have the choice of buying in innovations at an effective market rate or of researching themselves if they believe they can achieve a result more cheaply. There is no central research coordination, and the belief is that a market within the group will deliver sufficiently quickly and more cost-effectively than a bureaucratic control of research and innovation. Management culture appears to be equally concerned to control expensive innovative zeal that cannot make a real rate of return as to promote innovation, an entrenched attitude that implies some suspicion, at least, of innovators. It also implies the powerful hold which accountants have over the strategy of the group as a whole.

Each of these firms is successful in its own terms and its own ways. If failures were considered (IBM and the Philips group would be good candidates), there is also a body of evidence, which there is not space to consider here, on the many ways in which failures of technology diffusion within global firms contribute to their difficulties. The point is however to note the variety of ways in which diffusion takes place because of the distinctive interaction of experience, organisational culture and management strategies, as well as the different market environments in which each operates, and to argue the inadequacy of models which suggest that diffusion is a relatively uniform process. It also suggests the significance of the interaction of economic, social and cultural processes in leading to specific outcomes in technology transfer within global companies. And, as Cusumano and Elenkov (1994) also suggest, it emphasises the importance of management's strategic response to these conditions in shaping innovation diffusion patterns.

THE DIFFUSION OF INNOVATIONS IN THE NEW MATERIALS SECTOR

As well as looking at diffusion processes in the global economy in major firms, it is important to consider whether sectors have distinctive characteristics which shape diffusion patterns. This discussion will look at the new materials sector, and also introduce the idea that the exchange of knowledge and technology in the global economy is a function as much of the capacity of actors (states, governments, networks as well as firms, research institutes and whole sectors) to absorb innovative processes and products as it is of factors which promote their diffusion. The new materials under discussion here include a range of relatively new products in plastics, ceramics and composite materials, often including those which have been designed or researched for the specific properties which they possess at the level of molecular structure. In other words, they are based on nanotechnologies, strictly speaking scientific capabilities to predict the properties of molecular lattices and other structures (Cohendet *et al.* 1988; Van Griethuysen 1987). New generations of materials have been evolved in the 1980s which are capable of bearing particularly high loads in one dimension or a variety of twisting and irregular loads: so, for example, a wide variety of new ceramic materials can withstand heat and twisting pressures in a way that metals on the whole cannot. Much of this innovation has its origins in the aerospace sector, but has been spread, at very different rates, to industries as varied as sports products (including clothing), building and construction, automobiles, rail and other transport, and engineering and food processing technologies. New materials are not necessarily uniquely new products. They often substitute for 'old' materials. As a result, the new materials which have been coming onto the market in the 1980s and 1990s are useful either because they have distinctive intrinsic qualities, or because of their environmental value, or where they can fulfil an existing function more efficiently (at lower cost) than existing products. While the science of new materials has moved relatively quickly in the last generation, their application has moved much more slowly, again except for aerospace applications. They have also created fewer new job opportunities than many more optimistic forecasts have proposed. This is a problem to explain.

In a previous study (Farrands 1990), it was argued that absorption patterns were crucial to the understanding of the diffusion of innovation, and that this was especially so in the case of new materials. Global and local, as well as internal and institutional constraints, all interact to produce specific absorption patterns in different industry sectors. New materials are a diverse sector in some respects, but the core technologies are similar. In particular, new materials technologies require the capacity to handle relatively small batches of production in highly skilled ways – to critically control levels of temperature, pressure, etc. in order to generate to a very high standard of reliability the specific molecular structures which ensure the characteristics for which the product is desired (Cross 1989). This requires know-how on the part of process engineers and supervisors rather than science or business skill. Note that I am not claiming that the premium on know-how is unique to new materials, for it is clearly important in other advanced technology sectors. Rather, I am claiming that the demands on process engineering and quality control in new materials design and manufacture is distinctive of much advanced industrial activity. This puts a particular emphasis on human skills, and thus also on the training support which those skills demand if they are to be renewed and retained. Equally, the lack of flexibility and receptiveness to innovation as a result of weaknesses of training or a lack of skills – weaknesses of human capital – provide barriers in the system of production which make all the more difficult the adoption of new materials technologies (Storper and Harrison 1991; Parente and Prescott 1994).

These brief but, I hope, relevant descriptive accounts enable us to identify some of the key elements which shape diffusion patterns amongst large firms and across sectors (for a more formal economic account see Stoneman 1983, Chapter 6). They also remind us of the problems of interpretation which were raised early in this chapter, and which form a particular problem for students of technological change in the global economy. How far do economic explanations in themselves account for the patterns of diffusion described above? How far do the particular histories of individual organisations and the ideas and culture which shape them explain the experience of diffusion? How far is any relatively uniform account of diffusion processes possible? What are the implications of this for the study of global political economy? Leaving aside the very broad question implicit in these issues of how an interpretative social science is possible, it is possible to identify from the 'stories' of participants underlying theories and arguments which can be used to construct an account, and this will be how this paper proceeds (for views of this methodology in international business see also Faulkner and Johnson 1992, especially Chapters 8 and 10; and Huff 1990; for a strong case for its validity in IPE, see Cox 1992).

NETWORKING PATTERNS AND INNOVATION DIFFUSION

'Networking' is a slippery concept. Colleagues may claim to have been networking furiously when they have simply been out to lunch. Some organisational theorists may look for a substantive body of normative cohesion as well as a level of common action in order to allow that a network has come into existence, and others look only for some shared interaction. But the cases discussed above show that contacts through networked links are often important in the minds of participants themselves as an explanation of how technology diffusion works in practice. The idea of network links and exchanges has hung around the literature on international political economy (and indeed, on international integration, but that is another subject) for a long time. Murphy and Tooze (1991) have suggested that it is all the more important to look at transnational networks and groupings if the study of IPE is to move more solidly away from a narrow predominantly realist agenda focusing on states and multinational companies. Hall (1993) makes a similar point in the context of the growth of social science understanding in the 1990s. But there is not a very substantial IR or IPE literature on the role of networks and groups, despite one pioneering effort by Cox and Jacobson (1974).

However there is a burgeoning literature on networking in the international business studies literature which offers valuable ideas for IPE. Faced with three problems – how to explain cooperative behaviour amongst firms which is not self-evidently or directly profit-seeking, how to explain the growth of clusters of firms around pools of shared knowledge, including especially technical knowledge, and how to explain the behaviour of small firms in seeking competitive positions in global business through various kinds of collaboration – scholars in the business community have produced a considerable body of analytic literature on networks and strategic alliances. This literature is important not least because it challenges the orthodox economic explanations of multinational company behaviour, and converges with other, more socio-political arguments, including some recently developed by Strange (1994a), who has argued for a greater attention to the different kinds of firm–firm relationships in IPE. Jarillo (1988) has argued that strategic cooperation amongst firms is motivated by much more than profit seeking, and that the satisfaction of particular interests within firms, especially amongst managers, and the need for spreading costs associated with technical innovation makes strategic cooperation more likely amongst advanced technology firms, both large and small. Johannisson (1987) has also stressed the social dimension of collaborative behaviour. Both argue that particular networks formed and maintained by individual managers are important structures which create commitments which constrain future conduct by the firm, and both stress the link between particular business cultures, firm organisation, network history and the prospects for the survival of the networks. These ideas derive in significant part from Williamson (1975), who argued that firms would in effect make rational choices between forms of cooperation and forms of competition depending on perceived cost structures, including the costs of getting and sharing knowledge. But the more recent literature has tended to move away from the formal rational action assumptions which imbue

Williamson's very influential book, and tend to stress the diversity of ways in which networking comes to be important for firms and stakeholders in them (Lorange and Roos 1992). Fletcher (1994) has developed most fully the idea that international relationships even between small firms or amongst managers of relatively limited experience can be significant and can be explained through the use of a strategic networking paradigm. These ideas have started to filter into the more general international business literature (e.g. Dunning 1993), and to shape the way in which sectoral studies are undertaken (e.g. Sandholtz 1992), but they leave open the opportunity for further exploration in IPE.

The networks created within certain firms (notably HP) are deliberately designed to promote diffusion, while ILL was primarily conceived as a diffusion network. Networking activity plays a key role in technology transfer (Reddy and Zhao 1990; Midgley *et al.* 1992). Networks are clearly often difficult to manage and to sustain (Mytelka 1991; Fletcher 1994), and they are often not efficient in a formal cost calculation. But they are seen as minimising risks through giving the firm access to certain kinds of knowledge, as well as giving managers and researchers a certain sense of control and power within their area of operation. As processes of globalisation of knowledge and technical programmes have evolved, the reasons for networking activity – and the level of networking activity we can measure (Lorange and Roos 1992) – increases. What is not so clear is what impact this growth of activity has in turn on the shape and direction of globalisation, and this is a subject for further future research.

THE IMPORTANCE OF INSTITUTIONAL LEARNING

The empirical parts of this paper have stressed, among other things, the importance of how, when, and why institutions learn as a factor in understanding the diffusion of innovations across a global environment. I have argued that institutional failings are crucial elements in understanding why technical change happens in fact in a widely heterogeneous fashion. This is because the capacity to absorb innovations varies much more than some theories would predict. This is not so original an observation for anyone working in any large organisation, including the higher education sector, where a great deal of the daily gossip concerns in effect the inability to learn or the pretensions to learn of senior management. Differentiated absorption rates are not random, and in the longer run they will depend primarily on the quality of human capital. But in the short run they depend on the culture and structure of organisations (cf. Dunning 1993; Faulkner and Johnson 1992). Institutional learning capacities are also a key element in shaping long-run economic performance in societies based on knowledge industries of the kind Abernathy and Utterback (1978) suggested and Reich (1992) has described. Their importance is also central to the discussion of the framing structures of the global economy in Strange (1988).

In the HP and BOC cases, institutional learning is identified as an issue, although handled in very different ways, which managers seek actively to control. In the ILL case, a great deal of learning and sharing goes on, but the culture of scientists which makes it easy to transfer new knowledge or techniques amongst individuals and work teams makes it more difficult to embed new technologies institutionally, and a relatively rapid turnover of staff makes it more difficult for ILL to retain many of the innovations it may have contributed to. In the new materials sector, weaknesses of absorption capacity has made it more difficult both to transfer innovations amongst firms and across different sectors where possible applications may arise. Thus absorption capacities are seen as a fundamental element in the rate of diffusion of innovations which explain why diffusion happens at a rate much slower than would often be anticipated by conventional market or 'innovation as output' theory. The consequences of this view need to be integrated into an account of international relations for two main reasons. First, because many of the structured obstacles to absorption are international. Second, because the potential impact of these differentiated and varied patterns of innovation shape international relations, at least in a non-realist sense. Innovations which arise from patterns of process engineering demonstrate a dynamic pattern of change across firms, networks and public authorities. Change reshapes the distribution of knowledge and power, even though it also reflects an existing pattern of knowledge and power. This argument also demonstrates the importance of human capital and investment in the understanding of a particular aspect of technology change, and so has implications for policy and for the ways in which networks as well as public authorities respond to change.

INTELLECTUAL PROPERTY RULES AND DIFFUSION PROCESSES

The formal regulation of technology diffusion processes both within the inter-firm structure and in the global political economy is managed through the system of intellectual property rules (IPRs), in which are included not simply patents and licences, but also copyright and the practices and procedures through which they come to be enforced. There is a substantial literature on IPRs (see for example on legal issues Meessen 1987; Stone 1989; Litman 1991; and Seyoum 1993; and on consequences for firms and for competition De Woot 1990; Sandholtz 1992; and Dunning 1993). IPRs provide a framework which is designed to manage a trade-off between the interests of investors and innovators. This trade-off presumably lies in striking a balance between intellectual property owners and the community as a whole. Keeping results as innovators' exclusive property allows them an exclusive right to get profits from them, or to deny knowledge to competitors. To maintain the interests of the community as a whole entails a more rapid diffusion of innovations to as many people or firms as possible, increasing the pool of technology – and presumably the total earnings – of an economy.

IPRs ensure that the unique ownership of innovation can lie with innovators for a given period of time, which provides some assurance that they can get both proper recognition for their achievement and a proper return on their investment within that period. IPRs do not guarantee secrecy of inventions, and they have a fixed time limit, although in the case of copyright (which also applies to computer software) that time limit is fifty years from the death of the author. IPRs are managed through international conventions, and have been relatively uncontroversial elements of international diplomacy until fairly recently.

However the contentious nature of control over intellectual property in advanced technology industries which are seen as key to national economic development, together with specific disputes over the control and management of technology (especially between the US and Japan), has soured the climate of what looked like a relatively stable dimension of international relations. The globalisation of technologies and firms has led to the globalisation of disputes over IPRs. Especially since the agenda was defined for the 1986 Punta del Este meeting which initiated the Uruguay Round of the GATT, IPRs have become a principal bone of contention in international negotiations.

For firms to invest in innovation, they have to have stable expectations about IPRs. Where they cannot benefit directly – for whatever reason – there is a clear argument for public investment rather than for private research. This applies, for example, where the lead time to exploit an innovation would be much longer than the time a patent would allow for the recovery of that investment cost. The difficulty of getting an adequate return in time in more complex kinds of advanced technology investment has also led firms to conduct research in groups – strategic alliances (Mytelka 1991; Midgley *et al.* 1992) – where they have some hope of making a return more quickly. IPRs do not determine investment and innovation patterns, but they are crucial shaping factors. For regulatory bodies, the most difficult problems have been to try to keep up with technological changes, especially as the relationship between computer software and computer hardware has evolved, and to try to control piracy and imitation as educated but poor societies (such as India and Taiwan) have sought to exploit their comparative advantages in a world market by copying everything from compact discs to engineering software for bridges or for swimwear. The rules are supposed to be clear; as in any area of law, lack of clarity undermines the rules altogether. But in practice, there are centres of power in the interpretation of the rules and there are centres of weakness. And there are also cases where deals struck to try to manage relations between particular power blocs (especially between the European Union and the US, and the US and Japan) have the most serious implications for other countries and their firms although the third countries affected have no genuine legal remedy other than to collude in the piracy and deviousness of their more ingenious but less scrupulous citizens (Farrands

1995). This is equally true of relatively developed and of less developed economies.

CONCLUDING REMARKS

This chapter argues that an analysis of diffusion processes is essential as part of an attempt to understand the international political economy of technological change. It accepts that one vital dimension of diffusion is economic. But it argues that economic understandings of diffusion processes are inadequate in themselves, and that business strategies and social and institutional processes also hold a central place in any explanation. It suggests that there is a diversity of patterns of diffusion of knowledge and know-how, and that if the focus is moved from diffusion to absorption we must start to ask questions about the culture, institutional power and organisational procedures of participants in diffusion systems. We can no more assume in IPE that firms have a single set of clearly defined goals than we can anticipate that governments have a unique common purpose. In coming to terms with the social processes which shape diffusion, this chapter has identified four main elements: the organisational structure of diffusing bodies; networking activity; intellectual property and licensing rules and the practices which surround them; and organisational culture and the institutional learning capacity which it facilitates. The chapter has also explored some of the implications which a discussion of diffusion holds for the ways in which we understand international political economy, and has an important place in any account we try to offer of the ways in which technology change and the global economy interact, no matter how uniform or diverse we hold that experience to be.

7 Technology, globalisation and industrial policy

Margaret Sharp

INTRODUCTION

Industrial policy has frequently been overtly mercantilist. The aim in each country has been to promote national well-being by creating and supporting national production by national corporations. The jobs, the income and the profits are all generated from the home base for the benefit of nationals, and governments have openly connived with corporations to make this happen.

What happens then when the company concerned has production facilities around the world and deliberately locates important parts of the process overseas in order to take maximum advantage from the availability of low-cost labour, cheap capital or other governments' subsidies? Such a situation is aptly illustrated by the following quotation from Robert Reich's *Work of Nations*:

> When an American buys a Pontiac le Mans from General Motors he or she unwittingly engages in an international transaction. Of the $20,000 paid to GM about $6,000 goes to South Korea for routine labour and assembly operations, $3,500 goes to Japan for advanced components (engines, transaxles, electronics), $1,500 to West Germany for styling and design engineering, $800 to Taiwan, Singapore and Japan for small components, $500 to Britain for advertising, $100 to Ireland and Barbados for data processing. The rest – $8000 – goes to strategists in Detroit, lawyers and bankers in New York, lobbyists in Washington, insurance and health care workers all over the country and General Motors' shareholders – most of whom live in the US but an increasing number of whom are foreign nationals.
>
> (Reich 1991: 113)

In such circumstances, what is the point of nationally oriented industrial policies? Are industrial policies of any sort any longer relevant? If so, what sorts of policy are appropriate and how may they be implemented?

The purpose of this chapter is to give more detailed consideration to these issues. It considers first what is meant by industrial policy, arguing that the traditional market-failure arguments fail to meet the conditions of a world in which much production and trade is concerned not with bulk agricultural commodities but with complex manufactured goods such as cars and pharmaceuticals. Advanced technologies reshape manufacturing, design and quality systems as well as providing new products, and have come to be at the heart of the industrial policy debate. The next section looks at the issue of globalisation and comes to the conclusion that although the picture Reich paints in the quotation above is an exaggeration of the degree to which 'globalisation' has taken hold, nevertheless there are trends towards increasing internationalisation of industrial activities which raise questions of regulation and control which cannot be dealt with by national policies. The final section pulls the two previous sections together and examines the division of function between national and international policy. National policy, it suggests, should be dedicated to maximising national value added, while policy intervention is now needed at the international level both to constrain the ambitions of global oligopolists and to contain the scope for system friction.

INDUSTRIAL POLICY, TECHNOLOGY POLICY AND MARKET FAILURE

Industrial policy, as suggested in the introduction, has all the overtones of mercantilism and corporatism. It is traditionally seen as government intervention, prompted by and for the benefit of production interests, often offering subsidies as an alternative to protection and, like trade protection, open to capture by production interests. For all these reasons economists have always regarded it with suspicion. Yet industrial policy should not be seen merely as interventionism, for in its broadest sense it brings together a whole raft of policies, ranging from competition policy, trade policy and company law to regional and structural policies, much of which has been of central interest to economists.

The focus of interest within this range of policies has shifted over time according to the issues which rise to the surface and attract attention. In the 1950s when Europe was reconstructing its industrial base after the ravages of the 1930s depression and the Second World War, the focus of attention was the traditional issue of firm size and productivity, European firms being unfavourably compared with the mass-production regimes of the US. By the 1960s, attention had shifted to technology, with the French in particular concerned that, without state intervention, Europe would become unduly dependent upon US technology. In the 1970s this debate was eclipsed by the problems of over-capacity as industries such as steel, shipbuilding and chemicals hit the first major post-war recession, which came in the wake of the 1973 oil crisis. With GATT commitments by then limiting overt protection, these industries sought shelter in a plethora of subsidies and support schemes (non-tariff barriers) which the OECD euphemistically labelled 'negative adjustment policies' for the very reason that they often inhibited the rundown and rationalisation which needed to be encouraged.[1] By contrast, the OECD was anxious to promote what it termed 'positive adjustment policies' – policies which helped the development of new growth industries to replace those in decline. There was, it was argued, more sense in subsidising the development of new 'sunrise' industries than alleviating the death throes of the old 'sunset' industries (OECD 1977). The focus of policy shifted in the 1980s sharply towards technology, with micro-electronics and telecommunications in particular in the forefront after the spectacular breakthroughs in miniaturisation of the 1970s. But biotechnology was also beginning to make an impact, as were new developments in ceramics and new materials (Sharp (ed.) 1985). In such a 'technology rich' environment, it is hardly surprising to find technology policy achieving a central position within the spectrum of industrial policy even if attention shifted from technology *per se* to diffusion and subsequently to the generic conditions which encourage innovation. There is also an element of self-reinforcement – the focus on technology policy itself raises the stakes, and countries mimic each others' practice. For example, part of the impetus behind the development of European policies in the mid-1980s was the success of Japanese policies to develop microchips in the 1970s. In the early 1990s, the Clinton administration cited the influence of both Japanese and European policies behind some of its new technology initiatives.

The economists' traditional justification for policy intervention in industrial issues has been market failure, with the argument focusing on questions of indivisibilities and externalities, public goods and infant industries. Recently a new incarnation of the infant-industry argument has emerged in the form of strategic trade theory, developed, as Krugman has said, to take account of the fact that today much trade is concerned with products such as aircraft rather than commodities such as wheat (Krugman 1990: 1). Krugman's argument relies essentially on externalities and is not so different from the early Marshallian analysis of the economies to be gained from agglomeration (Marshall 1919). Both have their rationale.

The traditional base for public policy towards technology has also been market failure. Basic research and its related infrastructure have been deemed to possess many characteristics of a public good – most importantly, *non-appropriability*, because its 'output' consists of widening the knowledge base and is by its nature non-patentable; and *non-depletability*, in that use of the findings by one person in no way limits access by others. As a result the normal incentives of profit are absent (if you cannot patent, you cannot claim ownership rights on inventions and hence make a profit from them). Hence, if it is considered that such activities are beneficial to society as a whole (which they are), action by the state to make good these market failures is justified. Such actions include public subsidies for basic research; the adoption of common technical standards for interfaces and networks; and penalties or restrictions on technologies which damage (or might damage) health, safety and the environment.

However, the market failure approach has its limitations. In particular, it relies essentially on the economist's traditional static framework in which technology is treated as an exogenous 'bounty' available to all comers at zero cost. If, on the contrary, it is recognised that technology is often complex, multidimensional, expensive to implement and specific to a particular firm, that a large part of it is tacit knowledge (i.e. passed on by word of mouth and not written down) and derives from trial, error and learning, rather than from the systematic application of science, then very different conclusions follow (Dosi *et al.* 1990):

1 It means that *technological development becomes cumulative in nature,* because learning by doing is so important. Firms and countries differ in their paths of technological development (often referred to as their technological trajectories) to reflect the cumulative pattern of production and skills acquired over time, and this in turn means that the inheritance of skills and capabilities itself often defines the field of choice open for exploitation (Patel and Pavitt 1991b).

2 It also means that *technology transfer and imitation are costly.* R&D and related activities in firms are not only about getting ahead of the competition, but also about catching up and keeping up, and this process is not costless (Cohen and Levinthal 1989). It is notable, for example, that the two countries which for the last decade have been allocating most resources to civilian R&D, Japan and Sweden, both excel in applying technologies pioneered by others, as well as developing their own.

3 It means that *countries may differ not only in the direction, but also in the rate of their technological development.* Contrary to expectations in the 1950s and 1960s, industry-funded R&D in OECD countries has not converged towards a notional (US) best-practice level. There is no single correct 'model' that can be followed. Since 1975, there has been divergence, with the UK and the US being overtaken and progressively left behind by Germany, Japan, Sweden and Switzerland (Patel and Pavitt 1991b).

4 Finally, it is worth noting that these characteristics of technology imply that *one of the main economic benefits from basic research* comes not from useful information embodied in papers, but *in the form of useful problem-solving skills embodied in trained researchers* (Senker and Faulkner 1991). Since basic research skills are in general less internationally mobile than published papers, countries that finance high levels of basic research are more likely to benefit from a build-up of such skills (Hicks and Hirooka 1991; Pavitt 1991).

It is interesting at this point to note that while policy prescriptions deriving from both market failure and the technology-based 'evolutionist' (broadly Schumpeterian) approach are similar – namely, to support basic research and a research infrastructure which encourages industrial R&D – there is a significant divergence in the underlying rationale. Whereas the market-failure case is based on the essentially static arguments of misallocation of resources, the evolutionary approach looks to R&D and innovation as an essential part of system dynamics. As we have seen, following this approach, divergences in performance between firms and between countries are to be expected and are explained by the mixed inheritance of skills and institutions. Equally, such trends are not immutable. By encouraging greater investment in R&D in both public and private sectors, governments both increase the pool of skilled personnel on which industry can draw and help promote a system in which competition, divergence, catching up and keeping up are a necessary part of the system dynamics. We shall return to these issues in the final section of this paper (Farrands also explores the divergence of knowledge diffusion practice within and between firms in Chapter 6 of this volume).

INTERNATIONALISATION, GLOBALISATION AND THE NON-GLOBALISATION OF R&D

Internationalisation or globalisation?

The term globalisation is frequently used to describe current developments in international business. Yet it is often loosely used and ill-defined. In this paper the term internationalisation rather than globalisation will be used to describe the stage now reached in 'international production' – that is value-adding activities owned or controlled by firms outside their national boundaries (Dunning 1988; Cantwell 1989). These activities include the export and import of goods and services, outward and inward flows of direct investment and financial capital, outward and inward flows of embodied and disembodied technology, the international movement of skilled personnel, and trans-border information flows.

Given this definition, internationalisation has increased for the last century or more. Large multinational companies (MNEs) operating within the world supply system (and capable therefore of taking full advantage of the worldwide organisation of financial services) have driven the process. The 1980s were merely the latest stage in its development. The 1980s, however, were marked by a number of distinctive features:

1 a very fast rise in the flow of foreign direct investment (FDI) and the entry of Japan as a major source of capital, as the high value of the yen, the need to re-invest trade surpluses, and the increasing threat of protectionism in foreign markets combined to encourage such a move;
2 the end of the one-way flow of capital from the US to the rest of the world and the growth of the US as a major recipient of FDI both from Japan and from Europe. The major flows are now between the three main trading blocks of the world (the Triad) (see Table 7.1, but note that as yet Japan is not a major recipient of such flows, US and European

capital going to the other countries of South-East Asia rather than Japan);

3 the growth also of substantial flows of FDI within each part of the Triad. Closer integration of the European Community and the prospect of monetary union have led to major cross-border investments by European firms, often via merger or acquisition, and these in turn have played a substantial part in the later (i.e. from 1985) stages of this new phase of internationalisation. Similarly many of the newly industrialising countries (NICs) of South-East Asia now house Japanese subsidiaries as that country expands its operations within the area of the Pacific Rim. Likewise, the US has long been the major investor in Canada, and links have been tightened as a result of the free trade area, now extended to Mexico;

4 in addition to FDI, other new forms of industrial linkage have become common: joint ventures, subcontracting, licensing, cooperative research agreements, second-sourcing agreements. The result has been that many firms are now involved in complex international networks covering all the main areas of operation – research, production and marketing (see below).

The factors driving this new phase of internationalisation are complex and interrelated. On the one hand, the 1970s had seen the re-emergence of protectionism with the development of significant non-tariff barriers as the industrialised countries struggled to come to terms with prolonged recession. The threat of protection, particularly towards Japan and the newly industrialising countries (NICs) of South-East Asia, has been one of the main driving forces behind the upsurge of FDI. On the other hand, the 1970s also brought new technologies, and technology has also been an important factor behind the trend towards internationalisation.

The emergence of a number of large Japanese multinationals as a major competitive force in world markets in the last two decades has had particular effect, especially since their way of doing business is so different from the previously dominant Anglo-Saxon (Fordist) model that had characterised the American MNEs of the 1950s and 1960s. Intense competition in terms of new product models and model improvements from Japanese companies has made the ability to innovate a key factor in industrial competitiveness, with a premium on rapid model changes, customised products, and maximum flexibility. Many older MNEs have tried to copy their Japanese counterparts and in so doing forged close links with suppliers and customers.

Trends, however, vary from sector to sector. Industries such as chemicals and food manufacturing had long used FDI as a method of opening up new markets and localising production. The pharmaceutical industry, perhaps the world's first global industry, followed suit in the 1950s and 1960s. But, with the exception of the vertical linkages with new biotechnology firms, the degree of networking in pharmaceuticals (or for that matter chemicals) has

Table 7.1 Share of major OECD countries in outward and in... direct ... ...ment 1971 to 1989 (percentages of total OECD flows)

	1971–80	19...
United States	46.4	
Canada[1]		
Japan[1]		
EC[2]		
Belgium-Luxembourg[1]		
France[1]		
Germany		
Italy[1]		
Netherlands[1]		
Spain[1]		
United K...		
Swede...		

N...
Spa...
Unite...
Swede...

Memoranda...
Outward inv...
- as share of ex...
  goods and serv...
Inward investment...
- as share of imports...
  goods and services

Note:
1 Exclude reinvested earnings
2 Data for the European Commun...
  Data include intra-Community...
3 US $ billion, annual average.
Source: *Technology and the Economy: th...*

been very limited. In particular, unlik...
horizontal R&D collaborations with co...
as competition has intensified, so too hav...

Traditionally it has been industries with a...
in assembly operations which have forged lin...
with customers and suppliers and it is these firm...

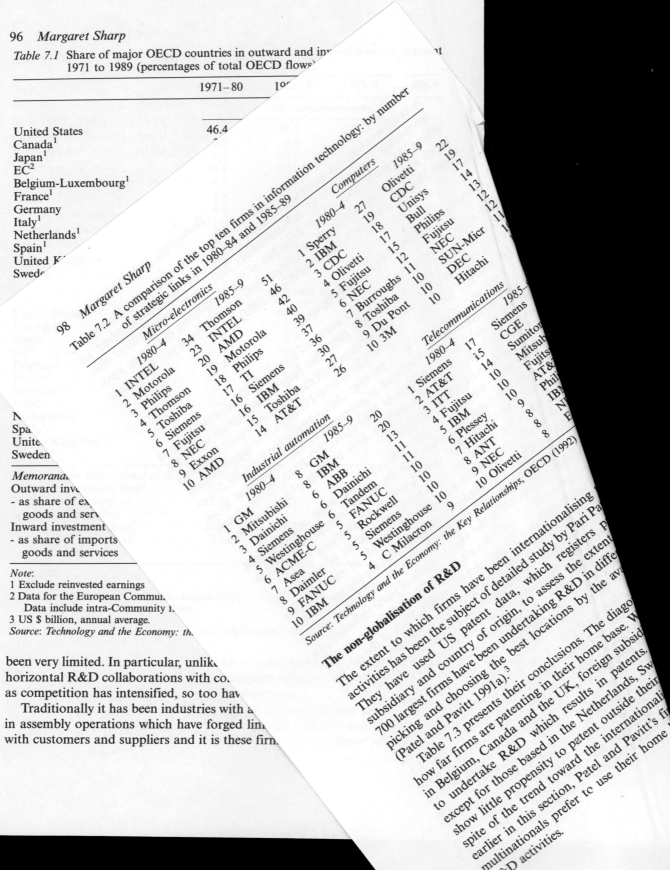

Table 7.2 A comparison of the top ten firms in information technology: by number of strategic links in 1980–84 and 1985–89

Micro-electronics

	1980-4		1985-9
1	INTEL	34	Thomson 51
2	Motorola	23	INTEL 46
3	Philips	20	AMD 42
4	Thomson	19	Motorola 40
5	Toshiba	18	Philips 39
6	Siemens	17	TI 37
7	Fujitsu	16	Siemens 36
8	NEC	15	IBM 30
9	Exxon	14	Toshiba 27
10	AMD		AT&T 26

Computers

	1980-4		1985-9
1	Sperry	27	Olivetti 22
2	IBM	19	CDC 19
3	Olivetti	18	Unisys 17
4	Olivetti	17	Bull 14
5	Fujitsu	15	Philips 13
6	NEC	12	Fujitsu 12
7	Burroughs	11	NEC 12
8	Toshiba	11	SUN-Micr 11
9	Du Pont	10	DEC 10
10	3M	10	Hitachi 10

Industrial automation

	1980-4		1985-9
1	GM	8	GM 20
2	Mitsubishi	8	IBM 13
3	Dainichi	8	ABB 11
4	Siemens	6	Dainichi 11
5	Westinghouse	6	Tandem 10
5	ACME-C	6	FANUC 10
6	Asea	5	Rockwell 10
7	Daimler	5	Siemens 10
8	FANUC	5	Westinghouse 9
9	IBM	4	C Milacron
10	IBM		

Telecommunications

	1980-4		1985-9
1	Siemens	17	Siemens
2	AT&T	15	CGE
3	ITT	14	Sumitom...
4	Fujitsu	10	Mitsub...
5	IBM	10	Fujits...
6	Plessey	10	AT&...
7	Hitachi	9	Phili...
8	ANT	8	IBM...
9	NEC	8	N...
10	Olivetti	8	E...

Source: *Technology and the Economy: the Key Relationships*, OECD (1992)

The non-globalisation of R&D

The extent to which firms have been internationalising ...
activities has been the subject of detailed study by Pari Pa...
They have used US patent data, which registers p...
subsidiary and country of origin, to assess the extent...
700 largest firms have been undertaking R&D in diff...
picking and choosing the best locations by the av...
(Patel and Pavitt 1991a).[3]

Table 7.3 presents their conclusions. The diag...
how far firms are patenting in their home base. W...
in Belgium, Canada and the UK, foreign subsid...
to undertake R&D which results in patents...
except for those based in the Netherlands, Sw...
show little propensity to patent outside their...
spite of the trend toward the internationali...
earlier in this section, Patel and Pavitt's fi...
multinationals prefer to use their home b...
R&D activities.

Table 7.2 A comparison of the top ten firms in information technology: by number of strategic links in 1980–84 and 1985–89

Micro-electronics				Computers			
1980–4		*1985–9*		*1980–4*		*1985–9*	
1 INTEL	34	Thomson	51	1 Sperry	27	Olivetti	22
2 Motorola	23	INTEL	46	2 IBM	19	CDC	19
3 Philips	20	AMD	42	3 CDC	18	Unisys	17
4 Thomson	19	Motorola	40	4 Olivetti	17	Bull	14
5 Toshiba	18	Philips	39	5 Fujitsu	15	Philips	13
6 Siemens	17	TI	37	6 NEC	12	Fujitsu	12
7 Fujitsu	16	Siemens	36	7 Burroughs	11	NEC	12
8 NEC	16	IBM	30	8 Toshiba	10	SUN-Micr	11
9 Exxon	15	Toshiba	27	9 Du Pont	10	DEC	10
10 AMD	14	AT&T	26	10 3M	10	Hitachi	10

Industrial automation				Telecommunications			
1980–4		*1985–9*		*1980–4*		*1985–9*	
1 GM	8	GM	20	1 Siemens	17	Siemens	45
2 Mitsubishi	8	IBM	20	2 AT&T	15	CGE	32
3 Dainichi	6	ABB	13	3 ITT	14	Sumitomo	29
4 Siemens	6	Dainichi	11	4 Fujitsu	10	Mitsubishi	28
5 Westinghouse	6	Tandem	11	5 IBM	10	Fujitsu	27
6 ACME-C	5	FANUC	10	6 Plessey	10	AT&T	26
7 Asea	5	Rockwell	10	7 Hitachi	9	Philips	26
8 Daimler	5	Siemens	10	8 ANT	8	IBM	24
9 FANUC	5	Westinghouse	10	9 NEC	8	NEC	23
10 IBM	4	C Milacron	9	10 Olivetti	8	Ericsson	20

Source: *Technology and the Economy: the Key Relationships*, OECD (1992)

The non-globalisation of R&D

The extent to which firms have been internationalising their technological activities has been the subject of detailed study by Pari Patel and Keith Pavitt. They have used US patent data, which registers patenting activity by subsidiary and country of origin, to assess the extent to which the world's 700 largest firms have been undertaking R&D in different parts of the world, picking and choosing the best locations by the availability of local talent (Patel and Pavitt 1991a).[3]

Table 7.3 presents their conclusions. The diagonal gives an indication of how far firms are patenting in their home base. With the exception of plants in Belgium, Canada and the UK, foreign subsidiaries show little propensity to undertake R&D which results in patents. Likewise, domestic MNEs, except for those based in the Netherlands, Sweden, the UK or Switzerland, show little propensity to patent outside their home base. In other words in spite of the trend toward the internationalisation of production identified earlier in this section, Patel and Pavitt's findings would indicate that most multinationals prefer to use their home base for strategic, patent-creating R&D activities.

developed a complex networking form of internationalisation. Electronics, telecommunications, automobiles and machine tools have been involved, all assembling components or sub-assemblies from parts manufactured elsewhere (Mowery 1988). Other branches of the engineering industries, aerospace and, perhaps above all, the major civil engineering firms, have done things this way for a very long time (Cook 1985).

Mergers, acquisitions and global oligopoly

One clear outcome from both the increased levels of FDI and the mergers and acquisitions movement of the 1980s has been the strengthening of the position of MNEs in relation to other parts of the supply structure. Estimates put the share of home-based US MNEs in total US exports at approximately 30 per cent, and in imports at 18 per cent (Julius 1990); the total for home-based and foreign MNEs combined is estimated to have amounted to as much as 40 per cent of US imports in 1985 (UNCTC 1990). By any count these figures are substantial and indicate how important intra-company trade can be within the total trade figures.

More important, however, is the role of these large multinational companies within the supply structure and the degree to which they are in a position to dictate to the market. Indeed, one of the worrying features of developments during the 1980s has been the concentration of production worldwide for most R&D-intensive sectors in the hands of relatively few major producers. The OECD, for example, estimates that the top ten firms in computers, telecommunications and semiconductors in 1987 contributed respectively 90, 85 and 61 per cent of the world output of those industries. In automobiles, the top seven firms in 1988 contributed 88 per cent of output; in tyres the top six firms contributed 85 per cent of output. Even in the service industries, areas such as advertising and management consultancy have seen a major concentration of interests – in management consultancy the top four firms (all US) took 54 per cent of the market in 1989 (OECD 1992: 222–3).

These trends towards concentration are a cause for concern in themselves. Work at MERIT[2] on the structure and pattern of the collaborative alliances of the 1980s shows that in the main information technology sectors many of the leading firms were also involved during the 1980s in alliances with their oligopolistic rivals (Hagedoorn and Schakenraad 1990a, 1990b). Table 7.2, derived from their work, gives some indication of the extent to which leading companies in each sector were involved in alliances and the changing pattern of these alliances between the two halves of the decade. This work shows a strong clustering element in these alliances, with a number of leading firms seemingly acting as nodes within the cluster. What emerges is a complicated patchwork of corporate networks anchored around a number of key firms who between them dominate the development of the information technology sectors.

Table 7.1 Share of major OECD countries in outward and inward direct investment 1971 to 1989 (percentages of total OECD flows)

	1971–80	1981–4	1985–7	1988–9
	Outward investment			
United States	46.4	20.1	25.3	16.9
Canada[1]	3.9	8.0	5.4	3.5
Japan[1]	6.2	13.2	16.2	27.6
EC[2]	41.8	56.0	50.1	47.6
Belgium-Luxembourg[1]	1.1	0.4	1.8	−1.0
France[1]	4.8	8.1	6.5	10.8
Germany	8.6	9.7	9.4	8.7
Italy[1]	1.2	4.6	2.7	2.6
Netherlands[1]	6.4	7.8	5.6	4.9
Spain[1]	0.4	0.9	0.6	0.9
United Kingdom	19.2	24.6	23.4	20.6
Sweden[1]	1.6	2.7	3.0	4.4
	Inward investment			
United States	33.8	62.8	59.3	51.4
Canada[1]	3.3	−2.4	1.3	2.7
Japan[1]	0.9	0.9	1.2	−0.6
EC[2]	61.5	38.3	37.3	45.8
Belgium[1]	5.5	3.6	2.3	4.6
France[1]	10.1	6.4	5.7	6.6
Germany	8.4	2.9	2.2	2.9
Italy[1]	3.4	3.5	3.0	3.7
Netherlands[1]	5.1	3.0	3.2	3.9
Spain[1]	4.2	5.7	5.9	6.1
United Kingdom	24.7	13.2	15.0	18.0
Sweden[1]	0.5	0.5	0.9	0.7
Memorandum items: Total of above countries				
Outward investment level[3]	28.9	36.0	83.0	142.2
- as share of exports of goods and services	3.6	2.3	4.4	5.3
Inward investment level[3]	16.7	30.4	56.2	127.0
- as share of imports of goods and services	2.1	2.0	3.0	4.7

Note:
1 Exclude reinvested earnings
2 Data for the European Community exclude flows of Denmark, Greece, Ireland and Portugal. Data include intra-Community flows.
3 US $ billion, annual average.
Source: *Technology and the Economy: the Key Relationships*, OECD (1992)

been very limited. In particular, unlike electronics, there have been few major horizontal R&D collaborations with competitors (Sharp (ed.) 1989). Rather, as competition has intensified, so too have mergers.

Traditionally it has been industries with an engineering base and involved in assembly operations which have forged linkage forwards and backwards with customers and suppliers and it is these firms *par excellence* which have capital going to the other countries of South-East Asia rather than Japan);

3 the growth also of substantial flows of FDI within each part of the Triad. Closer integration of the European Community and the prospect of monetary union have led to major cross-border investments by European firms, often via merger or acquisition, and these in turn have played a substantial part in the later (i.e. from 1985) stages of this new phase of internationalisation. Similarly many of the newly industrialising countries (NICs) of South-East Asia now house Japanese subsidiaries as that country expands its operations within the area of the Pacific Rim. Likewise, the US has long been the major investor in Canada, and links have been tightened as a result of the free trade area, now extended to Mexico;

4 in addition to FDI, other new forms of industrial linkage have become common: joint ventures, subcontracting, licensing, cooperative research agreements, second-sourcing agreements. The result has been that many firms are now involved in complex international networks covering all the main areas of operation – research, production and marketing (see below).

The factors driving this new phase of internationalisation are complex and interrelated. On the one hand, the 1970s had seen the re-emergence of protectionism with the development of significant non-tariff barriers as the industrialised countries struggled to come to terms with prolonged recession. The threat of protection, particularly towards Japan and the newly industrialising countries (NICs) of South-East Asia, has been one of the main driving forces behind the upsurge of FDI. On the other hand, the 1970s also brought new technologies, and technology has also been an important factor behind the trend towards internationalisation.

The emergence of a number of large Japanese multinationals as a major competitive force in world markets in the last two decades has had particular effect, especially since their way of doing business is so different from the previously dominant Anglo-Saxon (Fordist) model that had characterised the American MNEs of the 1950s and 1960s. Intense competition in terms of new product models and model improvements from Japanese companies has made the ability to innovate a key factor in industrial competitiveness, with a premium on rapid model changes, customised products, and maximum flexibility. Many older MNEs have tried to copy their Japanese counterparts and in so doing forged close links with suppliers and customers.

Trends, however, vary from sector to sector. Industries such as chemicals and food manufacturing had long used FDI as a method of opening up new markets and localising production. The pharmaceutical industry, perhaps the world's first global industry, followed suit in the 1950s and 1960s. But, with the exception of the vertical linkages with new biotechnology firms, the degree of networking in pharmaceuticals (or for that matter chemicals) has

Table 7.3 Geographic location of patenting by large firms 1981–8 (percentage distribution by country of origin and home base of firms)

Home country of large firms	Country of origin of patenting							
	US	*Japan*	*France*	*W. Germ*	*Neth*	*Bel*	*Swe*	*UK*
US	91.9	0.7	0.5	2.3	0.2	0.3	0.0	1.8
Japan	0.7	99.1	0.0	0.1	0.0	0.0	0.0	0.1
France	3.4	0.2	90.9	2.5	0.2	0.3	0.0	0.5
W. Germany	8.3	0.2	1.2	87.1	0.1	0.8	0.3	0.4
Netherlands	25.0	0.4	6.0	13.3	43.4	0.6	0.6	7.7
Belgium	27.0	0.0	1.2	16.7	11.7	39.4	0.0	1.9
Sweden	5.1	0.3	1.2	13.5	2.8	0.3	71.2	1.7
UK	21.5	0.1	2.4	3.8	0.9	0.4	0.3	65.9

Source: Patel and Pavitt (1991a)

The major exception to their conclusions is the pharmaceutical industry which had begun to internationalise its R&D activities in the 1960s and has continued to do so. The strength of the US science base in the life sciences and biotechnology is a major factor behind current trends, and many European companies have established R&D laboratories in both the US and Japan during the last decade and use these facilities for mainstream R&D on biotechnology (Sharp *et al.* 1993).

It is unclear how far the pharmaceutical industry will be a precursor for other industries in establishing a more intensive pattern of internationalisation of R&D. The Patel and Pavitt data quoted above relate to the earlier years of the 1980s and there is little doubt that the mergers and collaborative trends of the latter half of the 1980s have widened information networks and opened up new options which may be leading to much higher levels of internationalisation in R&D. But as Hu (1992) has pointed out, it is not just R&D that has remained home-based for MNEs. Corporate headquarters, finance and strategic planning have all remained predominantly home-based. As Hu puts it, a modern MNE is a national firm with extensive international activities.

The continuing importance of national systems of innovation

The evidence presented by Patel and Pavitt and Hu raises doubts about the degree of internationalisation among MNEs and confirms earlier suggestions that technology has developed differently within different environments. This tends to reinforce ideas that there exists what is described as a national system of innovation, that 'network of institutions in the public and private sectors whose activities and interactions initiate, import, modify and diffuse new technologies' (Freeman 1987b: 1). Historical circumstance and time mean that these systems differ markedly from one another. For example, the British industrial system, rooted in the Industrial Revolution, is very different from the German industrial system that developed at the end of the nineteenth

century under the paternal influence of Bismarck and the militaristic needs of
the Prussian state. Such differences are more than just interesting differences
in history. As Freeman has shown 'the rate of technical change in any country
and the effectiveness of companies in world competition . . . depend upon the
way in which the available resources are managed and organised both at
enterprise and at national level' (*ibid.*: 3). In other words, institutions and the
organisation of institutions matter and can have profound effects upon
performance.

   National systems of innovation do not always accommodate easily within
an international world. This is perhaps best illustrated by the current focus of
interest on the Japanese *keiretsu* organisation, the grouping of companies,
often around one or two major companies, into 'family groups' with inter-
group linkages through such things as finance and supply chains. Given the
demand for flexibility these groupings have proved highly adaptable and
effective in the current competitive climate. Yet what is fair play by one set of
rules becomes unacceptable by another. Is it reasonable for members of the
keiretsu to give fellow members preference in supplying new state-of-the-art
chip-making machinery? Or is such a practice unfair and in restraint of trade?
The Americans, for example, instituted as part of their continuing dialogue
on trade issues with the Japanese a set of talks known as the Structural
Impediments Initiative (SII) in which they put considerable pressure on the
Japanese to tighten their anti-trust procedures towards *keiretsu*. The
Japanese for their part resented the US attitude that their (i.e. the American)
way of doing things was necessarily better.

   The continuing importance of national systems of innovation with their
differing institutions and objectives led inevitably to clashes between systems,
or 'system friction' as Sylvia Ostry (1991) calls it. The danger, in the uncertain
but competitive world of the 1990s, is that the friction flares up and destroys
the very real gains the world has reaped from the process of internationalisation in the post-war years.

NATIONAL POLICIES FOR A GLOBAL ENVIRONMENT

What we have today, therefore, is a world in which large multinational firms
are playing an increasingly important part in production and trade; in other
words in many sectors, particularly high-tech sectors, what was national
oligopoly has become global oligopoly. Equally these same firms are firmly
rooted in traditions of enterprise and innovation which derive from their
national environments and both reflect and perpetuate these traditions.
Putting this together with the characteristics of technology discussed earlier it
is possible to suggest an outline of the sorts of policy which are appropriate in
such a global environment.

Support for the science and technology infrastructure

While the neo-classical view argues for support for basic research on grounds of market failure, the neo-Schumpeterian view adopted in this paper argues for it in terms of wealth creation. Given the person- and institution-embodied nature of public investment in basic research and training, we can view those trained to doctoral levels in science and technology as a small but essential part of competitive industry – the core of the R&D system. What is more, the economic benefits from investment in basic research come just as much from the problem-solving skills of trained researchers as from useful information codified in papers or patents. Benefit from support for the local research infrastructure thus remains surprisingly localised, embodied in people (most of whom do not migrate), and the jobs they do, many of which are relatively high value-added jobs. It is the jobs people do, not who owns the factory, that contributes to the value-added.

A major element of national and regional policy should therefore be geared to the provision and maintenance of what might be called the 'science and technology infrastructure'. This involves, on the one hand, promoting institutions which support a high-quality research and technological base – high-quality secondary education; a good vocational training system; a strong university sector; and a well-founded academic research base with a major postgraduate component. On the other, it implies support for institutions whose function is concerned with the diffusion (as well as the production) of science and technology. This includes support for such things as university–industry linkage, technology transfer, research associations, particularly those like the Fraunhofer Institutes in Germany which support technology dissemination to small and medium-sized business, and the encouragement of regional initiatives bringing together firms, universities and research institutions.

Support for strategic technologies

While public support for the science and technology infrastructure wins broad support, more controversy surrounds the notion of support for strategic industries. For one thing, there is no clear definition of what constitutes a strategic technology. Teece (1991: 36) encapsulates this well: 'The attitude of most observers is that they know a strategic industry when they see one.' At base the concept derives from its military origins – that withholding supply could inflict serious disadvantage to the nation as a whole, whether in a military or an economic sense.

In what circumstances might this happen? First, there may be monopoly power amongst suppliers of key components and equipment. This is what Flamm (1992) describes as the anti-cartel reason for promoting strategic industries. Such monopoly may not last for a long time in technologies with pervasive applications, precisely because pervasive applications tend to generate a large number of independent sources of supply. It does not preclude the possibility, however, that specific firms in specific sectors may withhold technology for competitive reasons and that this action can create considerable tensions both between firms and between nations. This, in essence, underlies the current US decision to back a US consortia for flat panel displays (FPD). The Pentagon maintains that although military use constitutes only 5 per cent of the FPD market, it is nevertheless a crucial military technology and the Pentagon cannot rely upon Japanese manufacturers for supplies.[4]

Second, a country may face the danger of its firms being excluded from a technological trajectory in cases where cumulative development over time generates a high rate of technological change (in products and processes), opening up yet further possibilities for change and growth. If these characteristics are also associated with first-comer advantages (i.e. steep learning curves), latecomers may not have sufficient incentive to enter and catch up. Baldwin and Krugman (1988) have analysed how Japan in the 1970s dealt with this difficulty in semiconductors and established its highly successful VLSI (very large scale integration) project. Airbus Industrie likewise has sought to develop a family of airliners in order to reap benefits of scale and scope economies and challenge Boeing's incipient monopoly.

The arguments here have to be used carefully. There is a great danger of every industry being labelled 'strategic' whereas the number is really very small, especially when account is taken of the fact that subsidiaries of foreign companies may create indigenous capabilities which, at the end of the day, are what is required. It also has to be borne in mind that most benefits derive from the *use* of new technologies, not production *per se*. Diffusion is therefore more important than production.

This suggests a policy approach which, although sceptical about the need for support on strategic grounds, does not rule it out. First, any such support should be subject to strict time limits and deliberately tapered over time (normally, say, to a five-year period). Second, collaborations associated with such support should be open to foreign as well as indigenous companies, unless the foreign company has been involved in cartel-like practices which have excluded indigenous firms from market entry. Again, what is important are the people-embodied skills and competences, and that local firms may benefit from such participation. Third, tough local content clauses for foreign direct investment make sense. Screwdriver plants bring minimal skills; what are wanted are the high-value-added jobs in R&D and management and the upstream and downstream supply-chain linkages. Fourth, diffusion is just as important as development, and diffusion policies should be given equally high status (cf. chapters by Farrands and Russell in this volume).

The promotion of competition

A third leg of policy relates to competition. The lessons from the failure of the period of national champions, when national governments collaborated with major firms to concentrate market power in the hand of particular firms –Bull and Thomson in France, British Leyland and GEC in Britain – should not be lost. All the evidence suggests that competitive oligopolies perform better than cartels or monopoly. Porter (1990) in his major analysis of the innovative record of different countries came to the strong conclusion that company innovativeness is stimulated by competitive rivalry in the home market. This is supported by further work at SPRU analysing the innovative record of the largest 660 firms that count for half the world's patenting (Patel and Pavitt 1992). They came to the conclusion that, first, mega-mergers are unlikely to increase the volume of innovative activities; and second, in Japan and the US, sectoral technological strengths are found when large firms are relatively numerous, rather than when they are relatively big; in Europe, strength lies in sectors where they are both relatively numerous and relatively big.

Given these findings, the trends towards global oligopoly described in the previous section are all the more disturbing. Nationally based competition policies have long had difficulty in coping with oligopoly – in defining the borderline between smart business practice and unfair behaviour. This becomes doubly difficult in dealing with multinationals which are able to switch resources and profits from one market to another within a horizontally and vertically integrated business, and which are able to use their power over intellectual property to create increasingly powerful barriers to entry to a market even at a global level. It suggests that the current efforts to set up an international competition authority within the framework of the new GATT World Trading Organisation (WTO) should be taken seriously. Such an organisation would, like GATT, need to be built upon the principles of mutual recognition and reciprocity and involve agreement at an international level of a mutually recognised code of practice for multinational firms. Transgression from such a code of practice by any MNEs would then be equally reprehensible in any signatory country and sanctions mutually imposed and reinforced.

In the longer run, as with the Single Market Programme, establishing the level playing field of fair competition may require agreement on a wide range of issues outside the bounds of what is traditionally regarded as competition policy, namely, the harmonisation of standards and regulatory regimes, agreement on public purchasing rules, etc. It needs also to be recognised that trade policy and competition are two sides of the same coin. If global oligopolies are to remain competitive there is little point in high levels of protection; the oligopolists have to be allowed, indeed forced, to compete with each other.

Making good institutional failure

This chapter has stressed the importance of local systems of innovation – the mix of institutions and attitudes which come together to 'initiate, import, modify and diffuse new technologies' (Freeman 1987b: 1). These two factors, institutions and attitudes, interact and reinforce each other. For example, German capabilities in the engineering sector are in part perpetuated by the training regime which emerged in that country in the nineteenth century. These institutions in themselves help to shape attitudes towards training, which in turn shape institutions. Abramowitz (1986), indeed, has suggested that differences in performance can often be explained not in terms of market failure, but in terms of institutional failure, and that policies need to take account of institutional failure.

The basic policy conclusion is clear – if the failure lies at institutional level, change the institutions as well as incentive structures. For example, low levels of industrial R&D funding may reflect industrial financing structures as much as entrepreneurial attitudes. It may be the banking or investment systems that need correction in that case. Introducing tax incentives to encourage R&D – attacking the symptom not the cause – is therefore only likely to have partial success. Equally, there is danger in thinking there is a quick institutional fix to problems that may be quite deep-seated. For example, establishing a state-funded investment bank will not necessarily cure R&D blues any better than an R&D tax credit. There are also obvious problems with trying to transpose institutional systems from one country to another without being able simultaneously to transpose cultures. This helps to explain why Britain is having such problems with its new German-style training institutions (especially the locally based Training and Enterprise Councils) – because it has not been possible simultaneously to import German attitudes towards training. But attitudes can only be bred slowly, over time and *with the help of* the right institutional framework. The conclusion therefore has to be that while changing institutions can help, such a policy needs patience and reinforcement by a strong 'cultural' (attitudinal) lead from government.

Coping with system friction

The existence of different 'systems' of innovation leads inevitably on occasion to a clash of cultures. There need to be mechanisms to help resolve and diffuse such 'system friction'. Setting up international codes of practice with mutual adherence and mutual sanctions helps. In effect it means attempting to create the 'level playing field' at an international level. It will not, however, solve all problems. For example, the US has identified the *keiretsu* system in Japan, with the cooperative relationships between firms within the *keiretsu* and the ready availability of patient money from the in-house bank, as one of the most difficult aspects of the Japanese system with which to compete

(Hodder 1991; Flamm 1990). The *keiretsu* system certainly incorporates some elements of unfair behaviour, yet it also has many efficiency-enhancing aspects and it would be foolish to lose these. Over the longer run, competition between systems stimulates evolution. Current concerns in countries of the Anglo-Saxon capitalist tradition in such areas as savings ratios, training systems, quality circles and 'just in time' already indicate some shift towards a different, more cooperative form of capitalism which has greater compatibility with the systems of Japan or Germany. In other words, convergence may eliminate the problem in the long run. What is required is a forum for the reconciliation of the short-term 'irreconcilables'.

CONCLUSIONS

We have come full circle. This chapter began by suggesting that industrial policy has long been mercantilist in intent. It has ended by putting forward a set of policies which might be called 'the new mercantilism'. Whereas 'the old mercantilism' focused on the location of *production*, the new mercantilism looks to value-added and seeks to maximise the value-added of local activities, irrespective of the ownership of the physical assets invested in the activities. This reflects a world in which the key resource in adding value is no longer hardware (physical assets) but software (human capital and accumulated human capital in the form of knowledge, 'best practice' and routines). As suggested in the first section of this paper, much of this knowledge-based software cannot be codified but is tacit knowledge, passed on informally by human interaction and learning by doing. While codified knowledge in the form of patents and publications is highly mobile, tacit knowledge is much less footloose. The new mercantilism is about policies which help capture the rents from tacit knowledge.

There is in addition a second strand of thought woven into this chapter which, building upon the growing importance of the role played by tacit knowledge, posits the notion of 'systems of innovation' – that mix of institutions, attitudes and behaviour which both reflects the cumulative development of ideas from the past and helps shape their future direction, leading, as we have seen, to distinct regimes or 'cultures' within different firms and different countries. Given the increasingly multinational nature of markets, there is inevitably conflict and friction between the different systems – especially in a world which continues to be dominated by mercantilist principles. Policy has therefore also to find ways of minimising this friction – of devising rules to be applied internationally which help to align the different systems sufficiently for them to be able to work in harmony with each other.

NOTES

1 Although many of these same industries, caught unawares by the severity of the recession, were at that time uncertain how far they were being hit by a temporary or permanent change in their competitive position. Many of the 'negative adjustment policies' actually helped a more orderly rundown of the industry over the longer term.

2 Maastricht Economic Research Institute on Innovation and Technology (PO Box 616, 6200 MD Maastricht, The Netherlands).

3 Patent data is not an ideal measure of innovation. Trends in patenting tend to vary from industry to industry (higher in the chemically based firms; lower in engineering, where learning by doing is more important), and from firm to firm. It is, however, readily available on a firm-by-firm basis in the public domain over a very large number of years and because firms are required to identify where the invention originated (i.e. in which of their plants) gives some measure of the relative contribution of these subsidiaries to overall performance. Within any sector over time the figures are consistent and therefore comparisons can be made.

4 Information given by Kenneth Flamm, now Deputy Assistant Secretary of Defence for Dual Use and International Programs at the Pentagon, at a symposium at the National Academy of Sciences in Washington, 20 July 1994.

8 Communities, networks, creativity and culture

Insights into localisation within globalisation

Claire Shearman

Local economies have substantially more significance in the international political economy than is generally acknowledged.[1] The first part of this chapter deals with the theme of localisation within globalisation. Here we argue that the increasing *political* salience of the local economy is linked to the two trends of globalisation and interdependence. These in turn have served to constrain the effectiveness of national policies. The experience of the 1990s, however, has shown European local policy-makers that achieving political significance is no longer a matter of a particular city and/or region being able to exercise substantial influence as a result of its comparative geographical, historical, technological, cultural and/or social advantages. Rather, it is a case of a number of disparate cities and/or regions *collectively* attempting to exercise political advantage through a series of (often) interlocking networks and alliances.

At the same time, *economic* aspects of globalisation are pushing localisation to the fore. The efficacy of national policies in globalised contexts has begun to be questioned. Survival within the evolving global economy is increasingly dependent on the quality and innovativeness of the people, skills, talents and institutions available at the local level. The capacity of a city or region to successfully innovate and compete is crucially embedded in the character and cohesion of its social and cultural context. Technology is adding a new dimension. The interaction between technology, culture and economic activity in the global marketplace cannot be understood along neatly defined national boundaries. That is not to say that within the context of evolving cultural and technological globalisation, there is no room for local diversity and creativity. In fact, for European cities the fusion of technology with cultural and historical experience may well prove to be a real window of economic opportunity.

The processes inherent in technological development and globalisation clearly present local economies with major opportunities. But there are also constraints. Much of the potential afforded by telematics technologies remains untapped. This results from the parochial nature of much local economic interest, the lack to date of applications developed in response to real user demand, and the social and economic trends inherent in the development of the so-called 'information society' which are resulting in the marginalisation of substantial numbers of people from economic and social activities. Public intervention as a means of addressing a distinct telematics 'applications gap' at the community level and encouraging infrastructural development and universal access to the new opportunities emerging is crucial to the successful exploitation of localisation within globalisation.

The second part of this chapter dealing with local policy signposts addresses some of the practical implications of managing localisation within globalisation from the perspective of the local policy-maker. Here we focus on the determinants of successful economic development and how they should be prioritised. We point to two policy insights in particular. First, the significance of social structures in facilitating or constraining economic and technological development; and second, the increasing relevance of the links between the productive elements of an economy and the cultural capacity of its society. The first combines insights derived from micro-level case studies of regional competitive performance and social models of industrial development to suggest that from the perspective of local policy-makers, what is at issue is the extent of the 'fit' between the nature of the existing local social conventions and community and the type and stage of industrial development they are seeking to promote. The second, drawing on the links between culture and production referred to above (and on some of the themes explored by Youngs in her chapter in this volume), points to the increasing importance of facilitating the development of a creatively driven 'imaginative milieu' as opposed to technologically driven innovative milieu.

Continuing on the theme of the practical issues for local policy-makers, the third part of this chapter uses the examples of information superhighways and the Internet to explore aspects of Palan's (Chapter 2 in this volume) identification of instrumentalist versus transcendentalist modes of technological expression. The transformative potential of telematics technologies is clear. For local policy-makers, the challenge is how to tap into this potential within the context of what we have termed an 'imaginative milieu'. Here we argue that it is not the technology *per se* that is crucial. While instrumentalist and transcendentalist or transformative modes of technological expression may not always be easy to differentiate at first glance, an essential component of the latter seems to be a *sustained* experience of openness of debate, radical traditions, intellectual novelty and creativity.

GLOBALISATION: PUSHING LOCALISATION TO THE FORE

Political dimensions

The increasing *political* salience of the local economy is linked to the two trends of globalisation and interdependence. Trends towards globalisation are diminishing the traditional powers and influence of the nation state.

National governments are responding to the erosion of aspects of their sovereignty by increasingly embracing various forms of supranational alliances and integration. New patterns of alliances are emerging at the local and regional levels too. Over the past decade, a combination of free-market rhetoric, economic recession, cuts in national funding sources and the need to seek common solutions to common problems (like urban regeneration and unemployment) have pushed cities and regions to abandon old allies in favour of new partnerships. Partly this is a direct response to supranational alliances. Supranational integration can trigger the fear of subordination of specific social interests to supranational institutions. But here again, such specific interests – including social policies, employment and labour market issues, the growth of multi-ethnic, multi-cultural societies and their marginalisation via urban dualism and racism in many cities – are now often expressed at the local and regional level, a trend which suggests a renewal of the role of regions and cities as loci of autonomy and political decision-making.

The more national states fade in their role, the more cities are emerging as a driving force in European society (Castells 1994: 23), particularly, as already noted, through a series of (often) interlocking networks and alliances. Recent examples include Eurocities, Telecities, Teleregions, IRISI and the Atlantic Rim Network. These partnerships are developing on a public/private sector basis both within a city itself and across networks developed in response to regional or sectoral imperatives. Eurocities, for example, is a European association of local government authorities from across the EU and beyond with sectoral working groups covering economic development, culture, the environment, social welfare, transport and technological co-operation. The aim is to provide a representative structure to enable key cities to participate in the development of trans-European projects in a direct and consistent way. The Atlantic Rim Network is a US East Coast-initiated global network of cities (including a number of Eurocities and Telecities members) aiming, amongst other things, to use international links to exercise greater political leverage domestically.

The field of telematics has seen the emergence of Telecities. This is a Eurocities-associated European network of cities which developed in response both to the imperatives of the information economy and the opportunities for funding engendered by the EU's Fourth Framework Programme. Focusing on technology to support economic and regional regeneration and social cohesion, it seeks to maintain an ongoing dialogue with the European Commission in an attempt to influence the shape and direction of future policy initiatives.

Technology policy has always been an area of contention between national governments and the European Commission, with the latter expanding its influence through alliances with industrial partners and new policy initiatives such as Esprit and the Single European Market. Indeed, EC science and technology policies played a key role in the 1980s in establishing a renewed momentum for European integration (Shearman 1986; Sharp and Shearman 1987). With a shift in the EU policy agenda which brought the issues of unemployment, social exclusion and sustainable development alongside those of competitiveness and globalisation, the Fourth Framework Programme emerged as the new political battleground. Its Telematics Applications Programme – developed in the wake of the Delors White Paper and the Bangemann Report – expanded the Commission's Esprit model of responding to industry needs to embrace a broader user community within society as a whole. With a major shift of emphasis from technology push to user pull, plans for new telematics initiatives were developed including – amongst those for libraries, transport, healthcare, the environment and so on – one for telematics in urban and rural areas.

Thus for the first time issues of economic competitiveness, employment and social exclusion were brought together in an EU technology-based programme in response both to the imperatives of the Bangemann Report and the urban needs quite clearly articulated by Telecities and other networks. The activities of the Telecities network gave cause for concern to some national governments and those vested interests inside and outside of the European Commission whose loyalties lay with the strong rural constituencies that had been created through previous European Commission Third Framework programmes. As city authorities prepared their bids for the urban and rural programme, some national government representatives were raising a formal objection against urban local authorities being allowed to coordinate bids on the grounds that the EC had no 'legal competence' on urban issues. The Commissioner for Regional Development (DG 16) ruled that trans-European networks of cities *were* eligible for EU support, but other factors meanwhile conspired to limit the cities' access to available funding.

Opportunities for Telecities and similar networks had been enhanced initially by the Commission's attempt to shift the focus of policy initiatives from the previous model of technology push to one of user and applications demand. Projects needed to be user-oriented, cost-effective and clearly based on market research into users' needs. Responding to user demand is clearly crucial to the effective development and commercialisation of telematics applications. Doing so within the first round of the Telematics Applications Programme call for proposals proved more difficult than anticipated. The programme was burdened by short time scales, oversubscription and relatively low levels of funding. The fact that the development and validation of appropriate applications projects – i.e. in response to actual urban user demand – does not necessarily involve R&D in the strictly conventional sense, made it difficult for Telecities projects to be accommodated within the framework of the specified Workplans. Moreover, almost all of the evaluators had a technical or R&D background with little experience of the economic, market and social aspects of technological development. Many of those working in DG 13 shared this R&D culture. Previous programmes had created strong constituencies of vested interests and new user groups were unrepresented in the Commission's evaluation process.

This is not to say that Telecities and other networks have gained no advantages from the EU policy-making processes. As new entrants to the technology policy arena, their success is likely to be limited. Some Telecities projects have been funded, but more importantly Telecities has established its status as a representative user group. Speaking at a Telecities General Meeting, the Assistant Director General of DG XIII stressed the importance of emphasising the 'social process' rather than the technological infrastructure, and acknowledged the problems experienced within the Fourth Framework Programme in shifting from past approaches. Fewer predominantly technology-based and more 'city-friendly' initiatives were likely to emerge from future programmes. Meanwhile, other parts of the Commission concerned with regional development, social policy and industrial policy are rapidly incorporating European cities into their policy dialogue.

Economic, social and cultural dimensions

At the same time, *economic* aspects of globalisation are pushing localisation to the fore. The local economy is a significant factor for a number of reasons. First, and most obviously, it is the sum of local experiences that makes up the national economic, social and technical infrastructures and competitive capabilities. Second, cities have long been recognised as a major driver of regional development. Third, often national policy solutions to problems of competitiveness prove to be ineffective. In response, economists are beginning to shift their focus of analysis. Reich (1991) and Sharp and Pavitt (1993) note that survival within the evolving global economy is increasingly dependent on the quality and innovativeness of the people, skills, talents and institutions available at the *local* level.

Such views underline Moss Kantor's (1994) analysis of factors influencing competitive advantage in the evolving global marketplace. She suggests that competitive advantage is increasingly located at the local level and argues that if cities and regions want to survive in the evolving global economy, they will have to develop what she describes as the 'Three Cs' – 'Concepts, Competencies and Connectedness'. 'Concepts' relates to the innovative capacity lodged in universities and other enterprises to be able to think imaginatively and develop new products, services and applications of high quality. 'Competencies' relates to skills and activities in manufacturing while 'Connectedness' builds on the old notion of trade links to encompass connectedness in electronic as well as trading terms. All three 'Cs' are local dimensions which can be enhanced through telematics technologies and need to be developed in the context of what Moss Kantor describes as 'social glue' or what we would term a fourth 'C' – Community.

This emphasis on social interactions brings us to one of the major themes of this chapter. As we argue in some detail below, the capacity of a city or region to successfully innovate and compete is crucially embedded in the character and cohesion of its social and cultural context. There is a clear and recognised link between technology, culture and economics (Youngs, this volume), and the rapid diffusion of relatively cheap and accessible telematics technologies linked to mass or popular culture is adding a new dimension. While the interaction between technology, culture and economic activity in the global marketplace cannot be understood along neatly defined national boundaries, within the context of evolving cultural and technological globalisation, there is clearly room for local diversity and creativity.

For European cities the fusion of technology with cultural and historical experience may well prove to be a real window of economic opportunity. The Information Society promotes a new and important association between the productive elements of the economy (knowledge generation and mechanisms for information processing – that is, the existence of know-how, skills, technology transfer mechanisms and organisational and local infrastructures) and the cultural capacity of society – namely the values, processes and historical experiences defining its potential and ability to accumulate and manipulate knowledge and symbols. One of the most important challenges to be met by urban policy-makers is the linking of the globally oriented economic functions of the city with the locally rooted society and culture. Some argue that this offers cities, in Europe particularly, a means of reinforcing their emerging political autonomy or influence. The historical and cultural experiences of cities, combined with access to and a facility with those new technologies enabling the fusion of popular cultural and economic activities, may well prove the key to creating those conditions most conducive to the management of the inherent contradictions of the local and the global, making the old urban traditions and cultures of major cities ultimately more strategically important than the high-technology complexes promoted by national governments (Castells 1994: 30–2).

Opportunities and constraints

The processes inherent in technological development and globalisation clearly present local economies with major opportunities. But there are also constraints. In theory, telematics technologies clearly add an important potential dimension to local economic activities in a globalised context, providing the opportunity for local political and economic agencies both to widen the 'boundaries' of talent, skills, entrepreneurship and innovation into which they can dip, and to enhance their sense of local and global 'connectedness'. Such potential, however, remains largely untapped due to the parochial nature of much local economic interest, an applications 'gap' at the community level, and the social and economic trends inherent in the development of the so-called 'Information Society'.

Let us look at the significance of the latter first. While all the dominant economic and political centres on which people depend are indeed integrated into the global economic networks, *the fact remains that only a minority of people are truly integrated into the global economy.* Development of the information economy – with all its associated structural readjustments – is bringing in its wake an increasing economic and social dualism within our cities which is reflected in the rising tensions emanating from the growing marginalisation, unemployment and poverty of significant numbers of people. As we argue below, the nature of local socialisation processes and the degree of social cohesion can be crucial determinants of economic effectiveness. Yet the very nature of the vision of the 'informational city' (Castells 1989, 1994) being promoted by many urban policy-makers militates against the development or sustenance of such social cohesion. Certain élites within cities are experiencing the cosmopolitanism (real and virtual) of Information Society life. Meanwhile, the majority of those belonging to disadvantaged groups find themselves ever more socially, economically, electronically and technologically disenfranchised.

This poses real problems for policy-makers seeking to manage the processes of structural adjustments at both the local and national level. Social considerations aside, there are strong economic reasons to counter this information economy dualism. Without a market, the information economy will not flourish. Without access to skills, resources and infrastructures at the local community level, the potential competitive advantage afforded local economies through the fusion of technology, culture and economics will remain unrealised. Uncontained, marginalisation results in social disintegration and tension and is not conducive to economic regeneration. As thresholds of unemployment, migration and poverty have risen across Europe and elsewhere in recent years, some form of containment has become a matter of contingency rather than choice.

Other constraints on local economies of relevance here relate to the need for some form of public intervention to address issues of infrastructure, applications and access. Asymmetries in the spread of technological development result from local and regional factors . Developing the capacity to compete in the global marketplace clearly makes demands on local policy-makers. Indeed Freeman and Soete (1994) emphasised the need for local authorities to create favourable infrastructural conditions. Policies promoting education and training, SME networking and public/private partnerships, for example, could be used to strengthen the attractiveness of the existing location, thus reducing the locational flexibility of both multinational and national corporations.

Further reasons for intervention at the local level are evident in the debate on information superhighways. Without suitable appropriate intervention to support the capacity of all individuals to have access to and actually use the new telecommunications infrastructures, the dualism referred to above will be reinforced through a largely irreversible pattern of 'information haves and have-nots'. The development of services to take advantage of upgraded and enhanced infrastructures moreover currently reflects a pattern of 'development from above'. If information superhigh-ways are to benefit the majority of individuals, households, and organisa-tions and businesses, there is a need for public support at the local level to promote 'development from below'.

This is a crucial factor. One of the main constraints on the current development of advanced communications services – nationally and locally – is the lack of new applications which can generate enough demand to pull through the installation of new infrastructures. This needs to be addressed via experimentation in the use of new communications technologies and infrastructural developments so that the indigenous potential of cities and regions can be better realised. Social innovation in the community – involving town halls, schools, voluntary sector groups, libraries, the health service, etc. – is as necessary as innovation led by industry, commerce and government departments.

The paradox is that the more globalised the economic context, the more important the localisation aspects. In a world economy characterised by knowledge and information flows, cities and regions are increasingly acting as critical agents of economic development, or to use Goodman's (1979) description, the last entrepreneurs. Regions and cities are often able to adapt to the changing environments of technology, culture and markets. They have less power than national governments but greater capacity to foster innovative environments in support of local development.

LOCAL POLICY SIGNPOSTS: SOCIAL CONTEXTS AND INNOVATIVE MILIEUX

So where does all this leave local policy-makers in practical terms? What are the determinants of successful economic development, and how should they be prioritised? Here, even seasoned policy-makers are floundering. The 1990s have brought a period of policy reassessment and evaluation. Technology-oriented frameworks are being supplemented, and at times replaced, by more sophisticated policy approaches taking into account such factors as historical experience, local environments and the ways in which skills and practices become socially and culturally embedded within our societies and institu-tions. Add to this the new opportunities engendered by the development and diffusion of interactive telematics technologies, and two policy insights are of particular interest. The first highlights the significance of social structures in facilitating or constraining economic and technological development. The second underlines Castell's identification of the links between the productive elements of an economy and the cultural capacity of its society, suggesting that the fusion of cultural (in the broadest sense of the term) and economic activities may well prove the key to creating those conditions most conducive to the management of the inherent contradictions of the local and the global.

Policy insight 1: social structures and economic development

Taking the socialisation aspects first, local experiences which at first glance appear broadly similar, may well turn out to reflect quite different patterns and structures of economic and industrial development. Much depends on the historical experience to date and existing social structures and cultural patterns. The capacity of a locality or region to respond effectively to global competitive pressures is quite distinct from access to the technology itself. As Saxenian's (1994) comparison of the Silicon Valley and Route 128 experiences clearly shows, similarities in terms of university competence, large firms, technology know-how and so on were not sufficient in themselves to ensure similar levels of *sustained* competitiveness in the two regions.

Much more important were the nature of the social contacts and socialisation processes inherent not only in the industries themselves but also in the broader local communities. Saxenian describes how Silicon Valley has a decentralised industrial system that is organised around regional networks:

> Its companies tend to draw on local knowledge and relationships to create new markets, products and applications. These specialist firms compete intensely while at the same time learning from one another about changing markets and technologies. The region's dense social networks and open labour markets encourage experimentation and entrepreneurship. The boundaries within firms are porous, as are those between firms themselves and between firms and local institutions such as trade associations and universities.
>
> (Saxenian 1994: 44)

Silicon Valley engineers developed stronger commitments to one another and to the cause of advancing technology than to individual companies or industries. Their working environment was one in which hierarchical structures were explicitly avoided and management styles were characterised by a high degree of professional autonomy. In Boston by contrast,

> Route 128 firms sought to preserve their independence by internalising a wide range of activities. As a result, secrecy and corporate loyalty govern relations between firms and their customers, suppliers and competitors, reinforcing a regional culture of stability and self-reliance. Corporate hierarchies ensure that authority remains centralised and information flows vertically. The boundaries between and within firms and local institutions thus remained far more distinct.
>
> (Saxenian 1994: 47)

Stability and company loyalty were valued over experimentation and risk-taking, and organisations were characterised by formal decision-making procedures and management styles.

These kinds of differences are reflected in other work on social models of industrial development which have sought to explain not only the organisational structures inherent in the development of industry structures, but also the underlying social processes reflected in a particular industry's development by considering management as part of a *social* network in which common perceptions, attitudes and behaviour are shaped and moulded. In particular, the differences between Silicon Valley and Route 128 represent what might be termed archetypal patterns in the social structures of industrial development, characterised by Shearman and Burrell (1987, 1988) in terms of community, informal network, formal network and club – the former managing to sustain the innovative dynamics of the community/informal network end of the spectrum, while the latter succumbed more to the patterns – and subsequent economic consequences – of the formal network and club.

What is important about Saxenian's insights is that the basis for comparison is extended beyond the boundaries of socialisation processes and patterns of social networks *within a particular industry or sector* to the *nature of the socialisation processes and inherent social culture of a particular locality or community*. Significantly, for example,

> ... none of Silicon Valley's founders had roots in Northern California; a surprising number had grown up in small towns in the Midwest and shared a distrust for established East Coast institutions and attitudes. Virtually all were young white males trained as engineers. Having left behind families, friends, and established communities, they were unusually open to risktaking and experimentation.
>
> (Saxenian 1994: 45)

Route 128, by contrast,

> ... was marked by a deep conservatism in both social and business practices. The social world of most New England engineers revolved around the extended family, the church, schools, tennis clubs and other civic institutions. Their experiences did little to cultivate the strong regional or industry-based loyalties that unified the members of Silicon Valley's technical community. Most engineers were from New England, and many had attended local educational institutions. They generally went home after work rather than getting together to gossip or discuss their views of markets or technologies. New England conservatism also shaped the organisation of local labour markets and patterns of entrepreneurship. Stability and company loyalty were valued over experimentation and risk-taking.
>
> (Saxenian 1994: 47)

From the perspective of local policy-makers, what is at issue then is the extent of the 'fit' between the nature of the existing local social conventions and community and the type and stage of industrial development they are seeking to promote. Earlier, more dynamic stages of industrial development flourish best in localities open to social fluidity, innovation and radicalism. Later stages of industrial development are sustained for longer in more conservative environments. A locality's previous experience can be of crucial significance. Silicon Valley, while seeking to replicate Boston's technology complex, 'unwittingly transformed it in the process. Unhampered by industrial traditions, the region's founders created a distinctive technological community' (Saxenian 1994: 44). But the particular nature of local social contexts can change over time. And, as Castells and Hall observe, California is not the only innovative place in the world nor does social interaction need to follow the Silicon Valley model. Social networking takes place in Japan – where conversations about technology too take place in bars, but under a different set of organisational and cultural arrangements (Castells and Hall 1994: 233–4).

Thus it is the combination of appropriate social networks and processes with an innovative milieu that is truly important. For, as Castells and Hall put it:

> social networks are indeed essential elements in the generation of technological innovation, and they are the backbone of the social organisation of any innovative locality.... Yet it remains the case that without an innovative local society, supported by adequate professional organisations and public institutions, there will be no innovative milieu. And without an innovative milieu the development of high-technology industries will contribute to regional development only within the heavy constraints set by the business cycles of industries that are likely to be highly volatile. There will be no possibility of truly indigenous growth, and thus no escape from the state of dependency on another region, another region's companies and another region's innovative individuals.
>
> (Castells and Hall 1994: 234–5)

This brings us in turn to the issues of creativity and culture.

Policy insight 2: production, culture and imaginative milieux

Castells and Hall (1994), in their discussion of the origins, structure and outcomes of emerging innovative milieux, cite the creation of synergy as one of the three faces of the technopole.[2] Here, the emphasis is on the generation of new ways of thinking, seeing and doing. The continuing development and diffusion of multimedia interactive telematics technologies, together with the policy context of Internet usage and information superhighway evolution, is shifting the locus of that elusive synergy away from high-technology technopoles towards the provision of infrastructural support via telematics applications and services. Here, we find an example of how *such generic technologies can open up the opportunity to make what we would argue is a crucial shift from the concept of a technologically driven innovative milieu to a creatively driven imaginative milieu,* for it is only when technology meets with creativity and imagination that synergy takes place. For local urban economies, that imaginative milieu is increasingly to be manifested within the cultural industries both as a result of, yet quite distinct from, the development of the technologies themselves.

Studies of culture as an economic activity are now recognising that rapid diffusion of multimedia, video, telematics and other technologies, combined with an emerging Internet and World-Wide-Web context, is leading to the development of a new techno-cultural sector where a wide range of activities possess commonalities in terms of technology, modes of production, high ratios of creative (as opposed to technical or other) input, Web potential and so on. This includes activities concerned with the production and distribution of cultural goods – broadcasting, publishing, recording, printmaking and animation – and those services which represent a creative input into production such as photography, graphic design, craft-based design in, for example, textiles, clothes and furniture, and more generic business- and knowledge-based activities such as advertising, marketing, promoting and software development.

Besides being a new medium of transmission, telematics also gives rise to new forms of the production and transmission of meaning – that is, new symbolic goods. Thus

> it is when a medium becomes the locus of the production of new meaning that technics becomes culture. This has two consequences. Firstly, it becomes crucial to the spreading of the culture of usage. Culture is not the 'hook' or the 'sweetener' that attracts new users to telematics delivery, it is the nature of the new medium itself.... Secondly, the provision of teleservices is becoming a cultural industry in itself... [underscoring] the need to encourage innovation within applications and software.... Culture and technology are now meshing closer together and one of the driving forces of innovative applications... comes from the cultural realm. Telematics business services are not only useful to cultural industries – they are increasingly being developed and provided as a branch of the cultural industries.[3]

At the same time, and quite distinct from technology development *per se*, the cultural industries play a significant if often unrecognised role in local and national economies. In the UK, for example, the music industry is one of the leading export performers with recording and publishing in particular making substantial contributions to the economy. More generally, as evidenced by their pursuit of such labels as City of Culture, cities now recognise the central role of culture in enhancing their image on the global stage.

Culture without creativity and imagination, however, brings little opportunity for synergy. Whilst in contemporary technology mythology Silicon Valley has become the archetype of the innovative milieu, historical analysis suggests that by far the commonest location of innovative milieux globally has been in the heart of the great metropolitan cities (Castells and Hall 1994: 227). Creativity, in turn, has always been the lifeblood of cities, essential to the operation of their markets, trading and production centres and the enticement of their entrepreneurs, artists and intellectuals. But it is not the isolated acts of such individuals that count. Rather, it is the dynamics of a cascading chain of innovations set in motion by some first act that historically underlies successful transformative experiences across the globe, from Lancashire in the 1780s to California in the 1960s. Moreover, while places like Los Angeles and Silicon Valley are relative 'urban upstarts', you do not have to be young to be innovative. In fact, it can be almost the reverse.[4] Indeed, within a number of Europe's older cities, the concept of the 'Creative City' is gaining ground both as a means of global publicity and a mechanism for economic development. Examples of cities tapping into the creativity theme – explicitly and implicitly – include Manchester, Edinburgh, Cardiff, Galway, Helsinki, Rome, Bologna and Milan. Increasingly, the creativity is being interpreted both in terms of cultural development and economic growth, and for some too there is a recognition of the links with technology itself.

Transcendentalism versus instrumentalism

Continuing our exploration of some of the practical issues for local policy-makers, we move on from imaginative milieux and local socialisation processes to consideration of instrumentalist and transcendentalist modes of technological expression. Adherence to Schumpeterian models and concepts of competitiveness produces an essentially instrumentalist process of technical change. But as Palan (Chapter 2 in this volume) notes, the impact of technology can be far more fundamental. In this transcendental process, technology moves beyond metaphor towards 'reality', conditioning how we view the world. Mechanical, biological and systems metaphors have all coloured and shaped our understanding of how society works, and now communications technologies are setting the tone.

Where Internet is concerned, for example, there is an important distinction to be made between the 'cyberians' who see themselves as part of a cultural revolution and the 'surfers' who are not. For the former, there is clearly a transcendental element to their experience. In the words of Rushkoff:

> Cyberia is... the place a shamanic warrior goes when travelling out of body, the place an 'acid house' dancer goes when experiencing the bliss of a techno-acid trance. Cyberia is the place alluded to by the mystical teachings of every religion, the theoretical tangents of every science, and the wildest speculations of every imagination. . . . The technological strides of our post-modern culture, coupled with the rebirth of ancient spiritual ideas, have convinced a growing number of people that Cyberia is the

dimensional plane in which humanity will soon find itself... But even those of us who have never ventured into (quantum) physics or a computer bulletin board are being increasingly exposed to words, images and ideas that shake the foundations of our most deeply held beliefs. The cyberian paradigm finds its way to our unsuspecting minds through new kinds of arts and entertainment that rely less on structure and linear progression than on textual experience and moment-to-moment awareness.

(Rushkoff 1994: 16–17, my emphasis)

For the 'surfers' then, the Internet and the information superhighway is an instrument to be used. For the 'Cyberians', it is the defining element of their lives – a paradigm shift in cultural terms. What is in the process of emerging therefore are new patterns of social, cultural, technological and economic activities which are essentially transformative in nature and, not surprisingly, have their roots in California. The very nature of the media, however, offers the potential not only to marry such diverse intellectual strands as quantum physics, virtual reality and shamanist philosophies, but to expand the pool of talent upon which local economies can draw, and within which ideas and innovation can thrive. Like all non-orthodox promoters, they are viewed by the status quo as being on the margins of society. Yet these people range in age from teenagers to ageing hippies, linked in their belief that they are the frontier pioneers in a new age, their progress unnoticed by those in the traditional conventions of society for whom the language and imagery of the techno-music world of young alienated people is as if it were another planet. Often technically highly skilled, and in search of a paradigm shift, in many ways they hold the key to future innovative and creative developments and may prove to be the bridge through which some of the inherent dualism of the Informational City can be addressed.

For policy-makers, the challenge is how to tap into this transformative potential as a means of linking the productive elements of an economy to the cultural capacity of its society within the context of what we have above termed an imaginative milieu. There is a tendency to equate technology itself with imaginative quality as in, for example, the way in which the imagery of the Net has captured the imagination of so many. But here, as in other cases, it is not the technology *per se* that is crucial. Technology without transformative development may be innovative but still intrinsically reiterating applications which are merely new variants on old themes. Technology plus transformation – by contrast – is transcendental in nature, representing a 'quantum leap' in vision, worldview and experience which has as much to do with the passions and interests of the people associated with its development as with any kind of commercial or technological imperatives.

Instrumentalism and transcendentalism are not always easy to differentiate at first glance, especially since the same technologies can represent quite fundamentally different processes. Looking back with the benefit of hindsight at Silicon Valley and Route 128, we can see that Massachusetts had all the hallmarks of an instrumental environment with the prime emphasis on the Schumpeter-type paradigm and competitiveness. It was in California that the imagery and language of transformation were to be found with risk-takers and visionaries engaged in the pursuit of private passions and interests stumbling, inadvertently almost, into global fame.[5] Moreover, the very words Silicon Valley have come to embrace and encompass all that might be understood in terms of new technologies and dynamic economic growth, engendering a myth and archetype so strong as to permeate the conscious-ness of politicians, policy-makers, industrialists and analysts across the globe, with even the Japanese – already competent and effective in their own terms – wanting to emulate it.[6]

So what makes a context appropriate for transcendental development? Here, *sustained* experience of openness of debate, radical traditions, intellec-tual novelty and creativity can be essential. Though California lacked the experience of industrialisation enjoyed by Massachusetts, significantly it had been for some time what Ferguson (1980) termed a 'laboratory for transformation'. While questions about the meaning of life and direction of progress are conspicuously absent from conventional analyses of industrial policies and economic development, and indeed from the lives of most of us preoccupied with the business of everyday survival, the same cannot be said of Californian society in general. Indeed, the current role of California as the 'New Age' mecca, embedded in alternative therapies and lifestyles, is only the most recent manifestation of a long tradition of 'frontier thinking' – that is, innovativeness and openness – reaching back almost two centuries.

Whilst not suggesting that 'offbeat' spiritual or philosophical awareness is a necessary precondition for effective, and fundamentally transformative, technological development, it is nevertheless true – especially given the importance of local socialisation patterns and processes – that the ambience of an environment open to radicalism and nonconformity generally is likely to spill over to technological and other areas. Accounts of the early Valley days and Internet development are peppered with the 'frontier' and 'evangelical' language of new breeds of pioneers empowered by a sense of mission (see for example Larson and Rogers 1985; Rheingold 1994). It is this very 'frontier' mentality that has served to foster the Silicon Valley myth. Equally important has been the ability of California to *sustain* the radicalism and imaginativeness of its innovative milieu over time.

MANAGING THE LOCAL WITHIN THE GLOBAL IN INFORMATION SUPERHIGHWAYS: SOME CONCLUDING REMARKS

For local policy-makers then, globalisation and technology clearly bring both opportunities and constraints. But experience to date gives clear indicators of policy directions to pursue. Much of the potential of telematics technologies remains untapped. Public intervention in support of local applications, infrastructural development and universal access is crucial. Successful economic development, however, is less to do with technology *per se* and more to do with acquiring a deeper understanding both of the socialisation processes at play within a particular locality or community and the links between the productive elements of an economy and the cultural capacity of its society. A determining factor is the nature of the 'fit' between the existing local social and community conventions and the type and stage of industrial development policy-makers are seeking to promote. Similarly, a creatively driven 'imaginative milieu' offers greater scope and potential than a technologically driven innovative milieu. The transformative potential of telematics technologies is clear. The challenge is how to tap into this potential. The capacity of a city or region to successfully innovate and compete is crucially embedded in the character and cohesion of its social and cultural context. Those with a history of open debate, radical traditions, intellectual novelty and creativity are more likely to prove successful.

So how might all of this relate to information superhighways? Today, the frontier myth is re-emerging in the rhetoric of information superhighways. As American Vice-President Al Gore put it:

> The linking of the world's people to a vast exchange of information and ideas is a dream that technology is set to deliver. . . . The creation of a network of networks, transmitting messages and images at the speed of light across every continent, is essential to sustainable development for all the human family. It will bring economic progress, strong democracies, better environmental management, improved healthcare and a greater sense of shared stewardship of our small planet.
>
> (*Financial Times*, 19 September 1994)

A Global Information Infrastructure (GII) will

> promote democracy by enhancing the participation of citizens in decision-making . . . and . . . promote the ability of nations to cooperate with each other . . . [and] be the key to economic growth.
>
> (*ibid.*)

This is a vision which not only reflects the global impact of technological development and structural readjustment, the economic promise of communications technologies and a concern with telecommunications policy issues of regulation, investment, interconnectivity, pricing structures and training, but also directly brings the local dimensions of economic development into play. The stage upon which the vision is to be enacted is both global and local. Thus

> the most important principle is to ensure universal service so that the GII is available to all.... [We] have called for positive government action in the US to extend the GII to every classroom, library, hospital and clinic in the US by the end of the century.... [Indeed] schools and libraries in every country could be connected to the Internet... in order to create a Global Digital Library... [which] would allow millions of students, scholars and business people to find the information they need, whether it be in Albania or Ecuador.
>
> (*ibid.*)

If, as argued in this chapter, the nature of local socialisation patterns, innovative environments and historical traditions of radicalism and culture shape the extent to which local policy-makers can exercise policy choices, then the patterns of information superhighway development and Internet diffusion in local environments – while similar on the surface – are likely to result in fundamentally different processes, essentially instrumentalist in nature for some and transcendentalist for others. This distinction can be a function of both actual (local) and virtual (cyberspace) conditions. Most policy-makers are pursuing an instrumentalist approach to information superhighway development. For those in the merging media, IT and telecommunications industries, information superhighways are about promoting new forms of entertainment industries. For the European Commission's DG 13, local (and to a certain extent national) policy-makers, the information superhighways are more like the electronic equivalent of local shopping malls. They reflect Bangemann's emulation of US preoccupations with teleworking, virtual learning environments, telemedicine, teleshopping and so on as a means of shaping the 'information space' they consider so crucial to future economic development and employment generation.

However, where superhighway activities are fused with techno-culture in an imaginative, creative and radical environment, new opportunities emerge for the development of innovative and potentially transformative entrepreneurial activities and improved social integration. As technology becomes culture (and counter-culture), it *is* helping to shape fundamental *mass* changes manifested in the personal experiences of a growing section of the population. But it is not the world of teleworking and business or the interests of thirty-something corporate managers that are in the vanguard of this techno-cultural revolution. Rather it is the world of music and multimedia technologies where young kids dance to electronic music at underground clubs. For the young people involved in today's subcultures, life may be in cyberspace, but cyberspace is not confined to the Internet (Rushkoff 1994).

What is clear now is that telematics have been incorporated into popular culture in a way not anticipated by the fathers of the 'Information Society'. The majority of current policies for information superhighway development offer little in terms of transformative development. Those urban economies most open to new ideas and creativity which, acting collectively politically and economically, are able to access, develop and use information superhighways to attract, exploit and synergise the potential afforded through new techno-cultural industries and paradigms, while at the same time extending the sense of community or 'social glue' to embrace greater numbers of people currently on the 'wrong side' of the social dualism, stand to perform better in the long term.

NOTES

1   The focus of this chapter is on information and communications (ICT) or telematics technologies, given the significant role they are perceived to play in global, national and local economic development. Telematics is here used to denote a range of technologies from basic electronic communications to Internet, multimedia, ISDN, etc. The comments made in this paper with respect to cities and local economies are broadly based on observations made as a result of the author's involvement with the recently established Telecities network, the Eurocities Association, the Atlantic Rim Network, a number of UK local authorities and the European Commission's DG XIII over the period 1993–4.

2   See Castells and Hall (1994: Chapter 9); 'technopole' is the generic term used by the French – and now increasingly appropriated by urban geographers and technology policy analysts – for high-technology developments and science or business parks to be found on the periphery of most dynamic urban areas.

3   Justin O'Connor, Institute of Popular Culture, Manchester Metropolitan University in Message 196, FW4-TURA-CHAT Bulletin Board, Manchester Host, Geonet. Examples in Manchester include 'City of Glass' – an SME (5 people) providing creative Internet and Web 'products' and services with entrepreneurs whose backgrounds include physics, design and telematics; 'Moonfish' – providing services combining computer programming with graphic design and fine arts; 'Music Net' developing interactive multimedia music Web sites; 'Idea' providing telematics, arts and video training; 'Basement Video' staging techno-cultural festival events; 'Cultural Transmission Network' working with multimedia, music, video and film. These are a selection of microbusinesses in Manchester's 'Culture Net' – a loose grouping developed in response to the establishment of a Creative Cities Network. Other cities involved in this include Edinburgh, Helsinki, Rome, Leipzig, Cardiff, Galway, Belfast, Strasbourg, The Hague and Livorno.

4   As Castells and Hall point out, the kind of place that Silicon Valley represents – new, previously unindustrialised and not fully urbanised at the point of first development – is by no means the only type of innovative milieu in history. They argue that the most common location for innovative milieux, especially in earlier times, has been in the heart of major metropolitan cities such as London, Paris, Berlin, New York, Tokyo, Los Angeles and Munich. While occasionally some of these might collapse as a result of war (Berlin) or have lost something of their synergistic capabilities (London), others – often 'old' – have remained highly innovative, especially Paris and Tokyo (Castells and Hall 1994: 225).

5   See for example, Rheingold (1994) and Larson and Rogers (1985). There were of course visionaries and risk-takers associated with Route 128 too. The difference

lies in the fact that Californian society has a non-conformist and risk-taking culture in general so that the 'fit' between entrepreneurs and society is easy to sustain. Massachusetts too has a longer urban history; Silicon Valley by contrast was still in the process of being urbanised at the point of first development.

6   As Castells and Hall (1994: 227–8) point out, the 'total centralisation of economic life in Tokyo...makes it difficult to comprehend the development of a "Silicon Valley" in an emerging Japanese region. Yet, this is precisely what MITI's technopolis policy is trying to achieve. The Japanese clearly yearn for the Silicon Valley archetype.'

9 A political economy approach to labour markets in knowledge-intensive industries

The case of biotechnology

Sally Hayward[1]

Recent years have witnessed growing interest in how contemporary economic systems have become increasingly more 'knowledge-intensive' (for example, see *Journal of Management Studies*, 1993 special issue). A number of writers across academic boundaries have argued that the creation and use of knowledge lie at the core of 'value-added' activities and that innovation rests at the heart of firm and state strategies for economic growth (Drucker 1983, 1993; Gorz 1991; Massey *et al.* 1992; Alvesson 1993; Archibugi and Michie 1995). For some analysts of social change and economic development, knowledge – and the rise of what has been variously called the 'knowledge society', the 'post-industrial society', or the 'information economy' (e.g. Bell 1973; Drucker 1993; Castells 1993) – exerts a powerful influence on understanding and explaining changing institutional structures. This presumed centrality of technical knowledge to the socio-economic organisation and political management of modern society has gained increasing attention across the ideological, intellectual and policy spectrum.

Within this broad interest in knowledge and technology, one area that has become a major topic of political debate is the role and the importance of skilled labour and its relationship to economic competitiveness. The economics and politics of education and training have become a key policy issue in many advanced industrialised societies, notably the US and the UK.[2] Underpinning this notion is the argument that the better trained the workforce, the better the performance of the economy as a whole (Reich 1991; IRDAC 1992, 1994; CEC 1993; *Realising Our Potential* 1993). This idea that investments in 'human capital' (skills, qualifications and labour-market experience) are a crucial input in the production process is not new.[3] However, it has recently re-emerged alongside the 'globalisation' thesis, which argues that in the face of powerful global, macro-economic forces, governments can only pursue supply-side policies – such as improving scientific and training infrastructures. Perhaps the most widely known proponent of this thesis is the Labor Secretary in the Clinton Administration, Robert Reich (1991), who argues that in a world where national barriers that inhibit firms and capital from moving are falling, nations now depend on the creativity and productivity of their labour force to improve their competitive position in global markets. Translated into industrial policy, this becomes a powerful argument for governments to do little else except invest in more education and training. This position has been heavily criticised on the basis that it is an oversimplification of the 'globalisation' thesis and that, notwithstanding the importance of education and training, the role for government is in fact increasing in other areas as well (see Krugman 1986, 1994; Lundvall 1992; Nelson 1992; Lazonick 1993; Humbert 1994; Amin and Tomaney 1995a; Hutton 1995).

Debates within and around 'new' IPE are a useful starting point for understanding the role of skilled labour markets in influencing the distribution of power and wealth in the global economy. Despite their salience, labour markets have been neglected as a direct area of enquiry in the study of IPE. It is this issue that provides the focus of this chapter. In broad outline, the chapter follows Daniels (1993) in arguing that, given the central role of knowledge workers in the production process of technology-intensive industries, the supply of advanced skilled labour and the successful management of skilled labour markets are significant factors in economic development strategies. The importance for IPE is that these labour markets are creating new arrangements both for the state and the firm where each is increasingly dependent on the other (Stopford and Strange 1991). As a consequence, this development is raising new points of enquiry in IR and IPE scholarship.

This argument is explored in four sections. The first briefly looks at the economic and social restructuring of labour markets, particularly with respect to highly skilled workers. The second section sets out a framework for studying labour markets in the broad area of IPE by drawing on Susan Strange's (1988) 'knowledge structure'. She, along with a growing number of other non-American scholars, challenges the orthodox approach to understanding political power and wealth in IPE by moving away from the dominance of the nation-state (see Murphy and Tooze 1991; Stubbs and Underhill 1994). This approach creates space for more critical attention to other patterns and types of interactions – such as international scientific labour markets – that characterise the contemporary global economy. The third section of this chapter presents some empirical research on biotechnology labour markets. The case-study illustrates the significance of advanced skilled labour to knowledge-intensive industries and also explores the broader range of problems related to labour market issues and performance in the biotechnology sector. The final section discusses the IPE of knowledge-intensive labour markets, their ramifications for public policy and firm strategies, and their importance for the way we understand theory and practice in IR and IPE.

CHANGING LABOUR MARKETS IN THE GLOBAL ECONOMY

Significant changes in the post-war global economy have led to equally profound transitions in labour markets. Heightened international competition for market share has had the effect of pushing industry towards cutting production costs and has led to the introduction of automation and the rationalisation of the workforce as well as to the systematic use of cheap labour (Streeck 1989). Consequently, much of the discussion of work organisation has tended to focus on de-skilling, rationalisation and the development of a peripheral workforce in labour market flexibilisation and segmentation (Edwards *et al.* 1973; Bravermann 1974). Labour-market analysis of professional workers has remained surprisingly absent in the literature (Armstrong 1993). Yet, as the previous section suggested, the demand for these 'quality' human capital inputs is rising as production becomes more knowledge-based.

One area in which this issue has been addressed is the 'flexible specialisation' thesis which is most closely associated with the work of Sabel (1982), Piore and Sabel (1984) and Sabel and Zeitlin (1985). The seminal text in this debate is Piore and Sabel's (1984) *The Second Industrial Divide*. The flexible specialisation thesis has been summarised by Ruigrok and van Tulder:

> Taking Alfred Marshall's industrial districts as a framework for analysis, Piore and Sabel proclaimed the rise of a second industrial divide, stating that craft and mass production could be reunited into a new synthesis... [and] that the rise of so-called flexible specialisation networks of interdependent smaller firms, for instance in the Italian region of Emilia Romagna or the German region of Baden-Württemberg, could serve as a best-practice model applicable to other industries and countries. Following this logic, others contended that flexible specialisation networks demanded high labour skills, leading to more worker autonomy and closer cooperation between end producers and their suppliers (Friedman 1988: 356). In this way, flexible manufacturing would be a stage beyond standardised (Fordist) production.
>
> (Ruigrok and Van Tulder 1995: 2–3)

Piore and Sabel's second industrial divide is characterised by a transition from one technological paradigm to another in which successful industries are increasingly dependent on the accumulation of local knowledge-assets such as local skilled labour markets, flexible small firms and accessible information to respond to rapidly changing consumer demand.

However, the flexible specialisation thesis has attracted wide criticism.[4] One significant limitation of this model of economic development is that it fails to address the influence of broader macro-economic forces. For example, it ignores the large body of work which views structural transformations in contemporary capitalism as a threat to localities as they become dominated by powerful international economic forces (Amin and Robins 1990). This leads to the assumption that skills and knowledge are only conditioned by local forces, and (in direct contrast to Reich) there is no recognition of the 'global webs of enterprise' and the emergence of international labour markets in certain sectors, of the relationship between multinational corporations and local economies, and of access to globalised knowledge structures. The poverty of the flexible specialisation thesis in recognising powerful global economic forces is a significant limitation of this approach for understanding economic development and contemporary structural change. To illustrate this point, it has been argued that in the era of 'footloose' capital, the provision of a pool of graduate and skilled labour is being used as a regional incentive to attract foreign direct investment into less favoured regions (Amin and Tomaney 1995b). In Ireland, the strategy of the IDA (Industrial Development Agency) has been to sell the benefits of a multi-lingual graduate labour force for attracting multinational call and teleservice centres (IDA 1995). In a case study of science parks in Britain, Massey *et al.* (1992) have commented on the need for local developers to create the right 'physical environment' to attract highly skilled workers (see also Castells and Hall 1994). Similarly, Reich comments on the physical environment of 'symbolic analysts' as 'substantially different to those of routine producers or in-person servers'. They usually work in spaces that are

> tastefully decorated [with] soft lights and wall-to-wall carpeting . . . calm surroundings . . . are encased with tall steel and glass buildings within long, low post-modernist structures carved into hillsides and encircled by expanses of well manicured lawns.

> (Reich 1991: 179)

The existence of 'footloose' global capital has similarly led many regional authorities to build into local economic development plans inducements for attracting highly skilled workers (Charles *et al.* 1995). These are issues for understanding the structure of the market for skilled labour which are ignored by the flexible specialisation thesis, and necessitate the kind of deeper discussion provided by international political economy theories on the relationship between production and power in the world system.

LABOUR MARKETS AND THE 'KNOWLEDGE STRUCTURE'

In an 'internationalised' economy, control of and access to knowledge have become key issues (Strange 1988). One aspect of 'knowledge' consists of the importance of the skills and insights embodied in the stock of scientific personnel. If 'knowledge' has become the primary factor of production, then the supply and mobility of skilled scientific labour are important factors for understanding IPE.

Approaches which move away from the state-centric model of IR provide a starting point for thinking about scientific labour markets. Susan Strange

(1991), for example, takes a heterodox approach and attempts to bridge the gap between international business literature and IPE. She positions firms as actors often equally and in some cases more importantly than states. Underlying this assertion is her analytical framework for understanding the 'inter-national' where international political economy is divided not into the political and the economic but rather into four interlocking structures in which politics and economics are inseparably intertwined. These structures are finance, production, security and knowledge – all mutually supportive (see Russell in this volume for further explanation).

For Strange, transformations in the knowledge structure are 'bringing new distributions of power, social status and influence within societies and across state boundaries'. She notes that 'power is passing to the "information-rich" instead of the "capital-rich" ' and that information 'unlocks the door giving access to credit' (1988: 133). The problem is defining who has power in the knowledge structure:

> The power derived from the knowledge structure is the one that has been most overlooked and underrated. It is no less important than the other three sources of structural power in the international political economy but it is much less well understood. . . . Analysis of the knowledge structure is therefore far less advanced, and has far more yawning gaps waiting to be filled, than analysis of other structures, even though they may be subject to less rapid and bewildering change. Ordinary people in their everyday wisdom have always recognised that 'knowledge is power'. But in a rapidly changing global knowledge structure such as we have today it is by no means clear to social scientists who has that power.
>
> (Strange 1988: 115)

Of all four primary structures, the knowledge structure is undergoing the most rapid change, with far less theorising about its significance than the others. Strange analyses the knowledge structure by conceptualising it in terms of the importance of know-how and access to information, and of the significance of belief systems which underpin the political and economic arrangements acceptable to society. It is these belief systems that enable power from the knowledge structure to derive less from coercion and more from consent. Power and authority are conferred on those occupying key decision-making positions in the knowledge structure, in other words on those who are

> acknowledged by society to be possessed of the 'right', desirable knowledge and engaged in the acquisition of more of it, and on those entrusted with its storage, and on those controlling in any way the channels by which knowledge, or information, is communicated.
>
> (Strange 1988: 117)

The market for skilled labour is essentially the market for specific types of knowledge. Consequently, the idea of the 'knowledge structure' provides a theoretical means of integrating studies of technology/industry-skilled personnel into broader work on international political economy.

THE LABOUR MARKET IN BIOTECHNOLOGY INDUSTRIES

Biotechnology provides an interesting empirical study for the argument on the significance of skilled scientific labour. It is based on small firm activity and it embodies both global and knowledge-intensive characteristics. Moreover, it holds the potential for revolutionising industrial systems (OECD 1982; IRDAC 1992, 1994; CEC 1993). It is argued that biotechnology is one generic activity that is transforming advanced industrial societies, in Strange's words, into 'information-rich' systems. Significantly, skills shortages have been cited as a major impediment to the growth of biotechnology in Europe. Equally, this has fuelled the assumption that increasing the supply of scientists and technicians will make a significant contribution towards improving Europe's competitive position *vis-à-vis* the United States and Japan (IRDAC 1992, 1994; CEC 1993; Realising Our Potential 1993; De Nettancourt and Magnien 1993). This argument resonates with Reich's overall thesis that industrial policies ought to focus on increasing the supply of highly skilled labour. However, a closer examination of the sector reveals that a broader picture emerges in relation to obstacles to the overall economic competitiveness of European biotechnology. Although the supply of skilled labour is central to the success of this knowledge-intensive activity, other factors play an important role in the choices made by states and firms in the biotechnology sector.

Historical background: American leadership

The commercialisation of biotechnology began in the United States in the 1970s with the rapid development of small firms. Benefiting from this headstart, the United States has gained a leading position in both knowledge and production. American know-how and expertise are unrivalled and are matched by government commitment to the funding of the life sciences (ACOST 1990).[5] This positive climate is supported by close links between industry and university, with many of the start-up firms emerging from university research. Sharp argues that as with micro-electronics, US leadership in the fields of genetic engineering, immunology and molecular biology stems from the catalyst provided by federal funding, not in this case for military and space research but for medical and biological research, and above all for cancer research (Sharp 1985, 1991b). Not surprisingly, at last count the United States had by far the largest number of biotechnology companies – 1,311 compared to 485 in Europe (Ernst and Young 1995).

The US has a clear industrial lead in biotechnology. Companies located in the United States have access to the world's largest biotechnology information infrastructure involving both databases and software as well as to the highest concentration of skilled labour. Equally, American companies attract the lion's share of financial investments – as the recent trend towards strategic alliances with European and Japanese firms demonstrates (*Financial Times*, 19 December 1991, 9 May 1994). A number of large European firms are establishing R&D operations in the United States to benefit from the advanced knowledge base and favourable conditions there (Van Tulder and Junne 1987). Moreover, the high cost and riskiness of research, particularly given stringent government regulations, has led many firms into looking for strategic partnerships with larger companies (*Bio/technology*, 12 April 1994). Sapienza (1989) argues that in a technology-driven industry the emergence of a new technology can trigger changes in the associated market structure and in the nature of competitive forces. Biotechnology, he suggests, has precipitated such a paradigm shift in the ethical pharmaceutical industry, and one consequence is a proliferation of R&D collaborations. Market success has come to those smaller companies (for example, Genentech, Amgen, Celltech, Cetus) that entered into various kinds of agreements with large, established (American) firms. With control of strategic databases and with the highest number of publications per annum (Orsenigo 1989), combined with domination over the lingua franca of the global scientific community, not to mention the availability of capital from both private (often charities) and public sources and more favourable regulatory conditions, firms in the biotechnology sector based in the United States are at a distinct advantage over competitors.

The importance of skilled labour

The preponderance of American firms has led to a number of concerns in Europe that the biotechnology industry is failing to rival its global competitors (Spinks 1980; SAGB 1990). One particular area of concern has been the vulnerability of the knowledge base (Pearson 1987a, 1987b, 1989). Towards the end of the 1980s, eminent British academics under the auspices of the UK Interest Group Working Party of Biotechnology Education organised several meetings (Bryce *et al.* 1989; Bryce and Bennett 1990) of economic advisors, policy-makers, industrialists and academics to confront the issue of a skills gap not only in Britain but across the European Union. From the onset the *raison d'être* was clearly that Europe needed to capitalise at the supra-national level on the potential of its best scientists and universities to compete against the dominant strength of the United States in biotechnology.

The breadth and range of biotechnology applications is highly multi-disciplinary and the industry requires a wide range of skills from its workers.[6] This is reflected in the general level of education of the workforce (over 70 per cent were educated to degree standard, with over 50 per cent educated to doctorate level). This requirement for a high level of skills is equally reflected in the responses on work-organisation patterns. Many of the workers were self-organised and relatively autonomous, having chosen not to subscribe to labour organisations as they felt little necessity to do so. Many, of whom over 70 per cent were male, were temporally and spatially flexible, working extremely long hours and often moving around a global web of science and technology networks in search of new ideas, capital and markets. On the whole, these sets of workers tended to be highly motivated towards their work. Recent studies on high-technology workers in science parks reach similar conclusions (Massey 1994). The knowledge that these workers accumulate from lengthy trial-and-error and from working on several specific projects leads to cumulative learning experiences which are valuable knowledge assets in sectors such as biotechnology. An investigation of science and technology inputs into the production process in biotechnology has shown that training 'on the job' and tacit skills accumulated over time are the most important 'science and technology input' into the firm for overall increases in productivity (Senker and Faulkner 1992). This is not new: 'learning by doing' and 'learning by using' have already been identified in the innovation literature as essential forms of knowledge-inputs in the advanced technology firm (see for example Dosi 1988b). In general the biotechnology sector requires workers with very high-level skills – in terms of both formal education and 'on-the-job' learning.

Recruitment difficulties or institutional failures?

Recent investigations have shown that there has been a general tendency for biotechnology firms to experience recruitment problems and that a fragmented and imperfect labour market has clearly emerged which has hindered mobility in Europe (Griffin *et al.* 1993a; Hayward and Griffin 1994a, 1994b, 1994c). Reasons for this imperfect labour market can be linked to the pervasive nature of biotechnology, which cuts across key industrial sectors such as pharmaceuticals, agrochemicals, healthcare and food and beverages, and to the lack of homogenous education and training systems across member states. Additionally, there is little evidence of permeability between industrial sectors for transferring skilled labour, and this may have been one reason why less advanced and less glamorous (in comparison to healthcare) biotechnology sectors such as environment and agriculture were suffering skills gaps (over half of the firms in the agriculture and environment sectors were unable to find relevant workers for specific activities). While variations between different countries did occur, firms seeking highly skilled engineers were unable to meet all their recruitment needs. This was less of a problem for biochemists or microbiologists – core subject areas, widely taught across Europe (Griffin *et al.* 1993b) – but in the highly specialised market areas in biotechnology or the relatively underdeveloped manufacturing fields such as immunology, staff were more difficult to recruit. It was especially difficult to find skilled scientists/managers at a time when many higher education institutions were not offering biotechnology courses with a commercial component (*ibid.*).

The recruitment and information process of many of the firms investigated consisted of ad hoc, personal networks within the global scientific community. Networking was considered to be the most important method due to the global scope of contacts made as a postgraduate student or postdoctoral researcher. However, the transaction costs of searching for suitable workers outside the nation-state could, in some cases, be problematic for the small firm. Thus national advertising for positions was frequently cited as a means for attracting skilled workers. Importantly, and as the flexible specialisation thesis asserts, local labour markets are still a significant factor in SME (Small and Medium Enterprises) success.

Labour mobility around the European biotechnology industry is still relatively small. The informality of spreading information about jobs across Europe has meant that there is a high level of uncertainty when recruiting. Fragmentation leads to decreased opportunities for attracting the right skills and ultimately disadvantaging certain firms (mainly SMEs) and regional economic performance in those areas (Griffin *et al.* 1993a). Combined with this, there is a general decrease in the number of graduates proceeding to postgraduate and postdoctoral training and a movement of labour from the south to the north of Europe as a consequence of underdeveloped scientific and technical infrastructures in the former (Walshe *et al.* 1992). Both have contributed to an under-maximised labour market in biotechnology and a concentration of an élite set of workers in certain geographical areas.

In biotechnology, it is clear that there is a distinctive and highly imperfect labour market. It is segmented by region, specific sector, patenting and intellectual property regulations (for example, what is considered acceptable in one country may not be in another; equally, quality-control expertise will differ considerably). This situation is in keeping with the conclusions from other studies of high-technology labour markets. Pisano (1991) shows how segmentation into vertical trajectories shapes research activity and innovative performance. McNabb and Ryan (1990) have explored the general characteristics of segmented labour markets in advanced-technology industries, while McNabb and Whitefield (1993, 1994) set out the ways in which segmentation in specialised labour markets shapes patterns of training and skill shortages. They show that investment in training systems can add effectively to the value of human capital and remove labour market imperfections, but that high-technology industries will remain segmented and diverse. Bosworth (1990) argues that in new knowledge-intensive industries, specific skill shortages limit the early growth of the sector and shape choices between different technologies, but are replaced by more general skill shortages as the sector grows and matures in its products and techniques. Biotechnology illustrates this diversity and segmentation (De Nettancourt and Magnien 1993; Griffin *et al.* 1993a). The case study of biotechnology reveals a complex labour market. A number of institutional factors underpin its behaviour, and these are related to the broader structure of firms, investment patterns and regional economic strategies and, importantly, to the national societal systems underlying the institutional arrangements of regions or states.

THE IPE OF KNOWLEDGE-INTENSIVE LABOUR MARKETS

The development of specific, fragmented, unstable labour markets in sectors such as biotechnology – but also including telecommunications, computing, materials, control systems and aerospace technologies (see Russell in this volume for comment on 'generic' technologies) – has important implications for the distribution of power and wealth. To give one example of the way in which a focus on such labour markets challenges orthodox ideas in IPE, the significance of the linkage between education and industrial competitiveness has been so important that the traditional North–South dependency debate has required detailed re-thinking as a consequence of changing power dynamics in the relationships between the newly industrialised countries (NICs) such as South Korea, Taiwan, Hong Kong and Singapore, and the first world, as a result of government commitment to the promotion of developing technical literacy levels, high technology and management skills (Carnoy *et al.* 1993). In consequence, the NICs along with Japan now constitute a dynamic growth pole of the global economy. The marketisation of Eastern Europe has also opened the technical riches of labour markets there (Carnoy *et al.* 1993). In computer software, the Japanese-owned British firm ICL manages most of its software design and maintenance from India, using a force of 2,400 highly skilled workers paid one tenth the average wage of a British software engineer (BBC Radio 4 'Today Programme', 13 April 1995). Equally, a reverse scenario is currently taking place where instead of jobs moving to newly skilled workers, the latter are moving globally to new jobs. Thus skilled workers recently made redundant from the Swan Hunter shipyard in the north-east of England have been actively recruited by companies in California who need their specific skills and insights (Tomaney *et al.* 1995). 'Globalisation' has opened the range of choices available to individuals, firms and states. But 'globalisation' also has negative tendencies, as the Swan Hunter case shows. Even in highly skilled labour markets, because of the fall in demand for such workers in the north-east of England, firms in California can offer far lower wages to highly skilled yet unemployed workers and without offering any formal labour representation.

If skilling the workforce and increasing control in the knowledge structure have become essential strategies for wealth accumulation, what ramifications does this hold for the relationships between relevant actors? And what are the wider implications for IPE of changes in the location of power? In the face of globalising tendencies in world markets, including those for skilled labour, it is tempting to follow Reich (1991) in discarding national economies as rapidly obsolescent entities. However, such analysis of macro-economic transformations has led to an oversimplification of the changes currently taking place (see Lazonick 1993; Amin and Tomaney 1995a; Hutton 1995). In particular, very little attention in IPE has been given to micro-economic processes and institutional dynamics, both of which are relevant to understanding scientific labour markets. In the biotechnology industry, state–firm bargaining can no longer be adequately explained in terms of the subordination of the firm to the nation-state. The 'rules of the game' are less clear, and the choices for the firm have in many instances become wider in a global marketplace. Certainly, Reich's thesis does support policies to generate more advanced skilled labour in a global marketplace. What is less compelling about his argument however, is that this is all governments can hope to achieve in industrial policy, in the face of the erosion of national identities.

On the contrary, a growing literature among economists and geographers emphasises how nation-state specific factors promote technological change (Porter 1990; Lundvall 1992; Nelson 1992). The main lesson to be drawn from these contributions is that technology is not easily transferable across borders but rather is country-specific and rooted in skills, capabilities and knowledge which are accumulated through time. Consequently, it is no surprise that in biotechnology, job advertisements as well as author indexes in journals are highly geographically concentrated. Specialised skills are more often located in territories which have recognised the importance and advantages of developing institutions that promote an advanced scientific infrastructure (Amin and Tomaney 1995c). Amin and Tomaney (1995a) argue that the evidence for the emergence of a disembodied knowledge network that transcends national boundaries is not convincing, and Archibugi and Michie (1993) suggest that in spite of 'globalisation', national systems of innovation continue to play a crucial role in the organisation of research and know-how. Firms appear to be heavily influenced by national capabilities when taking strategic decisions concerning joint ventures or the internationalisation of their R&D facilities (Archibugi and Michie 1993). Significantly, Teague (1995) argues that the nation-state retains an important role in relation to the labour market, particularly for the organisation of the social security system which can not be easily transferred upwards to a supranational body. The problem of regional labour market adaptation is further exacerbated by cultural, linguistic and other barriers to regional migration (Curran and Lovering 1994; Tomaney *et al.* 1995).

In addition, embedded social values and practices have affected the rate of economic development in certain areas of biotechnology. For example, in countries where the Green movement and the Church have significant popularity, pro-biotechnology lobbies have frequently met with fierce opposition on ethical grounds – for example with respect to Bovine Somatotropin (BST), patenting genes, human growth hormones and genetically modified foods. A Eurobarometer (1991) study showed that in countries where there was less information from non-governmental sources, public support for biotechnology was higher than in countries where there were powerful interest groups against it. In Germany, for example, the Green movement has successfully lobbied for a lengthy regulatory process before companies set up laboratories for scientific research in biotechnology (*Financial Times*, 9 May 1994). Economic development in some industries has become inseparable from cultural and political environments. In this respect, state actions have been constrained by the knowledge on the part of the state's agents of what is possible and what is precluded (Cox 1987). This has little to do with specific manipulation of state policies or actions of particular 'actors' but with general understanding about the tasks and limits of the state, given social preferences (*ibid.*).

However, the dialectic of globalisation is such that despite deeply entrenched national socio-economic value systems, governments are being compelled to accommodate global knowledge and production structures, or risk losing firms. For example, at a macro-economic level, the international-isation of R&D activities (Howells 1990) and of global scientific labour markets has contributed towards broadening the bargaining structure for some actors, with the consequence of limiting power for others. For global firms, there is much to be gained from this enlarged arena – they now have more choices than the limiting boundaries of the nation-state and have greater power leverage over the state in some areas. The strict regulations surrounding biotechnology research in Germany has lead many large companies – including Hoechst, Bayer and Boehringer Mannheim – to establish biotechnology R&D operations in the United States (*Financial Times*, 9 May 1994). German authorities are now looking to review the regulatory environment for biotechnology firms (Ernst and Young 1995). For core biotechnology workers there have been signs of migration to the United States (IMS 1983, 1987). The perception amongst the scientific community is that salaries and, perhaps more importantly, opportunities for technological development in biotechnology are greater in the United States. While the general principal at work is relatively simple – to those that have technology shall be given – the exact ways in which this process is worked out historically and geographically creates variations and patterns which are important to IPE and indeed to international relations in general. The consequences for long-term economic development are so important that governments feel compelled to keep strategic industries and accommodate them because the cost of losing them is too high in terms of employment and wealth generation. Such structural pressures were demonstrated by recent events involving Gensyme where lengthy regulatory procedures in Massachusetts threatened that state's position as a global biotechnology centre. The government in Boston responded by allocating ombudsmen to take biotech-nology firms swiftly through the regulatory procedures. The deal was made extra-sweet by the state authorities sanctioning tax breaks for Gensyme (*Financial Times*, 9 May 1994).

CONCLUSIONS

If it is part of the agenda of the 'new' IPE (Murphy and Tooze 1991) to consider individuals as agents in the global political economy, and to look not only at abstractions such as the state or structures such as the market, then it is all the more central to consider human capital and labour-market issues because of what they might suggest for the ways in which IPE is theorised. This chapter has attempted to construct a political economy approach to scientific labour markets and has suggested that there is a need within IPE generally to explore issues revolving around technology and knowledge. Certainly, there is scope for further work looking at how markets for skilled labour influence the behaviour of the firm competing in a competitive structure and of the state acting for national policy intent.

I have also sought to challenge the conceptual tendency to deal with transformations taking place at the macro-economic level as a homogenous process. On the contrary, globalisation has *not* led to national policy-making becoming ineffective. For labour market policy generally, increased international economic integration means – paradoxically – that the impact of successful national policy is greater.

NOTES

1 Until 1994, I was Senior Administrator for an EU COMETT-funded University Enterprise Training Partnership (BEMET). While I acknowledge with thanks BEMET's financial support, the views expressed herein are my own responsibility.
2 For further discussion, see Sally Hayward, 'Political Economy of Biotechnology Labour Markets', PhD thesis, The Nottingham Trent University, forthcoming.
3 See the work of Theodore W. Schultz (1963) and Gary Becker (1957, 1962, 1964). During the 1950s and early 1960s, they began to pioneer the exploration of the implications of human capital investments for economic growth and related economic questions.
4 For a critical discussion on the flexible specialisation thesis and 'post-Fordism' see the collection of essays in Amin (1994). Also see Pollert (1988); Amin and Robins (1990); Harrison (1991); Jessop (1992); Leborgne and Lipietz (1992).
5 For a fuller discussion on the development of biotechnology see Sharp (1985, 1989b, 1991b), Thomas and Sharp (1993) and Thomas (1993).
6 Over 230 biotechnology firms were used for this investigation. These were mainly small firms (less than fifty employees). See Hayward and Griffin (1994a) for details of methodology and sample size.

10 When technology doesn't mean change
Industrial adjustment and textile production in France

Geoffrey Underhill

Some of the most extravagant claims are made on behalf of technology with respect to contemporary and historical economic development, especially the process of 'globalisation'. It is portrayed as an autonomous variable forging a new society, a rogue historical force plunging us all into darkness or light, depending on the technology in question and one's normative preferences.

For many years, economic theories of technology tended to view technological progress as an exogenous variable outside the process of economic development itself (Rosenberg 1982: 17). Technological discovery and knowledge production, proponents of this position might argue, is the crucial factor driving the changes in contemporary industrial structure and the international division of labour (Mytelka 1991: Introduction and Chapter 1). The possession of technological capacities makes the wealth of the First World the exclusive preserve of a few advanced industrialised countries and condemns the rest to a marginal existence (Strange 1994a: 137–8). Multinational corporations, as owners and developers of technology, prowl the world conferring their bounty upon those who provide the appropriate infrastructure for foreign direct investment (Reich 1991). Research and development policies are aimed by states at developing independent and sustainable means for improving technologies in the search for competitive advantage in the international economy (Cawson *et al* 1990; Hilpert 1991). The productivity of labour and capital is closely associated with new technological developments, as are relative levels of national or corporate competitiveness (Strange 1994a: 136).

At the same time, transportation technologies have shrunk distances and expanded the scope of markets. What was once 'regional' or international in terms of market geography is now regarded as part of the same neighbourhood. Production units at some remove can service local markets as delivery costs and times are dramatically reduced and market information is relayed via electronic data networks. Expertise can be made available without the need for a localised presence.

The most extraordinary powers associated by the literature with technology are generally conferred on information technologies. Computerised information processing, digital technologies, and satellite and fibre-optic technologies which enhance the volume of information available and the speed of its transmission are, it is argued, behind the globalisation of economic space (Strange 1994a: 131). Service industries have been transformed, infrastructure enhanced, and political jurisdictions have been circumvented by the ceaseless march of new electronic information technologies. With respect to financial markets the case is often made very strongly (Edwards and Patrick 1992: 2; Cerny in this volume). The new technologies have made possible the integration of once disparate and distinct markets. The 24-hour global marketplace in foreign exchange has laid low the capacity of central banks to manage monetary and exchange-rate policies; capital controls belong to the past. The ability of regulatory agencies to monitor transactions and enforce their jurisdiction has been essentially undermined. The sovereignty of the state itself is at bay as multinational financial conglomerates move capital in response to changing policy climate in particular states. Rapid changes and volatility in new financial instruments leave regulators at a standstill (Underhill 1995).

If the argument that technology constitutes an independent variable, an exogenous force driving the process of economic change, is to be accepted, then a number of apparent anomalies remain to be explained. A few examples will serve the purpose here. Why, to cite a classic example, did the Chinese fail to take advantage of the enormous military potential of their invention gunpower? It remained for medieval Europeans to accomplish this retrospectively obvious (if not particularly laudable) feat. Why were fax machines, or 'telecopiers' as they were known in an earlier life, suddenly so abundant in the 1980s but used little in previous decades? The technology was there and changed little, and many offices had them. Yet curiously the telecopier remained under-exploited. And why, given great pools of capital and a strong historical tradition of research and innovation across many sectors of the economy, has British industry lagged so hopelessly behind with respect to investment in and application of new technologies to enhance a flagging competitive position?

While this chapter would not seek to deny the crucial role which technological developments play in the process of economic development and transformation, it will argue that technology needs to be placed in a larger context if its role is properly to be understood. In other words, we must pay attention to the complexities of the diffusion process (Rosenberg 1982: 19–23; see also Farrands in this volume). The diffusion of technology is governed by complex social, institutional and economic structural factors. Specifically, the chapter will argue that technology does not constitute an exogenous or independent variable in the global political economy. Technology is always married to social purpose: to some expression of self-interest, on the one hand, and that self-interest and therefore the application and development of technology is socially embedded, on the other. This makes technology the object of political interaction:

Since technological evolution represents opportunities for some groups and constraints and costs that must be imposed on others, it is immediately the subject of political controversies.

(Zysman 1977: 18)

This is not, it must be understood, a particularly original argument, but in view of the extravagant claims made on behalf of technology in the globalisation (globaloney?) literature, wherein it is *reified* (and indeed *deified*), some devil's advocacy might prove healthy to debate.

This paper will argue, then, that the role of technology is highly dependent on a number of factors. Important among these are the socio-political context, the economic structure of the market, and the patterns of perceived self-interest which emerge in political conflict at domestic and international levels of analysis. One must resist the temptation of technological determinism as much as I have argued elsewhere that one should resist the temptations of economic determinism (Stubbs and Underhill 1994: 17–44). Technology must be fused with self-interest to prove itself useful, and self-interest is socially and politically embedded.

The paper will analyse a case wherein available technology was *not* adopted as a solution to the difficulties of a particular industrial sector, the textile and clothing sector in France, at a time of severe crisis from the mid-1970s into the 1980s. There is clear evidence that investment by firms in capital-intensive technologies would have resolved many (though not all) of the sector's competitive weaknesses in the open economy. A number of firms availed themselves of the option and prospered commensurately, but most did not. The refusal to adopt the technological solution to the economic impasse was in part a problem of capital shortage for relatively small firms, but this does not explain all and also serves to reinforce the point that technology is a highly endogenous factor.

A broader argument is needed to explain the refusal of technological solutions by supposedly profit-seeking entrepreneurs. Such an argument should focus on the role of industry associations in mediating conflict amongst constituent members, on patterns of state–industry relations, and on the use of political resources to avoid economic adjustment. Textile and clothing industrialists pushed for policies which would enable them to avoid the disruption of traditional patterns of industrial organisation which the adoption of new technology implied. This strategy was not successful in the longer run, but it did succeed in appropriating considerable amounts of public funds in aid of the strategy and in catalysing a policy of trade protection in the industry across the European Union and the OECD in general. This case implies that technology is a highly *dependent* variable embedded in a larger picture of complexity. As technology may destabilise certain key social groups, it may successfully be resisted; for how long is a matter of circumstance. We must understand why technology is (or is not) adopted when it is, and for whom. Technology will be seen as formalised practice embedded in the socially accepted customs and values, or 'common ways of doing things', which we call culture (Franklin 1990: 15). The textile industrial complexes of Roubaix-Tourcoing, the Vosges, or the Rhône-Alpes constituted powerful cultures wherein common ways of doing things often overshadowed the competitive incentives of the market.

This paper will begin by looking at the nature of the crisis and the terms of competitive advantage in the textile and clothing industry, arguing that competitive pressures came more from advanced industrialised countries than low-wage LDCs. This implies that other countries successfully used modernisation through capital-intensive technologies to adapt to intensified competition in the wake of the establishment of the Common Market in the EU and GATT tariff reductions. Technology was a possible way out, and the crisis was not at base the result of an inexorable movement of textile production to low-wage areas. Next the paper will outline the political strategy adopted by French textile industrialists, working through their professional associations, to avoid the destabilising effects on the industry which modernisation would have entailed. In particular, modernisation of production would have disturbed the balance of interests inside the industry associations, a development which they sought to avoid at the expense of becoming an economic liability to the country at a time of generalised economic crisis in the 1970s and 1980s. This will lead to a brief conclusion which attempts to place technology as a variable in the context of this case of failed industrial adjustment which had considerable implications for the international trade regime (Underhill 1990).

CRISIS AND COMPETITION IN THE TEXTILE AND CLOTHING SECTOR

The French textile and clothing industry was a major source of value-added and a employer in the national economy, and it remains so, albeit in reduced form. In 1973 the sector accounted for close to 13 per cent of total employment in manufacturing industry or about 668,000 jobs (OECD 1983: 15; INSEE, unpublished series). The turnover of the industry was close to 8.5 per cent of total manufacturing production (*ibid.*), and was crucial to the regional economies of the Nord-pas-de-Calais, the Rhône-Alpes, Vosges, and Alsace-Lorraine (Battiau 1985), all regions which were eventually affected by problems of industrial crisis in a number of industrial sectors at once. It was also important to a number of regions in the country where there were few alternative sources of employment.

A combination of factors led to absolute and relative decline in the industry's fortunes in the context of the national economy. There was an absolute decline in national production levels from 1973 through to the mid-1980s and beyond (CES 1982: 213). The industry lost over 32,000 jobs in 1975, and an average of some 24,000 further jobs per year until a government programme slowed the process in 1982 (INSEE). Losses continued in the

1980s. If in 1973 the textile and clothing sector was 8 per cent of manufacturing production, this proportion fell to barely 6 per cent by the early 1980s (*ibid.*). The decline continued in the subsequent decade.

With such an economically important industry, it was difficult for its decline to avoid becoming a political issue, and the industry associations lost no time in putting their case as the crisis hit from 1974 (UIT 1974, 1975; UIH 1978). However, their priorities were revealed to be in contrast to those of government policy. The government had long articulated a policy which encouraged the concentration of industrial sectors, the better to compete, and an acceleration of investment to modernise production processes. The textile and clothing sectors were no exception to this rule. State intervention had begun with the Cotton Modernisation Act of 1953 (Berrier 1978: 142) and continued with the establishment of CIRIT – a merciful abbreviation of *Centre Interprofessionnel de Rénovation des Structures Industrielles et Commerciales de l'Industrie Textile* (Friedberg 1976).

From 1974, with the election of the Giscard government, these traditional French industrial policy objectives were combined with a more market-oriented policy emphasising competition and adjustment through international trade; the role of the state in industrial restructuring was to be reduced in favour of the market (*Le Monde*, interview with Michel d'Ornano, Minister of Industry, 11 June 1974). Such a policy implied the elimination of many small and medium-sized textile and clothing concerns, vertical integration of parts of the sector or the emergence of market niche strategies, and a breakdown of the traditional industrial structure and culture of essentially family-owned firms. The state aimed to push firms into industrial adjustment through investment in modern technology so as to ensure the continued export-competitiveness and national standing of the industry. Many firms would go to the wall or be absorbed in a process of mergers and acquisitions. The place of small, traditional *entrepreneur-notables* in the sector was in jeopardy.

As EU external tariffs came down following the conclusion of the Kennedy Round and eventually the Tokyo Round GATT agreements, foreign imports began to cause disruption to the industry. The organised interests in the industry were quick to point the finger at 'unfair' imports from low-wage countries such as the 'tigers' of Asia. Certainly the competition represented a considerable threat and imports were rising dramatically. From 1970–9, the domestic market share of French producers in virtually all textile product categories fell (Sénat 1981: 130). The market share of imports had in fact been rising since the late 1960s, a time of rapidly growing demand (*ibid.*).

Other factors contributed to the crisis. Consumption of textile products began to decline as a proportion of household expenditure (UIT 1982: 6), reflecting in part Engel's Law effects (OECD 1983: 29).[1] Growth in textile consumption levelled out from the early 1970s, thus taking a turn for the worse at a time of rising import competition (Sénat 1981: 212). Demand patterns were further affected by the social revolution of the 1960s and 1970s.

Traditional social patterns were often symbolised by patterns of dress at work (working-class smocks, men's grey suits) and leisure ('Sunday Best'). As these social habits broke down, tastes and fashions changed radically towards the casual and more personally expressive (*ibid.*: 228, 276–7). Changing fashions led to a more volatile clothing market as consumers turned away from the more traditional clothing products, changes to which importers apparently responded better than domestic producers. Increases in consumption disproportionately benefited imports. All in all, French firms responded poorly to competitive pressures from overseas and to changes in domestic market conditions.

What conclusions might one draw from this situation? Clearly French textile and clothing industrialists were responding poorly to both domestic demand patterns and trade competition. The growing pressure of the changing international division of labour appeared to be exerting itself, pushing the industry into decline. Few national producers could avail themselves of market opportunities as imported production undercut their cost structures and offered more desirable product ranges.

However, import competition was also affecting segments of the industry which were relatively capital-intensive, where LDC producers were scarcely present. In fact, competition from within the EU and the industrialised countries in general had a far greater impact on the industry's fortunes than the low-wage countries (Spoerer 1982: 7–10). From 1973 to 1979, the French trade balance lost some $400 million to LDC competition, but much more (approximately $700 million) to Italian firms alone, let alone the rest of the industrialised world (Meunier 1981: 398). In fact, Italy's export *surplus* in textile and clothing trade grew proportionately more in the 1970s than that of Korea or Hong Kong, and was of course much larger (*ibid.*). Import competition from the LDCs was, furthermore, limited to relatively simple products with low unit values, largely cotton, and did not affect more complex knowledge-intensive segments of the industry (Texier 1979: 46; Keesing and Wolfe 1981: 86). All in all, twelve industrialised countries accounted for 83 per cent of total French imports of textile and clothing products in the early 1980s, right in the middle of the crisis and at a time when LDC exports had been growing rapidly for some time (*Economie-Géographie* 1982: 14). France received about 25 per cent of its clothing imports from LDC sources in 1980 (France, Assemblée Nationale 1981: vol. 3, 172), whereas the EU average was as high as 65 per cent (EC 1981: 20). In other words, the French industry was less penetrated by LDC exports than other EU countries, and the French trade balance was weakest in segments of the industry dominated by the industrialised countries and capital-intensive production processes.

'Unbeatable' low-wage competition could not have been the culprit. The problem appears to have been the strategies of French firms. Investment levels, crucial to modernisation and the adoption of new technologies, were abysmally low and falling from the onset of the crisis in 1974–5 (France,

Assemblée Nationale 1981: vol. 1, 59). This appears to have been a particularly French problem: an analysis of cost structures and capital intensities in the textile and clothing sector reveals that in the industrialised countries they were about average for manufacturing industry by the late 1970s (OECD 1983: 84). Wage costs are not the only nor indeed primary factor, particularly if one examines the textile as opposed to the clothing sector. Technological developments in textile production in the early 1970s radically altered the available factor mixes in firm strategies (Wagner 1979; CES 1982: 245–50). Textile production therefore need no longer be labour-intensive with low skill levels, and the most modern technologies involved investment costs per workpost well above the manufacturing average (EC 1981: 10–14). By adopting new technologies and raising the capital intensity of the firm's production processes to levels well above the manufacturing average, it was more than possible to meet competition from low-wage producers in most product segments of the industry (Boussemart and Rabier 1983: 26): 'the industry offers scope for exceptionally large variations in the combinations of labour and capital' (OECD 1983: 84). It was estimated that for low-wage countries to gain a 20 per cent price advantage over western producers in consumer markets, they would need production costs *at least* 50 per cent below western levels, bearing in mind the high cost of capital in these economies and the need for reasonable levels of technology to produce sophisticated products (CEPII 1978: 65). Yet in France investment levels were stagnant or declining, and labour productivity growth lagged behind France's western partners (France, Assemblée Nationale 1981: vol. 1, 59). The country's firms were caught in a vicious circle of antiquated equipment, chronic investment shortages, demand shifts, poor marketing strategies (or utter lack thereof), and import competition. The textile and clothing sector was not a 'traditional' industry as such, but French industrialists in the sector were 'traditional' entrepreneurs wedded to outmoded production and commercial strategies.

WHY NOT ADAPT?

The question remains as to why the firms did not adapt by adopting the available production strategies which would have improved their fortunes. Government aid was even made available for this purpose. The state put considerable pressure on the industrialists to adapt to the intensified competition of the EU internal market and falling levels of EU tariff protection. The state-aid scheme encouraged larger firms and modernisation programmes. Yet the industrialists, using their professional associations as intermediaries, were able to capture the adjustment agenda and promote it for the defence of their sector's traditional structure.

There are several factors which cast light on this puzzle and explain the unwillingness of the textile and clothing policy community, including the labour force, to change despite apparent economic imperatives. A good starting point is what might be termed the 'traditional' industrial culture of the textile and clothing sector in France. By 'traditional' firms is meant those which are relatively small, family-owned and managed, using simple production technologies and with implications of decay and backwardness (Landes 1951; Sawyer 1951; Berger 1981). This is not to characterise the textile and clothing industry as necessarily 'traditional' in a general sense, but the majority of the sector in France could be characterised as such: small, numerous, family-owned and operated, and usually long-established with antiquated plant and management techniques. In 1981, at the height of the crisis, small and medium firms (under 500 employees or francs 100 million turnover) comprised nearly 95 per cent of total firms in the sector, and over 50 per cent of turnover (Boussemart and Rabier 1983: 31). Ownership and managerial responsibility usually passed from father to son across the generations. Family decision-making could frustrate efficient management, especially where considerations of personal prosperity, dependent on the fortunes of the firm, obliged directors to siphon off funds which would have been better employed as productivity investments. Family and business were 'inextricably united economically in the sense that business treasury and household purse [were] simply one, just as national treasuries were once inseparable from the King's personal fortune' (Landes 1951: 336).

The patriarchal independent industrialist jealously guarded his destiny, often to his peril. Rivalries among respective families might prevent profitable mergers and the eventual restructuring of important segments of the industry. The traditional entrepreneur faced competitive pressures with little or no grasp of integrated production and management strategies. Considerable effort at modernising industrial plant might therefore be expended to little long-term effect other than raising fixed costs in times of crisis: 'structures...equipment...mentalities...are archaic' (Labouerie [entrepreneur], quoted in Villeneuve 1977).

The jealously guarded autonomy of entrepreneurs may have prevented mergers and takeovers, but it also had repercussions when restructuring of the sector did occur. The concentration of industrial structure took place on a largely horizontal basis, yielding large conglomerates with little attention to internal rationalisation (Friedberg 1976). Government policy offered financial incentives to take over weak and failing firms (OECD 1983: 27, note 14) but the managerial autonomy of the newly acquired subsidiary firms was often preserved. Former owners were left in charge as subsidiary directors, and the result was often managers 'whose interest in their former firms [was] greater than in [the group] as a whole' (Berrier 1978: 227). Sick firms were essentially concentrated into large ones and in some cases family board members overruled professional managers to make unprofitable acquisitions (*ibid.*: 196) which salvaged the honour of failed industrialists in the textile community.

These local entrepreneurs who dominated the main textile regions such as the Vosges and the Nord were often political notables in their region

(Lambert 1969). Their prestige derived from their position as employers and establishment figures, entirely associated with their position as owners of capital. Family and firm had a perceived role to play in the local community, which included paternalistic attitudes towards workers, social welfare, and the economic prosperity of the locality (Lambert 1969: 95–7, 128; Pierrard 1978: 359–60). These perceptions affected the behaviour of industrialists towards market pressures (Berger 1981: 104–9, 144), and they sought 'extra-economic' solutions to the problem of intensified competition.

The crucial variable was the way in which these textile and clothing firms were aggregated within the employers' organisations, and the relationship of these professional associations (as they were called) to the state and the policy process. The textile professional associations were extremely dense in terms of organisation at the local and regional level. Organisation was based on specialised industry branch associations, representing the different activities of firms in the sector from woollen spinners to cotton dyers at the local level. These industry branch organisations were the pillars of the system, maintaining a vertical coherence and contact with the industrial base not matched by national umbrella organisations, in particular the Union des Industries Textiles (UIT) (Friedberg 1976: 119–21). Furthermore, firms were aggregated within their branch associations on the basis of one firm one vote. There was no adjustment for size of firm and obvious disparities in economic power. These local and regional branch associations were then *confederated* into national associations covering the breadth of the industry, preserving powers of veto throughout (*ibid.*: 125).

The national associations saw their role as essentially one of arbitration among the various competing interests of the member branches and the firms, large and small, antiquated or modern, each of which had equal status (*ibid.*: 319). Where economic issues were concerned, the professional associations were therefore anxious not to disturb the balance of interests within the sector. The strong sense of solidarity among association members contributed to this desire to maintain the equilibrium among member associations and firms. Even large and successful firms usually remained in family ownership and stayed loyal to the milieu. Although they might have an objective interest in breaking ranks, the heads of large firms were often the most important notables in the structure of professional associations, clearly identifying their interests with the compromises and arbitrage which the system incarnated (*ibid.*: 142). This was in sharp contrast to the Italian sector, where a fragmented firm structure similar to France nonetheless resulted in forms of 'centrally-controlled coordination of design, output, and marketing' (OECD 1983: 27) which led to one of the European textile industry's greatest success stories.

When it came to participation in the policy process, then, the objective of the professional associations was to preserve the balance of interests within these complex, confederal associations. These priorities effectively conflicted with those of state policy-makers, who wanted to see an acceleration of modernisation and concentration in the textile and clothing sectors (Plan 1971: 52). This liberal market policy orientation was much reinforced with the advent of the Giscard presidency in 1974. If the state got its way, then the balance of interests within the associations would be severely disrupted as modern management practices and takeovers would leave little room for the traditional entrepreneur.

However, policy-makers found themselves dependent on the employers' organisations as intermediaries when it came to implementing policy. The large number of 'traditional' firms in the sector meant that state officials had few means with which to circumvent the associations and establish direct contact with those owners and managers who favoured modernisation and restructuring. There was no convenient group of 'national champions' available, and this was a fatal constraint. The UIT (and its equivalent in the clothing industry), the national umbrella confederation, was seldom capable of decisive action separate from the interests of individual member firms. Patterns of state–industry relations were therefore essential determinants of policy outcome, given that state officials had little choice but to cooperate with the employers' organisations (Friedberg 1976: 160–1). To make a long story short, the priorities of the professional associations were therefore absorbed as objectives of state policies. The employers were able to determine in large part the direction of any redeployment effort and accompanying state aid, thus preserving the 'traditional' characteristics of the majority of firms in the sector (Boussemart and Rabier 1983: 156).

State assistance was as a result commandeered, the better to preserve the traditional structure of the sector. This pattern continued well into the 1980s when the Socialist government announced a comprehensive plan to help the sector (*Le Figaro*, 26 November 1981). This plan was much more an employment subsidy and an indiscriminate boost to company treasuries than it was a plan to introduce modern and successful technologies into the sector (see France 1982a, 1982b). This point was picked up by the EU Commission, which claimed that the plan did not represent a genuine restructuring effort and would unfairly subsidise French firms (*Le Matin*, 3 February 1982; *Les Echos*, 25 May 1982). Most firms could not hope to invest in the new technology. Many did not want to. They sought subsidies and controls on competition instead.

Matters were not helped by the characteristics of the labour force. It was poorly educated and organised. Many firms in the sector relied on either migrant labour or female labour from outlying regions. Stories abound of firms which invested in modern machinery and production processes that lay disused due to the inability or refusal of workers to adapt as necessary. A major study of the textile labour force in particular concluded that there was a link between the low level of worker qualification and the difficulties of modernising and reorganising production (CEREQ 1979: 175). Traditional firm strategies which treated the unskilled and marginal labour force as an expendable cost-variable to absorb cyclical downturns through unemployment (Berrier 1978: 253; Dubois 1981: 148) were ill-suited to the adoption of new technologies.

The modernisation of technologies would, then, have facilitated successful adaptation to rising competitive pressures in the French textile and clothing sector. However, genuine modernisation and restructuring would simultaneously have destabilised important elements of the textile and clothing business communities in France. Meanwhile, the industry associations mobilised on another front: trade policy. Trade protectionism was in many ways the panacea for all. It would avoid serious restructuring on the part of firms, and would spare the state spending large amounts of aid on the preservation of an economic liability.

Citing the low-wage import menace, the French government reluctantly bowed to pressure for import protection and championed a restrictive, protectionist quota system known as the Multi-Fibre Agreement (MFA). A mild version of this was sponsored in 1974 by the US (Farrands 1979), but once the French government got the full weight of the EU bargaining position in favour of tighter restrictions on LDC imports, the renewed 1978 and subsequent agreements were a foregone conclusion as instruments of protectionism (Underhill 1990: 192–201). A wider and wider band of products benefited from the so-called voluntary import quotas as France and key partners were able to organise a transnational coalition in support of a restrictive trade regime. This quota system is in theory to be dismantled as a result of the Uruguay Round GATT agreements, but the future remains uncertain (Underhill, 1997).

Of course, protectionism did not solve the problem for the French industry. Import competition from the far more significant high-wage, capital-intensive producers of the EU and OECD continued. GATT rules and EU law prevented any move to restrict these. The underlying problem remained: the need to adopt new capital-intensive production technologies and, one might add, information technologies for marketing and market data. Those firms which did adapt successfully reaped appropriate rewards in terms of profitability and expansion.

CONCLUSIONS

This chapter represents a cautionary tale with respect to the more extravagant claims made in the name of technology as the driving force of change. The backward economic structure and peculiar cultural and organisational context of business interests in the French textile and clothing sector yielded an industry impervious to the adoption of available, if expensive, technologies which might have ensured a prosperous future. The relationship of technology to economic change cannot be explained outside some notion of social 'embeddedness'. Technology, embedded in complex socio-economic systems, implies social purpose and requires a perceived self-interest if its undoubtedly considerable transformatory powers are to be harnessed:

Systems are evolving cultural artefacts rather than isolated technologies. As cultural artefacts, they reflect the past as well as the present. Attempting to reform technology without systematically taking into account the shaping context and the intricacies of internal dynamics may well be futile.

(Hughes 1983: 465)

This case study therefore contains some important lessons for policy-makers. Not all firms behave in the classic textbook manner. They respond to the opportunities offered by technology and modernisation in different ways. The exercise of political resources to avoid adaptation to new technologies may prove at least a short-term substitute for technological change, as the French industrialists demonstrated through their strategy of trade protectionism and appropriation of state aid. The market does not lead to a universal pattern of behaviour. Failure to understand this can lead to considerable miscalculations on the part of governments with market-driven priorities. Adjustment to changing technologies must be part of a larger social contract (Franklin 1990: 130) in a context of enhanced social and political legitimacy. The choice between weak industry and no industry is a difficult one to make.

NOTE

1   Engel's Law has to do with income elasticities for different categories of goods on the market. The law states that as income levels rise, consumer demand for 'inferior' goods such as basic food, clothing, and shelter, will grow more slowly (and perhaps even stagnate) than demand for newer 'superior' goods. In other words, one can only consume so much food or clothing before needs are satisfied, and so growing incomes will be spent in larger proportions on other goods.

Part III

Technology and change in the world political economy

11 The search for a paperless world
Technology, financial globalisation and policy response

Philip Cerny

The transnationalisation of financial markets raises several key issues concerning the relationships between technology, globalisation and public policy. The inherent flexibility of finance, as well as its central role in other economic processes, is dramatically increased by technological innovation in products and processes, making financial capital – the most mobile form of capital – an increasingly autonomous factor both in the dynamic of globalisation itself and in the erosion of state power. Technological change in financial services is thus the main independent variable in their globalisation – by reducing transaction costs and dramatically increasing the price sensitivity of financial markets across borders, while at the same time making possible a range of economies of scale. These developments have knock-on effects throughout the domestic and international economies. They in turn make obsolescent the governance structures which have characterised economic policy in modern nation-states, undermining the capacity of the state to produce public goods. At the same time, globalised financial markets interact with rapidly changing interest-group structures and divided state structures, especially through 'regulatory arbitrage.' Without the development of transnational regimes capable of regulating global financial markets, the structural basis of the national state itself is being undermined, and Polanyi's 'Great Transformation' is over.

Karl Polanyi saw international finance – *haute finance*, as he called it – as the linchpin of the ill-fated nineteenth-century attempt to create an international political economy rooted in a 'self-regulating market' (Polanyi 1944). In his analysis, social dislocations – including wars and depressions – caused by the failure of supposedly self-regulating markets inevitably lead to political upheavals. These are followed by attempts to institute new or refurbished regulatory systems in order to stabilise market systems, or even to abolish or replace them. Since the breakdown of the Bretton Woods system in the early 1970s, however, the concept of basing the international financial system on the model of a self-regulating market has once again dominated the agendas both of the major financial powers, especially the United States and the United Kingdom, and of the main economic actors in the international system, especially financial services firms and multinational corporations.

Market structures in the financial services industry have been transformed in this process, and at the core of this process of transformation, catalysing and accelerating other changes, has been technological change in finance in general and in the transnational financial services sector in particular. These changes have led to a quantum jump in the sensitivity of prices of financial instruments across the world, drawing market actors big and small – and their capital – into the search for paper profits. Changes in the global financial structure have in turn driven the evolution of a range of structural developments both in the wider economy – both national and international – and in economic policy. The centrality of finance and financial markets to economic change has been dramatically reinforced by technological change, and this is leading to a new hegemony of financial markets in a more open and interdependent world. This new global transformation has challenged gravely the capacity of the state to provide effective governance not only of financial markets themselves, but also of economic affairs generally.

THE THIRD INDUSTRIAL REVOLUTION AND CHANGING FINANCIAL MARKET STRUCTURES

In the absence of a world government, regulation of transnational financial markets can only be done in one of three ways: through workable international institutions; through a hegemonic state or group of states working through less formal mechanisms; or through the re-establishment of much closer and more direct state control over the markets. Serious weaknesses exist at each level. From a political perspective, with increasingly tightly knit global market structures, expanding international capital flows, and a context in which states (and public agencies within states) can be 'whipsawed' against each other in what is called 'regulatory arbitrage' or 'competition in laxity', any attempt at genuine transnational re-regulation of financial markets faces a vast array of structural and conjunctural obstacles. The conditions which made effective regulation possible in earlier eras no longer exist. State policies have tended to converge on a more liberal, deregulatory approach because of the greater structural complexity and interpenetratedness of the international economy – which in turn transforms the changing position of states themselves within that system. Competition between states is no longer simply a rivalry over market shares, but a race to participate in the benefits of transnationally interpenetrated and structurally integrated economic processes. In this context, the globalisation of finance has played a paradoxical role by cutting across structures of state power in such a way as to channel state power itself into reinforcing the structural power of private financial markets.

On the economic level, the debate has been dominated by the 'capital mobility hypothesis' or CMH (cf. Webb 1991; Andrews 1994; Cerny 1994a). Each country reacts differently to capital mobility (real or potential) because of its different size and state structure; however (the CMH posits), the increasing volume, speed and fungibility of capital movements on a transnational – if not yet homogeneously global – scale makes *all* states more vulnerable to what are clearly economic system-level changes (although some states are more vulnerable than others). Especially in the period since the breakdown of Bretton Woods, the volume of capital flows has grown exponentially, dwarfing the volume of merchandise trade flows (see Giry-Deloison and Masson 1988). If money and goods were indeed wholly commensurable – i.e. if use value were identical with exchange value – then the fact that financial flows have regularly been estimated at 20–40 times the volume of trade (and with that gap increasing from year to year) would speak for itself.

Major changes in the character of financial exchange itself, some having emerged from long-term developments in areas such as information technology, some involving shifts of scale which have transformed the structure of transaction costs in financial services, have now become so consolidated and interwoven that they operate to a large extent autonomously of traditional forms of political action and state intervention. Of course, the development and impact of technology does not involve merely the machinery of (in this case) financial transactions – the electronic equivalent of nuts and bolts – but also the culture of production, competition, and innovation in the financial sector and, indeed, in all of the other sectors of economy and society. It is the way that financial flows are structured, not just the volume of those flows *per se*, that gives global financial markets their autonomy and their capacity to impose 'embedded financial orthodoxy' (Cerny 1994b) on governments and societies. It is the structure of competition in financial markets which gives rise to financial innovation.

It is the character of financial innovation, in turn, which gives the markets a complexity – involving 'circular' rather than 'linear' forms of causal interaction (Kitschelt 1991) – which states and limited intergovernmental regimes cannot match. Furthermore, it is not simply the speed of capital flows but the fact that they flow through market structures characterised by what Kitschelt calls 'Mark V' technological structures (*ibid.*: 461, 471–4)[1] – with the innovation strategies which are thereby enabled and the almost infinitely variable economies of scale which result – which allows the markets to stay ahead of the regulators. And it is the rapidly evolving capacity of companies and market actors to manipulate the structures of firms and organised markets through complex and flexible mixtures of market and hierarchy which makes the territorial state and its international extensions structurally unsuited to the task of effective regulation. Financial regulation is becoming more and more difficult in the face of the flexibilisation of financial markets. What that flexibilisation has most dramatically increased is the transnational *price sensitivity* of those markets, and this new global-level price sensitivity constitutes the main driving force of the wider structural transformation.

The economic structure of the world today is not only in the process of changing rapidly. It has already changed dramatically since the 1950s. Globalisation has altered the scale of the 'structured field of action' (Crozier and Friedberg 1977) in which the relationship between the provision of different kinds of goods and assets is shaped. The globalisation of finance has increasingly divorced finance capital from the state. In this context, political control, stabilisation, regulation, promotion, and facilitation of economic activities have become increasingly fragmented. This has, for example, fundamentally altered the nature of so-called 'public goods' (Olson 1971; Cerny 1994a, 1995). Regulatory goods – crucial to the financial issue-area – are an obvious case. In a world of relatively open trade, financial deregulation and the increasing impact of information technology, property rights are increasingly difficult for the state to establish and maintain. Cross-border industrial espionage, counterfeiting of products, copyright violations and the like have made the multilateral protection of 'intellectual property rights' a focal point of international disputes and a controversial cornerstone of the Uruguay Round negotiations.

International capital flows, the proliferation of 'offshore' financial centres and tax havens, etc., have made the ownership of firms and their ability to internally allocate resources through transfer pricing and the like, increasingly opaque to national tax and regulatory authorities. Traditional forms of trade protectionism are both easily bypassed and counterproductive (Nivola 1993). Currency exchange rates and interest rates are set in rapidly globalising marketplaces, and governments attempt to manipulate them often at their peril. Legal rules are increasingly easily evaded, and attempts to extend the legal reach of the national state through the development of 'extraterritoriality' are ineffective and hotly disputed. Finally, forces and actors seeking to evade, counteract or constrain the state are becoming more and more effective. The ability of firms, market actors and *competing parts of the national state apparatus itself* to defend and expand their economic and political turf has dramatically increased. Activities such as transnational policy networking and 'regulatory arbitrage' have both undermined the control span of the state from without and fragmented it from within (see Cerny (ed.) 1993: Chapters 3 and 6).

This transformation, however, has not merely involved the changing scale of public goods *per se*, but the changing technological and institutional context in which *all* goods are increasingly being produced and exchanged. The so-called 'Third Industrial Revolution' is characterised by several profound and far-reaching structural changes which have been major factors in the globalisation of economic structures. The Third Industrial Revolution has a wide range of characteristics, but the ones which are most relevant to our concern include five trends in particular. The first is the development of flexible manufacturing systems, and their spread not only to new industries but to older ones as well. The second is the changing hierarchical form of firms (and bureaucracies) to what has been called 'lean management'. The third is the growing capacity of decision-making structures to monitor the actions of all levels of management and of the labour force far more closely through the use of information technology and thereby to use such methods as performance indicators far more widely. The fourth characteristic is the increasing segmentation of markets in a more complex consumer society. Finally, the Third Industrial Revolution has been profoundly shaped by the emergence of more and more autonomous and global financial markets and institutions, which is our concern in this chapter. The abstract nature of finance – the link with trade in commodity gold having been broken in the 1930s – makes trading in financial instruments virtually instantaneous. In the period since the 1950s – and especially since the breakdown of Bretton Woods in 1971–3 – finance has once again become globalised, with newly deregulated markets increasingly absorbing money from the real economy (Allen 1994).

Indeed, finance embodies, reinforces, and catalyses all of the other characteristics of the Third Industrial Revolution mentioned above. In product terms, it has become the exemplar of a flexible industry, trading in notional and infinitely variable financial instruments. Financial innovation has been rapid and far-reaching, affecting all parts of the industry and shaping every industrial sector (see Crawford and Sihler 1991). Furthermore, product innovation has been matched by process innovation. Management structures have evolved a long way from the traditional staid world of domestic banking, and traders and other financial market actors and firms are expected to act like entrepreneurs (or intrapreneurs) as a matter of course. The expansion and globalisation of the financial services industry in recent years has been virtually synonymous with the rapid development of electronic computer and communications technology, which transfers money around the world with the tap of a key (for some of the implications of these changes, see Strange 1990). The ownership and transfer of shares and other financial instruments are increasingly recorded only on computer files, without the exchange of paper certificates – what the French call 'demater-ialisation' – although a 'paper trail' can always be printed out for financial controllers, auditors or regulators (in principle, at least).[2] With the increasing globalisation of production and trade, market demand for financial services products is also continually segmenting.

But probably the most important consequence of the globalisation of financial markets is their new structural hegemony. In a more open world, financial balances and flows are increasingly dominant. Exchange rates and interest rates, essential to business decision-making as well as to public policy-making, are increasingly set in world markets (see for example Fukao and Hanazaki 1987). Even more important, however, is the fact that as the trade and production structures of the Third Industrial Revolution go through the kinds of changes outlined earlier, they will be increasingly coordinated through the application of complex financial controls, rapidly evolving accounting techniques, financial performance indicators (because non-financial performance measures are more and more complex and difficult to apply in a globalising world), and the like. The development of new information and communications technology is probably most important in this context. With no physical commodities to find, to move, to transform, or to sell, in finance – in contrast not only to the primary and secondary sectors, but to much of the tertiary sector too – electronic messages are the sum and substance of what is produced and traded in the markets themselves.

O'Brien (1992) has called this the 'end of geography'. Although the firms whose stock or bonds are traded may be physically located in one place, the actual exchange of their securities no longer even requires the physical transfer of paper certificates, and can take place anywhere in the world. Where governments attempt to regulate such trading by prohibition or protectionism, the trading can just as easily be done offshore – undermining not only the regulatory power of the state, but also causing capital to flee and the benefits of investment to accrue elsewhere, thereby undermining the state's taxing and spending powers as well as its ability to foster economic growth and competitiveness. Banks, too, when they make loans, are able to 'book' those loans virtually anywhere in the world – that is, to record those loans on the books virtually anywhere and thereby to choose what regulatory jurisdiction to operate in, depending on the size and scope of their operations and their connections with other institutions and markets – offshore as well as onshore (for a key recent example, see Beaty and Gwynne 1993, especially pp. 114 and 144–5). With the 'securitisation' of many traditional operations – in the narrow sense, the transformation of bank loans, mortgages, credit card loans, etc., into negotiable securities[3] – the new flexibility of both financial markets and banks is combined into ever more potent global bundles (Stone *et al.* 1993).

TECHNOLOGY AND CHANGING FINANCIAL MARKET STRUCTURES

Of course, financial transactions have always had something of this character. It has often been argued, ever since the invention of the telegraph and the telephone, that the process of financial innovation has always had the potential to become de-linked from geography – both in the sense of being geographically detached from the location of material resources and productive facilities and in terms of being constituted, in the most essential sense, by information and communication itself (Strange 1990). In treasury functions, foreign exchange, and securities operations – the main branches of financial management – the new information and communications technology has revolutionised the way that financial products are designed, systems are developed for supporting financial operations, high-risk as well as low-risk transactions are managed, managers and traders understand and interact with each other and interface with the technology itself, transactions are followed up and systems maintained, and a whole host of other functions are carried out. The development of artificial intelligence, expert systems, intelligent networks, and knowledge engineering are merely some of the more complex potential aspects of this process (Chorafas 1992). In this context, the mathematical complexity of financial innovation and transactions has been running ahead not only of the ability of regulators to follow (much less to control *a priori*) but also of the ability of many firms and financial firms to understand. Markets and institutions are still at the beginning of the learning curve. For example, recent experience with derivatives trading – running at $12 trillion globally in 1994 – indicates that it is this very complexity which makes derivatives so attractive not only to investors and borrowers, but also, of course, to the financial firms that design them, sell them, and profit from the rise in turnover.

The tasks which financial institutions have to face in the current climate are extraordinarily complex, and require some of the most complex technological infrastructure available, both in terms of hardware – e.g. supercomputers and global communications networks – and software – e.g. expert systems and artificial intelligence. The largest institutions must be present in all markets – with the number of markets for new financial products expanding rapidly – and they must be able to do customer-led research, design products, trade instruments, manage complex portfolios, settle transactions, etc., on a twenty-four-hour basis. The larger firms have to decentralise myriad operations while maintaining the closest information and trading linkages, while smaller firms need to work harder in their specialist areas to keep up with the huge information flows and modelling systems available to the larger ones. The most central change is a *qualitative* one – i.e. in the *tasks* which are undertaken by the new technology. Most existing computer architecture in the banking industry has consisted of 98 per cent of a computer system's integrative support dealing with the structure of data itself, with only 2 per cent dedicated to answering queries about the data; the current standard is for 60 per cent at the 'intelligent query' level (using complex software and networks) and 40 per cent at the data management and data structure level; and this 60 per cent is eventually expected to reach 90–98 per cent of the functionality of the total system (*ibid.*: 232).

Probably better known, however, are the *quantitative* changes which technological change and globalisation bring. Nomura Securities alone has around one million retail customers using personal computers connected to databases through Nomura's network (*ibid.*: 233). In portfolio management operations, such queries increasingly entail 'long transactions', involving 'many subtransactions addressed to different, often incompatible databases'; research by Sweden's Skandinaviska Enskilda Banken in 1992 found that such long transactions required around '1,000 database accesses each –

versus about 10 accesses needed for the simpler, more traditional transaction'
(*ibid.*: 230). In addition to the operations of securities markets and
investment banks, more and more commercial banks now finance many of
their own operations from the financial markets rather than from deposits.
And with a global marketplace open twenty-four hours a day, even smaller
'niche' firms cannot afford to close down. Chorofas (*ibid.*: 77) outlines one of
the most basic technological problems which faces the trader, portfolio
manager, or indeed the customer, in relatively simple foreign exchange
transactions – the basic mass of information which increasingly has to be
processed in parallel. (These problems are multiplied exponentially when
different markets for a wider range of financial instruments are taken into
account.)

Let us look at what an analytical approach may mean in terms of *number
crunching*. We will do so by taking into account historical data that extend
over two months (46 trading days), and by realising that data vary on an
hourly basis – twenty-four hours per day for global trading. By multiplying
these items together, we get 1,104 information elements. But we should also
account for the need to address at least five key currencies: dollars, sterling,
German marks, yen and Swiss francs – if not more; incorporation of
treasury-type bonds (gilts), with at least 8 per currency; and inclusion of
variable exchange rates and commodities. All this adds up to a significant
data load. These last three items provide among themselves over 350
combinations, which, multiplied with 1,104 information elements, gives
about 400,000 data points. We should also realise that at least ten markets
change simultaneously (New York, London, Tokyo, Zurich, Frankfurt, Paris,
Milan, Toronto, Singapore, and Hong Kong) and at least five financial
markets trade parallel over the twenty-four-hour timeframe. The result is a
minimum of two million rapidly changing information elements to be
number-crunched in order to get some knowledge from them. Furthermore,

> [A]s Wall Street and other financial markets employ supercomputers, it
> will be progressively more necessary to move from the coarse one-hour
> interval to *minute* intervals, and then to *seconds*. The minute level of
> reference will multiply by sixty the 2 million information elements to be
> handled in parallel, making them 120 million ... [and with seconds the
> total becomes] 7.2 billion – and they will have to be number-crunched at
> subsecond speed.
>
> (Chorofas 1992: 77)

Finally, finance is the basis for linking together all of the other economic
processes in the global marketplace. The most fundamental characteristic of
markets is that they are arenas for the setting of prices. Prices, in capitalist
society, embody the only measurable *value* which can be placed upon an
asset, good or service – what Marx called 'exchange value'. 'Efficient' prices
clear markets – i.e. everything that is offered for sale is sold at mutually
agreed prices between buyers and sellers. 'Self-regulating markets' can only

work if the price-setting mechanism is sufficiently efficient to clear those markets. The key to setting efficient prices is the clarity and precision of the price signals conveyed and exchanged between buyers and sellers. Market actors must be *aware* of the impact of changing price signals too, for rapid response to those signals – as in an auction – is necessary for those signals to converge on an equilibrium which will clear the market. Market actors must also be aware of the marginal utility to themselves of complex and rapid price changes. In theory, then, the more *price-sensitive* a market, the more efficient it will be. Many traditional critiques of capitalism have concentrated on the inefficiency of markets in producing desired outcomes – not only in terms of economic utility, of course, but also with regard to moral values, social utility, 'use value', etc. But in mainstream economic theory itself, the search for more efficient markets is the key to maximising utility, and the development of increasing price sensitivity is the key to making markets more efficient in the narrowly economic sense.

Price sensitivity is much easier to foster and expand in financial markets because of the *abstract* character of those markets. No physical goods need be produced or exchanged; numbers on a piece of paper, or, nowadays, on a computer screen which can be linked into almost any market in the world at any time of the day or night, are all that are needed. At one level, genuinely price-sensitive financial markets will attract holders of capital because of the ease and scope of participation in those markets, compared to the slog and the longer-term risks of actually making things; the wider their net, the better. At another level, even those who wish to make things need capital, and are forced to go to the financial markets to find that capital; there, they are subject to the rules and the marginal utilities of those who operate on those markets full-time or who have a high level of financial market power or market share. The price sensitivity of the increasingly 'paperless world' of the global financial marketplace is increasingly controlling market – and political – decisions elsewhere.

The so-called 'Euromarkets' (which began to take off in the 1960s) were the first to produce, out of competitive necessity, two more features which shaped structural change: first, complex types of *financial innovation* which went far beyond the traditional instruments of bank loans and fixed-rate bonds, including a range of currency hedges, variable-rate bonds, perpetual notes, interest-rate swaps, and 'off-balance-sheet' instruments such as revolving credit facilities; and second, the introduction of *new information and communications technology* to process orders and trades. In this fiercely competitive environment, profits came increasingly from volume and volume-related fees and spreads rather than from safe, regulated returns. Commissions on transactions were fully negotiable, not fixed as in most domestic financial stock and bond markets at the time. There were no interest-rate controls, but interest-rate competition – nurtured in the unregulated Euromarkets and other offshore markets of the 1960s and 1970s – led to the convergence of market rates; spreads between bid and offer prices narrowed. Profits would increasingly come from the volume available from global trading, rather than from the larger but more static – protected – profit margins available under the old system. Although the larger institutions were the spearhead of the deregulation movement, it infected the smaller institutions too with the view that their only future was to be able to compete on price with the big boys for their specialised services.

The competitive deregulations of the 1980s have been compared to the competitive devaluations of the 1930s. An international 'ratchet effect' has been at work. Each deregulation led in turn to increased structural complexity, making a return to tighter national-level regulation less possible. The same process can be seen in the 'securitisation' and 'disintermediation' of finance – i.e. the trend away from traditional bank loans (particular contracts between specific bankers and borrowers, based on the former's knowledge of the latter's creditworthiness) towards the selling of *negotiable* securities (which can be bought and sold by any 'bearer'), from certificates of deposit to complex mixes of debt and equity. The crucial feature is that these instruments can later be traded in a secondary market, and the most attractive and efficient of such markets – i.e. the most liquid and price-sensitive – are international markets.

This process has also led to financial innovation – the design of new, complex and often specially tailored instruments. A notable example is the development of 'derivatives' markets – mainly futures and options – in which imaginary financial instruments are traded, ostensibly to hedge against loss in volatile markets. Derivatives markets developed mainly in Chicago out of the longstanding commodities futures markets. They first focused on currency options and futures to compete with the Euromarkets. Indeed, futures and options markets, because they are the most 'abstract' markets (they do not require the actual buying and selling of the 'underlying' securities), are rapidly becoming one of the most globalised financial markets. However, the interaction of derivatives markets and markets in real financial instruments has also been seen as a source of volatility, especially in the way that stock market futures and options are 'arbitraged' against the basic stocks. Thus new and volatile international circuits of capital reminiscent of the 1920s mushroomed, but through a much more complex system than that of the interwar period.

POLITICAL PROCESSES AND POLICY RESPONSES: THE EROSION OF STATE CAPACITY

These far-reaching changes in financial market structures have generated equally far-reaching challenges to the capacity of national governments to make and implement public policy. The essential mechanism of change is *regulatory arbitrage*. Once the dikes of domestic regulatory compartmentalisation and international capital controls have been breached in key sectors and the centrality of money and financial markets reasserted – as in the breakdown of the New Deal system in the United States and of Bretton Woods (Cerny 1994c) – other market sectors seek to reduce existing regulatory barriers in their own areas in order to compete for business. Governments and regulatory agencies desire to promote the health and profitability of their 'own' national financial systems (in the global context) and their 'own' sectors (in domestic terms). To this end they will seek to 'level the playing field' (to remove competitive disadvantages) and even to provide their own clients with *new* competitive advantages *vis-à-vis* rival nations or sectors. Globalisation and deregulation are thus inextricably intertwined aspects of a virtuous – or vicious – circle, undermining attempts to regulate price-setting in such an acutely sensitive and interdependent context.

However, states acting unilaterally *do* still possess the capacity to take decisions which *open* financial markets rather than attempting to keep them closed. This *political* cycle of market opening constitutes the essence of the 'competition state' in the financial arena (cf. Cerny 1990, 1994b). But as that opening process has, in turn, increased the complexity of those markets in transnational terms, states are finding it more and more difficult to take the kinds of decisions which *control* those markets – decisions which can effectively and systematically shape, stabilise and control not only the workings of the markets themselves but also the wider economic and political ramifications of their operation. In the world of more open financial competition characteristic of the 1980s and 1990s, then, it is the complex (circular) linkages between markets – and prices – rather than the simple (linear) volume of capital flows which drive and facilitate ever-expanding processes of regulatory arbitrage. Competition between states – and between different branches and agencies within states – interact with structural changes in international financial markets to promote processes of deregulation and re-regulation.

This crucial feature of the markets also reflects the growing domination of money and finance over the 'real' economy – the production and trading system. Without a much denser transnational regulatory order with the capacity to impose systematic controls on the financial markets, narrowly financial criteria will continue to play an ever-larger role in the allocation of capital across the world. In terms of financial structures themselves, there has been a complex process of both concentration *and* flexibilisation of markets and institutions. Of course, this process has not been wholly homogeneous or even. The most short-term and liquid markets like those for foreign exchange and US Treasury bills are by far the most transnationally integrated, while equity (share) markets are probably the least integrated in terms of the proportion of transnational capital flows to the volume of overall turnover in these sectors (Giry-Deloison and Masson 1988). However, not only has the transnational price sensitivity within each of these markets dramatically increased, but the arbitrage *between* them – represented, for example, by derivatives trading – has arguably been the main feature of their development in recent years.

Securitisation – the shift of financial services from traditional 'relationship banking' to the trading of negotiable securities – is probably the most important single characteristic of the reshaping of different markets and institutions into a single system. The key advantage of securitisation is that it provides geometrically increased prospects for flexibility and price sensitivity. Securitisation is quite simply not possible without new technology to deal with the complex data and mathematics it involves. Securitisation cuts across what were once distinct sectors of the overall financial marketplace, making prices in each sector more sensitive to price changes in the others. Market actors can 'arbitrage' their funds almost instantaneously between different types of financial instrument in order to take advantage of such price changes.

With regard to securitisation in particular, the capacity of institutions to avoid being burdened over long periods with specific assets and liabilities, i.e. their ability to *trade* those assets and liabilities in liquid secondary markets at a discount, has always played a role in the development of banking as well as being at the heart of stock and bond markets. But the possibility of selling literally anything – from huge 'block trades' of standardised securities to packages of small bank loans to specific customers (Stone *et al.* 1993) – on to other institutions is growing vaster, and a whole range of new markets has grown up in and around traditional stock and bond markets to service this demand (Crawford and Sihler 1991). Many of these new securities can only be sold on because they are attractive to buyers – and they are attractive to buyers because they can be sold on again, and again, if need be, in liquid secondary markets. It is therefore likely that international finance will become even more concentrated, because only the big institutions – often dealing with only the biggest non-financial firms – will have the economies of scale to be both flexible and profitable in a highly competitive environment where profit margins will be cut to the bone. Perhaps the most striking example of this tendency is the recent rapid growth of massive pension funds and mutual funds (unit trusts), known as 'institutional investors', which increasingly dominate the high end of the markets (O'Barr and Conley 1992).

But this raises another question: whether the sort of continuous trading we have been describing merely privileges a structural *short-termism* of the kind that, for example, pension funds have been widely accused of. For securitisation, in the broad sense in which we have been using it, does take some of the risk out of the markets by providing a wider range of hedging possibilities, and therefore might be said to encourage speculation. And after all, the supposed benefits of price sensitivity lie precisely in the way that it enables decisions to be taken more and more quickly. Will, as Keynes argued, globalisation and concentration merely crowd out long-term investment, especially 'productive' investment in the 'real economy'? Will they increase profitability at the expense of manufacturing production, real standards of living, and jobs? Will they open the way to more booms and slumps, more financial bubbles and panics? And if governments can no longer control this process in an effective, strategic way, will it not lead to an increasing 'democratic deficit'?

Some believe that globalisation is not yet sufficiently comprehensive and inexorable to prevent governments from taking back control, at least to the extent of mitigating the worst possibilities. Cooperation between Finance Ministers of the developed world in keeping the financial markets liquid after the October 1987 crash is often cited, as is the 1988 Basle Agreement on capital adequacy standards for banks. However, such international cooperation is both too little and too limited. The Basle Agreement has not been followed up by significant further international regulatory cooperation of such a basic kind, and the disagreements between governments on capital adequacy regulations for securities markets demonstrates the limited scope for further progress in this area. With the exception of Basle, most international – intergovernmental – cooperation has been in the form of crisis management, often following the most egregious regulatory failure, as in the case of the Bank of Credit and Commerce International (Beaty and Gwynne 1993), rather than in terms of effective *a priori* regulatory control. The high costs of new regulatory barriers and enforcement procedures are likely to be prohibitive in a world where so-called 'footloose' capital, epitomised by financial capital, can relocate so freely. Governments can try to manipulate global capital flows, of course, for example by the creative use of deficit financing and some limited manipulation of industrial policy, education policy, etc. But this is a question of attempting to ride the tiger.

CONCLUSIONS

These questions will be increasingly determined by competitive forces in the *global* marketplace, and governments will have either to adjust or see their options narrow even more. A country without efficient and profitable financial markets and institutions will suffer multiple *dis*advantages in a more open world. It will lose yet more investment, it will suffer worse real interest rates in the attempt to attract capital, and its government will not only be limited in its general economic policy by the threat of capital flight but will also see a long-term erosion of its tax base. In today's world, the global markets and the big institutions are 'where the money is' – as nineteenth-century bank robber Willie Sutton said of banks – and there is no government with the 'extraterritorial' power to control its allocation. Indeed, the very nature of the 'competition state' drives this process forward as state actors attempt to *free-ride* on financial globalisation through increasing market liberalisation (Andrews 1994). Financial markets, not states, represent the closest thing to a new hegemony in the contemporary international system. A new Great Transformation will be required at a global, supranational level if values other than the establishment of a global self-regulating market are to be realised.

NOTES

1 Kitschelt follows Charles Perrow (1984, 1986) in classifying technological systems along two axes, the one being how tightly coupled their elements are and the other being how complex their interactions are. The elements themselves are 'concrete legal and economic organizational entities' (Kitschelt 1991: 461). Mark V technological systems are characterised by loose coupling and high complexity. The main examples of Mark V technological systems are 'computer software, customized microprocessors and workstations, genetically engineered products and pharmaceuticals, and specialty chemicals' (*ibid.*: 474).
2 The collapse in 1991 of the Bank of Credit and Commerce International and the conviction of leading traders like Ivan Boesky and Michael Milken show, however, that the temptation to fraud, and the capability of keeping it hidden for a long time, still exists.
3 This term is also used, including in this chapter, in a wider sense, to mean the general decline in recourse to traditional bank loan financing ('intermediated' financing) and the increasing predominance in finance of both securities trading and financial innovation in securities markets (see below).

12 Technology and globalisation
Electronic funds transfer systems in Europe as a case of non-globalisation

John Howells

A version of this article appears in the journal *Technology Analysis & Strategic Management*, 8, 4: 455–66. In this chapter I address the 'process' of globalisation in Europe in the case of 'retail' financial network design with specific reference to the case of EFTPOS – Electronic Funds Transfer at the Point of Sale. The central issue is the role of technology in the process of globalisation and whether the implementation of network technology necessarily increases the global standardisation of financial services. Technical language will be explained as it is introduced, but the reader who finds the technical acronyms of the subject hard to remember may want to refer to the glossary at the end of the chapter.

In any EFTPOS system, paper transaction records are replaced with electronic records; but such a network can be built in many ways. The evidence from EFTPOS in Europe is that there has been a great deal of variety in the way networks have been constructed, and that this variety is a result of national institutional structures, including banking industry firm structure, the socio-legal framework, and the political system. This chapter argues that these differences in network design hinder attempts to establish a European Payments System (EPS). The establishment of an EPS, whether this is attempted by interlinking the national services now in existence or through agreements to standardise national service provision across countries, would be a step in the direction of further 'globalisation' of provision of this type of financial service. The case of EFTPOS allows analysis of national-specific institutions and structure and how they interact with network technologies. It will be argued that if an EPS is created it will be as a result of the activities of the European Commission, one of the few truly European institutions involved as an actor in EFT developments. Rather than there being an 'intrinsic' trend towards globalisation, there is at best a dynamic interaction between institutions with the power and interest in furthering the process of globalisation and the technologies which they shape for this purpose.

EFTPOS POSSIBILITIES

If EFTPOS is on-line only, then it can become an instrument for control of bad debt, because cards could be rejected if attempts were made to breach agreed overdraft limits. As far as it includes off-line modes of operation, this 'value' of the electronic service to the banks is reduced – off-line terminals make no communication with the customer's primary account and process transactions below a fixed 'floor limit'. If a personal identification number system (PIN) is used instead of signature, it is widely assumed in the industry that encryption is required to protect the electronic transaction message (which includes both PIN and account number). This raises communication costs and terminal processing time to a degree, but may be considered worthwhile if the PIN system provides more security than signature alone. If there is to be encryption there are a number of algorithms that could be used (for example DES (Data Encryption Standard) and RSA (Rivest Shamir Adelman)) and these may be implemented in ways which again differ in their effect on cost and security in the electronic network. Another source of variety is the card scheme or schemes that use the physical network.

In their decisions on all the above design features of an EFTPOS network, the banks are strategically constructing a future competition game. At one extreme they could all decide to build competing physical networks, each with its own independent card scheme. At the other extreme they could build a single physical network with one shared card scheme, in which case competition would be limited to areas such as the efficiency of customer account service and the marketing differentiation of services. The process by which banks decide on the level of competition they wish to build into their networks is essentially social, institutional and political. There are also possible 'mixed' positions, but, as this chapter will show, there are real costs and obstacles associated with possible combinations of technologies.

UK EFTPOS[1]

In the early 1980s, the UK banks organised joint working groups with the remit of finding an EFTPOS strategy. They first conceived of EFTPOS as on-line only, PIN-based and with DES encryption of transaction data, with an associated debit card scheme to which all banks would belong and with common conditions of operation. It was intended that the topology of the network would consist of all banks and all terminals linked to one central processing centre. When the banks began to implement their 'pilot' system in 1986, the design had changed to allow a limited degree of off-line functionality and the 'unified' card scheme had been abandoned. PIN numbers were used in the pilot and encrypted by using the RSA algorithm rather than the more usual DES. The topology of the network was changed so that banks linked to terminals directly, and only linked to a central communications 'switch' for the purpose of inter-bank communication.

Despite the £160m that was spent on the pilot scheme, it was abandoned in favour of a third EFTPOS system. There are now two physically distinct network designs in the UK, one that supports Switch transaction processing, the other based on the Visa network and associated operating conditions. There is a higher percentage of off-line than on-line processing, no encryption is used in the Switch network and DES-encryption in the Visa network, while signature is everywhere used in preference to PIN as a means of verifying transactions. Not only is there not a central processing centre, there is no common central switch (for simple routing of transactions). Instead, the Switch banks clear EFTPOS transactions via a system of bilateral links, while the Visa banks use the established Visa central processing centre.

A historical circumstance that affected the UK EFTPOS outcome was the widespread use of credit cards (a result of Barclays' activities in the late 1960s) and the associated rising levels of card fraud in the 1970s. This led Barclays (as the major credit card issuer) to first introduce on-line EFTPOS as a means of controlling card fraud. Later, in response to retailer demand, Barclays began to expand the service into a national EFTPOS service (called PDQ). Barclays' stake in the design of their proprietary EFTPOS service made them ambivalent about the national scheme and keen to mould its design to suit their other interests. Deep distrust developed within the national scheme's governance structures, which led to the breakdown of cooperation and the establishment of the present UK EFTPOS system. The present system embodies this distrust and is close to the high-competition extreme outlined in the previous section, where competition takes the form of building rival, physically separate networks and designs.

The technology raises new ownership and control issues over the point of sale (POS) – most importantly who controls the design and functionality of the terminal, but also who owns the terminal and how to distribute costs between bank and retailer. These were important enough to retailers that throughout the inter-bank competitive struggles, UK retailers attempted (with success) to influence outcomes, for example through boycotting certain debit card schemes and bank-designed equipment intended for the point of sale.[2] This was the first time retailers had organised collectively to increase their power *vis-à-vis* the banking industry and to force a change in bank behaviour. The historical relationship between the two sides was one where the banks had collectively imposed their decisions on a fragmented retailing industry and so besides the inter-bank competitive struggle, and partly because of it, they were faced with rethinking their strategy towards retailers.

All these shifts in strategy occurred within a new (1986) deregulated financial framework which gave building societies greater access to the banks' clearing systems. This introduced the problem of how to relate to the newcomers. It also undermined faith in the tradition of a cooperative relationship based on the 'big four' banks.

However, the state has traditionally practised a more direct form of control over banking through the Bank of England. From the point of view of many of those representing their bank within the pilot project's governing structures, the nature of this relationship had become confused (Hine and Howells 1993). Bank of England control was not exercised openly but through an informal set of relationships at the most senior levels of the banks. The most senior appointment to the board of the company charged with developing the EFTPOS pilot project came from the Bank of England. This could be interpreted as a desire on the part of the Bank that the clearing banks should support the cooperative venture, or as a simple desire to signal the neutrality of the development company. The rhetoric and intention of the deregulatory banking bill was of competition and markets. So a number of interpretations of the significance of the Bank of England appointee were able to coexist among the clearing bank representatives on the pilot project and the perspective that the Bank of England was still in control or 'surveying events' obstructed the development of individual bank strategies on EFTPOS matters.

This synopsis of events in the UK shows that EFTPOS presented the banks with many strategic, interconnected issues, and that there was often little historical experience the banks could draw upon in their attempts to maintain a coherent approach to design and implementation of the new network. The options for restructuring the inter-bank relationship that the new technology offered made a coherent approach difficult and some degree of power struggle likely. The same set of problems were encountered in other European countries and if the outcome in the UK is compared to that in these countries it will be evident that there is not a pre-determined or 'optimal' design for EFTPOS networks.

EUROPEAN EFTPOS

In other countries there have been quite different outcomes to EFTPOS design which show that, given different initial conditions and relationships between banks and retailers, a variety of EFTPOS designs are possible. In Denmark a PIN-only, on-line only network supported by a unified debit card scheme and with retailer service provided through a central organisation, has been in operation since 1986, and there is no alternative choice of card scheme or terminal technology available to retailers besides the design chosen by the banks. The banks appear to have succeeded in establishing their preferred design because they offered terminals free to retailers and only charged for transactions after a period of grace had elapsed. Both in Denmark and in Belgium, where banks introduced a similar network design, retailers have begun to fight back as EFTPOS transaction volumes, and therefore charges, have risen with increased card use: in Belgium retailers have collectively attempted to refuse to pay transaction charges (Anon 1986).

In France another network design created by a collaborative bank approach succeeded with the creation of an organisation to oversee the national electronic payment card system, the Groupement des Cartes Bancaires. Banks compete with each other to issue cards and acquire retailers, and they are governed by a set of national standards. Woodman (1991: 5) quotes the President of Cartes Bancaires, Jacques Masson, speaking at the 1991 Monetique conference: 'We are in favour of competition, but . . . not too much competition.' This would serve as an apt characterisation of the UK banks' attitude when they first created their early EFTPOS designs, or the German banks with their 'Electronic Cash' scheme (see below). According to Woodman, Cartes Bancaires differs from the intended UK banks' scheme in not being open to non-banks (in the UK, deregulation gave Building Societies access to the banks' collective EFTPOS scheme) and being responsible for the electronic card schemes' rules, such as interchange fee rates (the charge made between banks when they process each other's cards). French retailers have attacked these rules in the courts as uncompetitive and obtained some favourable rulings (*ibid.*). It is particularly interesting that the French banks have decided to tackle card fraud by jointly developing dual magnetic stripe/smart cards, i.e. cards with a memory chip. A quarter of the 19 million French cards issued have smart card functionality and 75 per cent of the 150,000 French EFTPOS terminals can read these cards (Loubiere and Riché 1992). The object in 1990 was to replace magnetic stripe cards with smart cards by 1992. This unique approach is made possible by the cartelistic approach to EFTPOS, which reflects also other aspects of the French financial services sector and its relations with government; but the result is further divergence between European EFTPOS systems.

In Germany the cheque never became a major payment instrument because the banks avoided the establishment of an equivalent to a cheque-guarantee card. This changes the cost-benefit analysis for EFTPOS since cheques are expensive to process and the prospect of displacing large-scale cheque usage increases the variety of network designs for which the investment will appear to have positive returns. German banks have been trying to introduce a centralised EFTPOS system since the early 1980s and have clashed frequently with the retailers.[3] By the end of 1991 they had launched a 100 per cent PIN and on-line network called 'Electronic Cash' with a standard 0.3 per cent charge on all transactions. The banks had installed 2,000 terminals and processed more than two million transactions per month (Heinz 1991). However, the retailer Peek and Cloppenburg successfully introduced purely off-line EFTPOS in 1990, prompting Deutsche Bank to break away from the collective EFTPOS system to provide the clearing function for that system. The features of the Deutsche Bank/ Peek and Cloppenburg system are no PIN, no third-party network operator organisation, and no necessity for a particular level of on-line authorisation. According to Heinz, more retailers have signed up with the Peek and Cloppenburg system than with the banking industry-supported Electronic Cash system. So the Electronic Cash scheme is being undermined, and although the final outcome had not yet been decided, at least by 1992, with a split in the ranks of the banks, events in the UK would suggest that Electronic Cash will not survive.

Sweden provides a particularly interesting case because the largest three retailers, KF, ICA and Axel Johnson, have developed on-line, PIN-based EFTPOS (Sparen 1991) for their own purposes. These retailers have taken the favoured design route of banking oligopolies all over the world. However, this is a very powerful combination of retailers, together accounting for more than 70 per cent of the Swedish food market and more than a fifth of petrol retail sales. The Swedish clearing banks are less concentrated. They attempted to develop an EFTPOS service consisting of separate terminals with on-line authorisation and signature, with the retailer responsible for filing and retrieving copies of signed receipts and paying for the terminal and all communications costs. The three retailers were aware that under such a system, if card volume grew they would suffer the costs and the banks would capture the benefits. The retailer KF had developed a proprietary PIN-based EFTPOS system for a petrol-retailing subsidiary which processed a similar number of transactions to that collected by the Danish national Dankort system. In 1988 the Swedish retailers' experience with PIN-based EFTPOS, their knowledge of the fate of retailers in Denmark, and their dissatisfaction with EFTPOS as designed by the Swedish clearers, formed the rationale for developing EFTPOS on a larger scale. The Swedish clearing banks declared that the retailer-preferred design route (which minimised transaction processing time at the checkout) was impossible, but the retailers had the size and market power to develop their potentially national EFTPOS project called RASK with the Swedish savings banks.

According to Sparen,[4] the economics of PIN-based EFTPOS are good in the Swedish situation because the retailers are developing proprietary X25 protocol networks for reasons other than EFTPOS – EFTPOS communication costs could be zero-rated on internal cost-benefit analysis. Another advantage of RASK is that it will rationalise the processing of KF's own card scheme transactions; 1,200,000 KF cards will be acceptable in the RASK terminals. In Sweden the large retailers have acquired an incentive to rationalise money transmission that the banks apparently do not have:

> The [Swedish] banks have to decide whether they want the card to be an alternative payment media or a supplementary payment media to cash. For the Coop the answer is easy. We need card reading for the fidelity (proprietary) card and can't accept a slow-card handling system in our checkout lanes. If the banks can't build an efficient card payment system

adapted to the needs of the retailers, we have to strongly promote our own payment card.

(Sparen 1991: 5)

As they proceed they clearly threaten the core business of the clearing banks – control of money transmission. KF has bought a Swedish clearing bank to gain access to the clearing system and so overcome what would probably be an insuperable obstacle to retailer-inspired EFTPOS in other countries. This was facilitated by the fragmentation of the Swedish clearing banks and the existence of so many small banks who nevertheless had access to the electronic inter-bank clearings.

Another source of variety in EFTPOS in Europe is the attitude to debt in the different countries. Sweden, and the Scandinavian countries generally, are known for an institutionalised and 'harsh' (in UK terms) view of debt. One of the UK bank interviewees pointed out that Swedish law required 60 per cent of credit card debt to be cleared each month, while information laws allowed public access to credit card accounts. This has discouraged large-scale use of credit cards in these countries, which alters the economics of EFTPOS.

THE SIGNIFICANCE OF DESIGN VARIETY IN EFTPOS

The development of EFTPOS in all these countries shows that the systems that exist in Europe differ in their use of PIN, encryption, communications standards, terminal functionality and payment card conditions. There are patterns in this development. Where the clearing banks are few in number and have a tradition of acting as a cartel, and where there is little concentration or cooperative tradition within the retailing industry, the banks are more likely to have imposed their 'ideal' EFTPOS system satisfying a maximum of internal banking industry problems rather than meeting retailing industry interests. So the power balance between banks and retailers as well as within the banking and retailer groups influenced the EFTPOS outcome. In addition to the power of the private interest groups to impose or negotiate advantageous outcomes for themselves, we can summarise other influences on outcome: the historical evolution of the paper-transaction environment (use of cheques, plastic cards); the degree to which attitudes to debt have been institutionalised; and the extent of deregulation (whether non-banks have access to the national clearing systems).

This variety in EFTPOS designs across Europe demonstrates the power of the national-specific context to shape design and development. The significance of this has been captured by the chairman of the UK Retail Consortium, also a member of the European retailers interest group, CECD (Confédération Européene du Commerce de Détail):

If anyone were attempting to create European card inter-operability, establish a consistent approach, or still less, unify payment schemes across

Europe, you would certainly not start by choice from European payment systems as they are today.

(Woodman 1991: 3)

The national EFTPOS networks that are currently in place were designed with little reference to activity in other European countries, and the development of such systems has complicated the prospects for a European payments system, not facilitated it.

THE COMMISSION AND THE BANKS

Just as combinations of institutions with shifting sets of sub-alliances shaped the creation and form of national EFTPOS, some kind of institutional arrangement will frame decisions on an EPS. Foremost among these at present (1994) are the European Commission (EC) and the European banks.

However, the concept of what constitutes a market for payment systems may be at issue in the development of an EPS, as it was for the UK banks in their development of EFTPOS (Howells and Hine 1993a). If investment in new infrastructure cannot be linked clearly to projected returns, and if different banks conceive of the benefits from an EPS differently (and their ability to capture those benefits), such investment may not take place at all. With the European payments service market neatly partitioned between the nation states it would appear unlikely that the banks will invest in and pursue an EPS with vigour.

Until the early 1990s there was little sign that the UK banks were developing a policy on EFT in Europe. But as the UK national bank rivalry generated over EFTPOS faded, and once the Commission had signalled its interest in an EPS in the document entitled *Making Payments in the Internal Market* (CEC 1990), the electronic banking/shopping/EDI/EFTPOS conferences which the UK banks run twice annually gained a European dimension.

In contrast to EFTPOS, the European Commission (EC) has been highly active in the setting of standards for Electronic Data Interchange (EDI) – because it believes that EDI is important to the operation of companies within the European Union single market. An interesting case of what can happen when there is no agreement of standards in advance of implementation is provided by EFTPOS. In the UK, the British Standards Institute (BSI) had begun a process of attempting to set European EFTPOS standards based on the UK 'national' EFTPOS system characteristics. Little progress was made and the attempt was abandoned with the collapse of the UK national system. However, it was the belief of various suppliers, retailers, security consultants, standards committee convenors and even banks that this amounted to an attempt to block the routes to cheaper and incompatible versions of EFTPOS in Europe.[5] The process of setting standards, far from being the dry and dusty business of defining technical attributes, can be as political a process as the issue of whether banks or retailers control the point of sale (see above). Given these circumstances it would appear that the European Commission, acting as referee and arbiter to the national banks, will nevertheless be the vital institutional player in the development of an EPS, as only it has an explicit policy objective of creating a trans-European payments service.

Although in the 1991 UK EFTPOS conference the banks were attacked for the poor quality of service they delivered to customers on cross-border payments (Mitchell 1991), the head of the Commission Directorate-General, Financial Institutions and Company Law, Troberg, departed from his prepared talk in an attempt to reassure banks that the Commission did not intend to coerce them, despite the Commission's desire to see a rapid establishment of a trans-European electronic banking payments network:

> The Commission's work to date has sometimes been misinterpreted as being aimed at eliminating such competition [between private providers of payment services] and at imposing on all involved from above a single monolithic Community-wide payment system. The opposite is the case... the Commission sees its role primarily as that of a catalyst, as a body which causes market participants to pool their thinking about future developments and opportunities for integration.
>
> (Troberg 1991: 5)

The role the Commission might take was indicated by the following:

> there will in future be some division of labour between the central banks and the EC Commission. The central banks will lay the foundations for the role of the 'Eurofed' [a European central bank] in the EC-wide payments sphere... the Commission... will concentrate more on the needs of the individual customer and on the smooth and inexpensive functioning of the individual payment procedures.
>
> (Troberg 1991: 3)

It is the Commission that is interested in the process of creating a European-wide EFTPOS network for European citizens, but there will be no directives compelling banks to cooperate on the provision of an EPS. With this approach, some of the more radical measures taken in other industrial sectors are unlikely. For example, with national government agreement it would be possible to imagine a process of amalgamation and takeover leading to provision of an EPS by single European clearing banks. While there is some evidence of a relaxation by European countries of policies of supporting 'national champions' (Freeman and Oldham 1991; Sharp 1991a) in some industrial sectors, the banking industry has yet to see such a national policy shift. In its absence, it is not surprising that the national banking industries have not autonomously adopted strategies for the creation of an EPS.

CONCLUSIONS – TECHNOLOGY AND THE PROCESS OF GLOBALISATION

Much discussion of the idea of 'globalisation' presupposes a trend towards the global company providing some product or service that is standardised in some way (see Levitt, this volume). With regard to an electronic EPS,[6] there are a number of methods by which the banks could have become more 'global'. They could have planned the European dimension to their electronic financial transactions strategies from their inception – but none of them did so. They could now begin to build networks and carry services cross-border – but none of the UK banks has plans to do this. There is patchy development of card and terminal inter-operability across Europe, but the networks in place will make the achievement of a uniform service difficult because the national-specific socio-legal contexts of the paper-based transaction systems have dominated the design of electronic systems.

However, one must be careful to distinguish between the different contributions to an EPS. It can be argued that the unequal diffusion of EFT payment services decreases the standardisation that already exists within the paper monetary system. Unequal diffusion of terminals means an unequal, non-standard payment service on a European scale. The situation of inequality is made worse in the period when the physical networks are being established but before card schemes are made inter-operable.[7] Inter-operability restores a degree of standardisation. However, even where inter-operability is possible, different cost structures will exist because of the physical network design, rendering the unification of charge structures across European countries highly unlikely.

The new technology has the potential advantages of making payments faster, more convenient and cheaper to process, and these arise from the automation of information flows that is characteristic of information technology. A clear contribution to an EPS associated with increased speed of processing is the time-saving of avoiding a separate foreign currency exchange (although the paper Eurocheque also allows the user to avoid the time-cost element). As the banks use EFTPOS to displace cheque and cash use (because it decreases processing costs) this benefit could become widely diffused throughout Europe. Of course this and other benefits would be achieved without information technology if the political achievement of a single European currency was realised.

EFT network technology is highly 'plastic' and 'configurable' (Fleck 1991): it is moulded by existing social-political contexts, and the 'direction' it has is largely given to it by socio-institutional arrangements. The 'social shaping'[8] of networks that has been described here has been by national banking industries, retailers and the EC in conjunction with the banks. Other important 'constituents' (Molina 1989) in the shaping process are the equipment and service suppliers such as Tandem, IBM, British Telecom,

Omron and Nokia, who influence the range of options open to the other constituents through their policies of technology development.[9]

Perhaps the above argument can be usefully and briefly compared with Levitt's original 'globalisation thesis' (Levitt 1983). If we wish to understand the *process* by which a European Payments system may become reality, I believe Levitt's thesis has little to offer and is indeed misleading. For example, he claims that

> A powerful force drives the world toward a converging commonality, and that force is technology.... The result is a new commercial reality – the emergence of global markets for standardised consumer products on a previously unimagined scale of magnitude.

> (Levitt 1983: 92)

This is an example of what I shall call the 'strong' argument, where globalisation is seen to have a simple cause (technology) and to involve discontinuous change. The example of EFTPOS in Europe allows us to conclude that, for networks at least, 'technology' is not an independent 'powerful force', that social and institutional values are clearly influencing the construction of network technologies, that many routes to different network configurations are possible and are being followed, and that another, pan-European institution (the Commission) is attempting, albeit indirectly, to influence the creation of a European Payments System. It may be useful to characterise this position as the 'weak' argument. This maintains that the connection between technological change and a 'trend to globalisation' is complex and has a great deal to do with institutions and policies.

It can be argued that other formulations of the 'strong' argument have been weakened by recent work. Some of the 'classic' issues of globalisation have been most fully argued with respect to manufacturing and in the context of a predicated 'New International Division of Labour' (NIDL), where stages in production can be 'disarticulated' spatially and located around the world wherever there are local advantageous combinations of factors (Fröbel *et al.* 1980). Here it is pertinent that strong empirical investigations of the NIDL have revealed its assumptions as simplistic and have pointed to the complexity of influences at work (Henderson 1989). Henderson in particular clearly shows how the state policies of the NICs (newly-industrialising countries) have served to attract foreign direct investment and have facilitated technology transfer to indigenously owned firms. The tendency towards 'globalisation' apparent in the often-quoted finding by Julius (e.g. Howells and Wood 1993: 153) that FDI in the early 1980s grew at four times the rate of world GDP growth can be interpreted as partly the result of the mode of *industrialisation* of a select group of (especially) East Asian countries.

The surge in inter-firm strategic alliances in the 1980s (see Sharp, this volume), could also be taken as evidence of a 'trend' towards globalisation, but as Dosi *et al.* argue in their exploration of technical change and international trade:

such a 'new' globalisation trend is more a reflection of new ways which firms are increasingly using to try to overcome the firm- and country-specificity and cumulativeness of technological change.

(Dosi *et al.* 1990: 270)

In other words this globalisation 'trend' is the result of new firm technology strategies, which may or may not persist and which are a reaction to new inequalities in the location of technology. It would appear dangerous to take the 'trend' towards globalisation as inevitable or as the basis on which to build sweeping generalisations about the future. An example where judgements on policy are made on the basis that the 'trend' towards globalisation has causative power rather than being an effect is found in Howells and Wood:

Even if it is becoming harder to maintain and more of an anachronism, 'techno-nationalism' ... still remains a major constraint on the process of globalisation. The use of government-supported R&D programmes ... technical standards; quota restrictions; limitations on foreign investment ... all act as restraints on the globalisation of production and technology... the process of globalisation ... is ... making them increasingly invalid and difficult to apply. Sooner or later governments are going to have to accept that many of these mechanisms can no longer be effectively implemented and new mechanisms and strategies will have to be found.

(Howells and Wood 1993: 155)

The policy response of withdrawing from the use of strong technology-policy instruments at a national level is not an inevitable result of the globalisation trend, nor is it necessarily an appropriate 'response' to such a trend. This argument is reinforced when it is realised that the high-growth NICs and Japan are countries which have used the most extreme and manipulative forms of 'techno-nationalism' to force the pace of industrialisation and economic growth.[10]

In conclusion, the 'strong' globalisation argument that there is a 'trend' to globalisation with simple technological causes or with easily forecastable consequences, is untenable. The discussion above of alternative interpretations of the evidence for a globalisation 'trend' and the detailed evidence on European EFTPOS support the view that trends in globalisation are the result of processes that are strategy-led or policy-driven at state and firm level.

GLOSSARY

ATM	Automated Teller Machine
BSI	British Standards Institute
DES	Data Encryption Standard
EC	European Commission

EDI	Electronic Data Interchange
EFT	Electronic Funds Transfer
EFTPOS	Electronic Funds Transfer at Point of Sale
EPOS	Electronic Point of Sale (electronic cash tills)
EPS	European Payments System
FDI	Foreign Direct Investment
NICs	Newly Industrialising Countries
NIDL	New International Division of Labour
Off-line	A terminal which stores transactions for terminal collection at a later time, usually by a computer dialling the terminal overnight
On-line	A terminal which contacts an issuing bank's host-terminal computer processor to authorise the creation of a transaction and then usually transmits it immediately
PDQ	Pretty Damn Quick – the Barclays EFTPOS service
PIN	Personal Identification Number
POS	Point of Sale
RSA	Rivest Shamir Adelman algorithm

NOTES

1 Much of this chapter is drawn from Howells and Hine 1993.
2 The Retail Consortium (an association of the largest retailers) refused the conditions attached to Barclays' Connect card when it was first issued in 1987. Large retailers informally boycotted the pilot scheme for the banks' PIN-based, encryption and on-line version of EFTPOS. This was part of the power struggle over control of the POS which continued throughout 1986–90 (Howells *et al.* 1993).
3 At one point retailers threatened to introduce their own card schemes (Anon 1987a) while the German banks replied that transaction charges would rise steeply if this happened (Anon 1987b).
4 Personal conversation.
5 Unpublished interview data.
6 EFTPOS is only one of the component EFT networks that together could form the basis of an electronic EPS. Others include Electronic Data Interchange (EDI) and Automated Teller Machines (ATMs). Progress in linking or standardising the payment services delivered by these networks would be progress towards an EPS and part of the 'globalisation' of retail financial services.
7 For example, for a time plastic cards that operated in the ATMs of one European country (for example Switch debit cards) were useless in another.
8 The point about the social construction of technology has been made repeatedly elsewhere, for example Hughes 1983; MacKenzie and Wajcman 1985; Bijker *et al.* 1987.
9 For example, EPOS retail tills are routinely supplied with the ability to be adapted to take smart cards, should the banks decide to launch a smart card payment service. By equipping tills in this way the suppliers are facilitating such a choice.
10 For example, see Anchordoguy 1989 on the Japanese state and its development of the computer industry; or Kim and Dahlman 1992 on South Korea's use of technology policy instruments for development.

13 Aviation's technology imperative and the transformation of the global political economy

Vicki Golich

In April 1994, Boeing rolled out its latest aircraft – the 777. New-generation aircraft, by definition, incorporate virtually everything innovative in terms of *product* technology. The 777 employs fly-by-wire operational systems, uses three times the amount of composite materials of previous Boeing aircraft, and features an extraordinarily flexible interior which can be configured to meet the needs of nearly every market. Nevertheless, the roll-out ceremony was remarkable for at least two other reasons. First, the 777 promises 'to be the last all-new western heavy transport to take flight this century' and ranks as 'probably the largest current endeavour in the world funded by a single commercial company' (AWST 1994: 36). Second, and perhaps more importantly, the research, development and production (RD&P) of the 777 represents a 'profound conceptual shift' in Boeing's organisation and management of production *processes* (*ibid.*).

Boeing introduced digital design techniques, an impressive number of automated assembly methods, as well as lasers to align and level body panels and fuselage sections. Alignment is so precise that variance is 'less than the expansion resulting from sunshine heating one side of the transport' (AWST 1994: 42). In addition, Boeing built a $370 million new Integrated Aircraft Systems Laboratory (IASL) where extensive testing is aimed at eliminating expensive production-floor changes, cutting warranty costs, and reducing the need for the significant learn-by-doing advances which have characterised aircraft production in the past (Rosenberg 1982). While all primes – the firms responsible for assembly and delivery of the final product – have typically exceeded the testing required to meet safety certification standards, the new facilities and testing procedures are designed to deliver the first, completely service-ready aircraft on time the first time (AWST 1994: 43–4).

Still, the boldest breaks with tradition may have been the use of cross-functional design-build teams and of foreign manufacturers from Japan as 'Program Participants'. Large commercial aircraft (LCA) consist of two major parts, the airframe and the engine. Each comprises thousands of components. The 777 incorporates some fifty-seven major systems which depend on 'over 3,500 line replaceable units plus 20,000 additional standard parts' (AWST 1994: 56). Although eventually this huge number of complex systems and components must be assembled, research and design have traditionally been fragmented. Evolving blueprints were prepared by separate sets of scientists and engineers; floor design was distinct from kitchen designs, and each was separated from cargo space even though the design of each affected the operational efficiency of the other. As each group completed its work, the plans were 'thrown over the wall' to the next; little sharing of mutual or connected problems occurred.

For the 777, over 238 'Working Together' design teams included representatives from virtually everyone who will use the plane, including pilots, flight attendants, mechanics, baggage and cargo handlers, and passengers. The system was so interconnected that teams working to integrate engine and airframe with airline maintenance needs could 'access the enginemaker's blueprints' (AWST 1994: 51). Improvements range from push-button access panels to ease maintenance, especially during cold weather, to stronger and more user-friendly floor design. The teams used computers – at one time encompassing over 2,200 CATIA workstations networked to a cluster of eight mainframe computers manipulating nearly three terabytes of data from suppliers around the world – to share their ideas and insights regarding the evolving aircraft in real-time, 'early and often', thus avoiding costly change-of-error and rework incidents and creating the first 100 per cent 'paperless' aircraft (AWST 1994: 36).

To acquire the requisite components, Boeing contracted with 241 vendors; nearly one-third were firms from Australia, Brazil, Canada, France, Ireland, Italy, Korea and Singapore. Japanese firms enjoyed a status new to Boeing, that of 'Program Participant...a transitionary arrangement between a conventional subcontractor and a full partner role' (Benke 1987). Japanese representatives were members of the executive council and programme committee. Although programme management and control resided with Boeing, the Japanese reviewed the status, progress and outlook of the programme and participated in some design and development decisions early in the R&D process. In return, the Japanese accepted significant risk participation, assuming responsibility for both the non-recurring and recurring costs of the hardware items they produced.

It is difficult to overstate the dramatic change in production organisation and technology which this shift in Boeing's corporate culture represents. Although neither the use of foreign suppliers nor the tighter linkages among some of them is particularly innovative,[1] Boeing and the United States have resisted the trend toward globalised production in this industry sector with impressive tenacity and success until now. Therefore, Boeing's shift may signal the institutionalisation of a transnational production structure once considered anathema for a strategic industry sector (see for example Lorell 1980; Hayward 1983; Golich 1991).

The transformation has not followed a linear path. Rather, more of a '"stochastic" element [is] at work here – a situation where the random or unpredictable interaction of elements produces outcomes which are "sticky"'

(Cerny 1994a: 335). The factors impelling change in global political-economic structures and processes vary in degrees of importance and role – sometimes acting as the dependent and sometimes the independent variable. They are coupled – sometimes loosely, sometimes tightly (Perrow 1984, 1986) – in 'causally complex interactive systems' (Kitschelt 1991) marked by what I have referred to elsewhere as dynamic reciprocity (Golich 1992).

This chapter explores the role of technology as one catalyst to change in the global political economy, as well as the dynamic reciprocity among technology, politics, and economics as manifested in the commercial-class aircraft manufacturing (CCAM) industry sector.

An analysis of this sector is relevant for two reasons. First, its evolving organisational structure and related production processes reflect changes in the global political economy. CCAM began in the 1920s with a large number of competitive firms which often participated in transnational joint production efforts and sometimes shared technology. By the mid-1930s, with strong encouragement from key states, it shifted to a set of oligopolistic domestic firms which jealously guarded technology secrets. Since then, CCAM has been considered a strategic industry;[2] a multitude of political and economic incentives have compelled states to protect and to dominate it. Nevertheless, as the 1980s dawned, sector production patterns shifted again to a new style of globalisation and with some timid technology sharing.

Second, CCAM is at the centre of a much broader aviation system. It is both an integrator of thousands of components – many of which are the products of complex technologies and production processes themselves (for example, airframes, engines, and avionics) – and a supplier of *the* critical capital good which makes air travel possible. Furthermore, aircraft and the services they facilitate require an incredibly complex infrastructure of airports, air-traffic control systems (see Keith Hayward in this volume), and computer reservation networks, each of which again incorporates intricate and sophisticated technologies in its delivery and management. Thus CCAM both symbolises many of the dramatic changes in the global political economy we observe today (dependent variable) and continues to facilitate changes through the introduction of faster, more comfortable planes which can fly further more reliably (independent variable).

STATES, FIRMS AND TECHNOLOGY

The relationship among states, firms and technology is complex, reflecting 'circular' rather than 'linear' interactions (Kitschelt 1991); each contributes unevenly to the metamorphosis of the global political economy. The three variables combine in a complex, reciprocal cycle of persistent change which eventually compels radical transformations of political economic structures and processes (see Figure 13.1).

Political decisions are influenced by demands from both domestic and

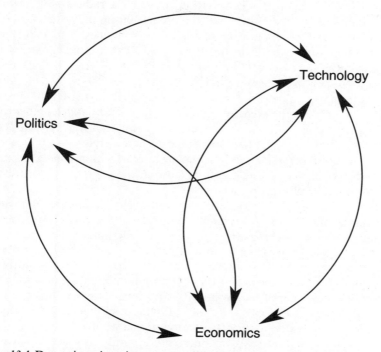

Figure 13.1 Dynamic reciprocity among politics, economics and technology

global constituencies; they involve policy selection and implementation designed to maintain sovereignty and security. Decisions are informed by policy-maker *Weltanschauungen*, which are shaped by perceived structures of power – both internal and external to the state – and status of global and domestic economies, as well as the consequences of technological innovation on product and manufacturing processes. State policies create the parameters for corporate activity; they may be designed to promote an industry sector or to achieve other goals – for example, national security, employment stability, or economic diversity.

Whereas states technically have the authority to pursue a particular policy path, changes in technology, as well as in political and economic dynamics not subject to their control, can constrain their ability to follow that path (see for example Hayward 1983: 8–9; Underhill 1991). The 1978 American decision to liberalise global air transport provides a powerful example. Policy-makers believed that US airline sophistication in service delivery would ensure their domination of this critical and potentially profitable industry sector (Kasper 1988), and implicitly assumed that larger, more profitable US airlines would create greater demand for US aircraft. Instead, a set of unintended and unanticipated consequences (Kahn 1988) yielded significant financial losses for US airlines and dramatically decreased demand for new aircraft. Deregulation triggered a radical shift in airline route structures and redefined aircraft preference from the widebodies under development and production to smaller, narrow bodies. The 1980s global recession depressed overall air traffic demand, further reducing airline need and ability to buy aircraft. Surplus capacity in all civil aircraft market segments (Lopez and Yager 1987: 5; Kelly *et al.* 1991: 84–5) was aggravated, perhaps ironically, by technological advances which increased the potential lifespan of an aircraft from twenty-five to fifty years and lengthened the replacement cycle. Aircraft manufacturers were negatively affected since production is not easily slowed or shifted to new aircraft types. Frustrated primes, to get rid of 'white tails' – complete aircraft with no buyer – initiated long-term, 'walk away leases'; as they ran out, these aircraft were added to the pool of relatively cheap transports.

Political decisions help shape the pace and style of technology innovation, since this is subject to government approval via standards and licensing systems. Governments have actively promoted technological advances – such as the jet engine to increase speed and range – to serve both security and commercial objectives. Historically, security has been a primary motivating factor, given the prominence of two world wars and the subsequent long Cold War which have paralleled aviation's advances. Two examples warrant mention. By the mid-1930s, virtually all states, suspicious of Germany's intentions, actively discouraged the transnational production arrangements which characterised aircraft manufacturing, and encouraged firms to retrench production strategies within domestic boundaries. The French created *groupements*, an industrial structure which allowed members to maintain their autonomy, 'preserving their own fixed capital, production facilities, research laboratories, and administrative services'; a central bureau parcelled out orders to members and negotiated contracts (Chapman 1991). The incredible demand for aircraft during the Second World War helped shape another aspect of the evolving structure of commercial aircraft manufacturing. Subcontracting for specialised components began in earnest at this time to take advantage of the resulting economies of scale and other efficiencies. When firms eventually returned to a style of globalised production toward the end of the twentieth century, these two aspects of industrial organisation helped make the transition possible. The *groupement* structure decreased fears related to lost state or firm identity because it allowed for autonomy; the low-vertical integration between suppliers and primes allowed for a wide variety of separate firms around the world to participate in aircraft production (see Figure 13.2).

AVIATION'S TECHNOLOGICAL IMPERATIVES – A CATALYST OF CHANGE

Technology advances as scientific discoveries are applied to products and processes. Specific innovations may be adopted by corporations to decrease

Figure 13.2 The aircraft industry production pyramid
Source: G. W. Bernstein in Pinelli *et. al* (forthcoming 1997).

production costs or increase market share through the introduction of technologically enhanced, discrete products. Alternatively, advances may be encouraged by states seeking to maintain global stature and sovereignty, and to satisfy domestic demands. Technological innovation in either the military or commercial sector depends on psychological or cultural receptivity to them (see Youngs and Underhill in this volume). For example, the transformation of aircraft from tools of military reconnaissance to fighter planes had to overcome the original respect pilots from both sides had for each other. The First World War was well under way before pilots strapped guns to their aircraft wings and began shooting at enemy aircraft (Winter *et al*. 1969). On the commercial side, a three-engined aircraft flown by a three-person flight deck crew was technologically feasible long before it was introduced in the widebodies of the late 1960s; neither the public nor the state was willing to give up the perceived balance and failsafe back-up power of four engines tucked under the wings and of four crew members in flights across the Atlantic or over the Rockies. Now, of course, we fly across both in two-engined aircraft with two-person deck crews.

Once civil aviation proved its commercial and military value, governments served as primary agents of change in technological innovation and industrial organisation. Policy-makers have used direct subsidies as well as indirect promotion of exports, basic research, launch aid and related industries.[3] Until the 1970s, most government aid and even some of the earlier phases of European collaboration were aimed at gaining, regaining, or maintaining unilateral dominance of the industry.[4] The seemingly secure availability of RD&P capital in perpetuity contributed to a consumer expectation of virtually constant increases in performance and comfort. The drive to incorporate technological innovation became an imperative. It was economically feasible since ready cash was ever present and because passengers responded positively to increased flight comforts by increasing air traffic demand, hence expanding the market to be shared. It was politically possible because no expense would be spared in the provision of national security and because, until recently, commercial aircraft development benefited from R&D for military aircraft so there was little added cost.

Advances came in rapid succession during the two world wars. Aircraft speed, range and reliability were dramatically improved as was the aviation infrastructure through advances in radio communications, navigational aids and other instrumentation. As a result, the general public became 'airminded', more frequently choosing air transportation when travel distances exceeded 200 miles (Davies 1964: 238–40, 271–2); from 1929 to 1954, the passenger-kilometres generated by the world's scheduled airlines increased at an average annual rate of 25 per cent (Hochmuth 1974: 154). Two critical advances include first, the 1931 first all-metal, monocoque airframe passenger transports – the Douglas DC-2 and DC-3 and Boeing's B-247 – which marked the 'end of the wooden-wing plane' (Solberg 1979: 155; Mowery and Rosenberg 1982: 105); and second, jet engines, simultaneously discovered by Germany's Hans von Ohain and Britain's Sir Frank Whittle. The new engines offered significant savings in time provided by the 500 mph capacity and previously unknown regularity of service. Though the British introduced the first jet aircraft with the 1944 Gloster Meteor, and the first commercial jet with the 1952 DH106-Comet, Boeing was the first to introduce a commercially successful jet-powered aircraft with the 707.

The introduction of wide body aircraft in the late 1960s marks an equally dramatic shift in aviation technology. Payload capacity jumped from just over 100 passengers in a plane powered by four engines and flown by four crew to some 300 passengers in a three-engined aircraft (except the Boeing 747 which retained four engines) piloted by three. This dramatically decreased the cost of service delivery for airlines and increased passenger comfort; widebodies had the potential to be wildly successful in the commercial market.

There was just one hitch. Corporate decisions focus on how to make a profit in a competitive market defined by state policies and preferences as well as by customer demands and expectations, which are influenced by changes in technology. Aviation's technological imperative resulted in skyrocketing RD&P costs (see Table 13.1) and lengthened return on investment cycles (see Figure 13.3), making it increasingly risky to initiate new-generation projects. As a result, the ratio of launching cost to equity rose from 42 per cent with the 1940s Douglas DC6 development, to 155 per cent with the 1970 DC10 (Taneja 1980). Moreover, 'an increasing proportion of the costs of introducing a new aircraft [were] incurred during the phase of greatest uncertainty concerning market prospects and technological feasibility' (Mowery and Rosenberg 1982: 167).

Table 13.1 Aircraft development costs

Aircraft	Entered service	Development cost, US$ (millions)	Development cost in 1991, US$ (millions)	Development cost/seat in 1991, US$ (millions)
DC-3	1936	0.3	3	0.1
DC-6	1947	14.0	90	1.7
DC-8	1959	112.0	600	3.75
B747	1970	1,200.0	3,300	7.3
B777	1995*	5,000.0*	4,300*	14.0*

* = Estimate
Source: US Congress, Office of Technology Assessment (1991: 343)
Note: The 1991 values are computed using aerospace industry price deflators for 1965–1989 and GNP deflators and estimates for other years.

During the 1940s and 1950s, a return on investment cycle required four to five years; today it can take that long just to develop a new airframe or engine, while the return on investment is closer to ten to fifteen years. Higher RD&P costs increase manufacturer cashflow needs as it seeks to sustain a production line until it becomes profitable, and to pursue the constant process of researching and developing new-generation aircraft. In addition, higher costs simultaneously multiply the number of planes which have to be sold to earn a return on investment, while raising airframe prices, making sales in the volume necessary to achieve profitability more difficult. While aircraft costs soared, the customer base continued to shrink and the list of commercially successful aircraft remained very short compared to the list of LCA produced; today twenty-five airlines purchase over 70 per cent of commercial aircraft.

Just as technological R&D costs reached nearly prohibitive levels and payoffs were uncertain and long-range, government coffers were no longer flush, competition within the industry had increased, and cashflow from airlines to manufacturers via purchases decreased to create a capital vacuum. Suddenly access to RD&P capital was no longer guaranteed. In the US, state treasuries were drained from prolonged participation in the Vietnam conflict and efforts to build a 'Great Society' – each a response to perceived foreign-and-domestic political and economic phenomena. Overall industry sales to the Department of Defense dropped 24 per cent from 1968 to 1971, while jet transport sales plummeted 68 per cent. Public disenchantment added to the problem as they voted to 'cease development of a supersonic transport, to

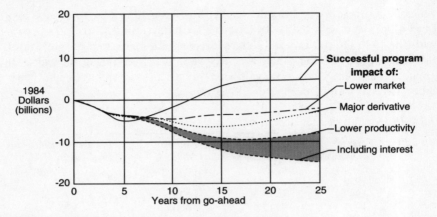

Figure 13.3 The aircraft return-on-investment cycle
Source: Bacher (1984: 14).

end the B-70 manned bomber programme, and to reduce B-1 bomber funding' (Golich 1992: 919).

The situation was aggravated by the greater economic parity among advanced industrial states and the growth of aerospace manufacturing capabilities in Europe and several newly industrialising countries, including Brazil, Israel and Indonesia. Large foreign debt emerged as a structural problem, falling hardest on the developing countries which traditionally import a significant share of civil aerospace products, since they produce none of their own in the commercial class category and ageing aircraft fleets needed to be replaced and expanded to accommodate predicted traffic increases. Persistent debt also decreased US airline profitability at a time when domestic fleets needed replacement and enhancement.

Companies were forced to seek capital elsewhere, including from foreign firms. Lockheed and General Electric (GE) were among the first to access foreign capital in exchange for significant participation in product delivery. Lockheed built its L1011 to be compatible with Rolls-Royce engines. GE joined forces – despite strenuous objections from the US Congress (Golich 1992) – with SNECMA (Société Nationale de Construction des Moteurs) to produce the very successful family of CFM LCA engines. In so doing, GE shared some B1 bomber engine technology. In another effort to access cash, this time through sales, manufacturers pursued offset agreements initiated in 1972 with a planes-for-hams swap between McDonnell-Douglas and Yugoslavia, which evolved into a guarantee for production participation (Schaufele 1988).

Within this context, Boeing, Lockheed and McDonnell-Douglas were each developing new-generation wide body aircraft. Boeing, having lost a military transport contract to Lockheed, and with it substantial R&D funds, literally 'bet the company' to bring the 747 to market (Newhouse 1982: 113–

22). While Boeing's gamble was successful, what turned out to be the deadly competition between the producers of widebodies with comparable payload and range – Lockheed's L1011 and McDonnell-Douglas's (MDD) DC10 – sent a chilling message to the aviation community. It was no longer possible to build a number of comparable aircraft, let the market select the winner(s), and move on to the next aircraft competition. Both Lockheed and MDD were negatively affected by the competition: Lockheed was forced to cease production of the L1011 in 1981; after lackluster earnings, MDD announced in 1996 it would not pursue the development of its next generation civil aircraft.[5] The number of LCA primes contracted to the current three – Boeing, Airbus Industrie, McDonnell-Douglas – with British Aerospace active in the smaller aircraft market. This marked a dramatic departure from the thirty or so primes once in operation.

The perceived need to access capital via joint ventures with foreign firms was reinforced by the increasingly global market for LCA. The international market was no longer considered a series of distinct national markets linked by trade, but rather a single market where regulation variation was only marginally more significant in many cases than that which exists between any two US states. Moreover, the US was no longer the largest commercial transport market. Approximately two-thirds of the market was located outside the United States (Taneja 1994). If passenger traffic demand forecasts are accurate, this is a trend that is likely to continue for some time to come (see Figure 13.4).

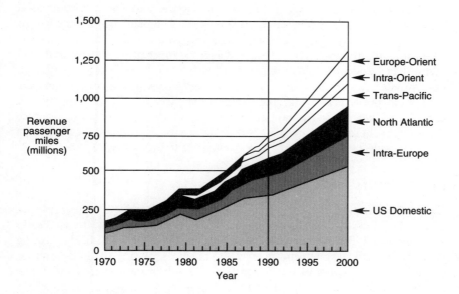

Figure 13.4 Historical forecast of international air transport traffic
Source: O'Lone (1991: 77).

Meanwhile, European aircraft manufacturers decided they would have to collaborate to compete with US firms (Servan-Schreiber 1968). Pushed by concerns about US intentions to dominate, the inefficiency of its fragmented markets in a global industry, and the high cost of RD&P; pulled by the desire to maintain a presence in the sector, Europe created Airbus Industrie (AI). AI could be successful because of technological advances in communications, in transportation of components (i.e. the Guppy), and in production processes. AI's success has also been attributed to lessons learned during the production of the Anglo-French technological marvel, the Concorde supersonic transport.[6] Given the strategic nature of the industry, states and firms seek involvement, in part, because of the associated prestige; hence no-one wishes to be assimilated in a production effort where participants become invisible. The *groupement* industrial organisation model could allay these fears and was appropriate to the low-vertical integration between suppliers and primes (see for example Mowery and Rosenberg 1982; Hayward 1983, 1986; Golich 1992).

Despite the tremendous risk associated with the pursuit of technological innovation in aircraft, with the list of possible enhancements seemingly infinite, LCA manufacturers have clearly indicated they will continue to incorporate new technologies no matter what the cost. More recent technological innovations have included even further reductions in engines and flight deck personnel, along with ever increasing amenities for passengers, such as the ability to show movies and serve hot meals, the availability of telephones, etc.,[7] as well as increased payload, range, and speed capacities.

Most recently, responding to the oil shocks and the environmental movement – both of which encourage decreased dependence on the use of fossil fuels (Talalay, this volume) – technological advances have focused on increasing flight efficiency through decreased operational costs and fuel savings. In addition, public demands to reduce noise pollution resulted in government regulations requiring quieter flight, to which corporations have responded positively. By far the greatest expenses for airlines are human capital and fuel, hence fly-by-wire and avionics technologies that can reduce the need for flight deck crew members or reduce weight[8] (which requires extra fuel) are highly valued, as are more fuel-efficient engines.

CONCLUSIONS

During the aviation age, the international system has passed through phases of relative stability: *Pax Britannia* and *Pax Americana*; and chaos: World Wars One and Two. It has adjusted to or 'muddled through' fairly striking changes in the way states and markets do business: closing the gold window, oil shocks, the collapse of the Soviet Union. Each of these events, much like an earthquake, marks the end to a build-up of tremendous pressures compelling the creation of new structures and processes, and sends aftershocks through the system that affect virtually all sectors and societies. In the case of aviation, technological innovation came as a response to war (anticipated or real) which urged the availability of superior equipment. Oil shocks triggered the search for fuel efficiencies gained from lighter-weight aircraft and advances in engine design.

CCAM have also responded to less earth-shattering political and economic shifts in the global political economy. Consequences of more gradual change – such as the creation and expansion of the European Union, the emergence of greater parity among advanced industrial societies, and proliferating interdependence among actors and across issues – have also instigated and reflected change. The strategic nature of the industry means all states seek participation at some level. By the 1980s, policy-makers believed that denying a potential foreign partner's access to a production market might propel them to become competitors in the future (Fuqua 1989: 3; National Academy of Engineering 1985: 63–4). Alternatively, they were concerned that rejected partners might form competitive alliances. Perceived benefits were equally compelling: risk could be reduced by pooling resources and talent so that no single entity bore market-failure costs. Suppliers of specialised goods and services could market to primes in different countries and achieve economies of scale associated with increased sales volume, thus driving down costs. Some production arrangements, such as offsets or turnkey, could be linked to aircraft purchase. Critical financial support could be obtained from programme-participant governments, even under the new GATT rules.

Firms have adapted by creating a variety of flexible strategic alliances, many of which are transnational (see Figure 13.5). Several resemble global *groupement* where members may partner with others, but where success within the partnership generally leads to increased collaboration. Technological advances have been as critical to the feasibility of transnational production arrangements as they have to changing aircraft performance capabilities. To date few have ventured far into the territory of sharing technology and knowledge bases. However, it appears almost inevitable that the nascent steps currently taken in that direction will continue and proliferate. The tight communications linkages necessary for a team approach to R&D as manifested in the production of Boeing's 777 exemplifies this trend. Since no partner – corporation or country – wants to be considered a weak link in a production chain, since perceived equity in the value of contributions appears to be critical for strategic alliances to endure, and since the risks associated with advancing technology show no indication of decreasing in potential costs or gains, the pressure to move toward the sharing of technology and design decisions seems likely to increase.

A major consequence of this transformation of a strategic industrial organisation may be the continued diffusion of a variety of national capabilities generally associated with state abilities to achieve preferred outcomes, including wealth, knowledge and production capabilities.[9] Despite

192   *Vicki Golich*

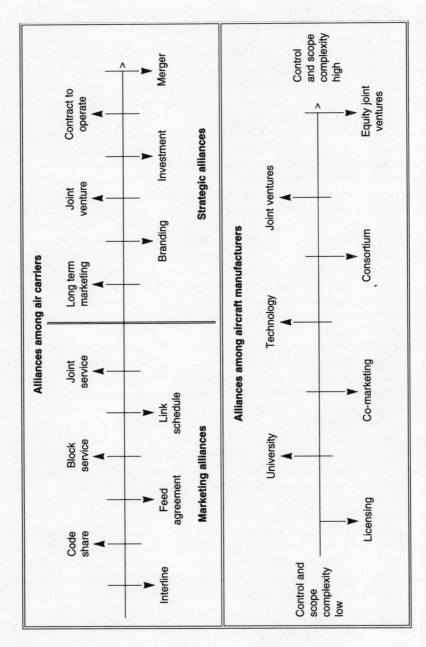

Figure 13.5 Aviation alliances
Source: Derived from Golaszewski (1993) and Raphael (1993).

its oligopolistic structure, commercial-class aircraft manufacturing remains highly competitive. The three primes have demonstrated every willingness to meet the requests of their decreasing pool of consumers through creative financing, leasing and production arrangements. As the potential for monopsony power increases, particularly where states are involved in decisions about aircraft purchases (which is virtually universal), greater demands for participation in the production, and eventually the research and development phases, seem likely. Airlines prefer to purchase aircraft from competitive firms to avoid monopoly costs, hence they are likely to perpetuate the presence of at least a few primes with widespread production that distributes costs and benefits among a variety of firms and states (AWST 1994).

Another major consequence may be observed in the prevailing attitudes and ideologies of dominant élites, be they corporate or governmental. These changes may not appear dramatic at first, but may eventually spawn a new *Weltanschauung*. They are manifested in a redefinition of security and a reconceptualisation of how to achieve desired outcomes. In the first case, policy-makers more readily acknowledge that the once-prevalent distinctions between security (high politics) and economics (low politics) are becoming less and less useful. They recognise that security encompasses a wide array of issues – military, economic, political, social – at a number of levels – global, national, local, family.

In the second case, a new consensus appears to be emerging regarding how best to achieve preferred policy outcomes. It was once considered reasonable and effective for the strongest to impose its will upon the weak. Twenty-first century realities may cause international relations scholars and practitioners, following the lead of business experience with transnational joint ventures, to re-examine this approach. The notion that imposing one's will on another is satisfactory and desirable simply because it is possible and might generate short-term gains, may be revealed for its lack of vision, as well as its inability to achieve long-term gains. These ideas may be replaced by a way of thinking which recognises that shared power generates more benefits for the larger community over a longer period of time. Hence policy-makers may adopt a new strategy for achieving policy goals which incorporates all stakeholders in the decision-making process (Gray 1989). To the extent that the new transnational production structures serve to blur political boundaries between states and to reinforce (and be reinforced by) similar conversions in a variety of other industry sectors – for example, in this volume: finance (Cerny), aviation systems (Keith Hayward), entertainment and culture (Youngs) – this transformation in strategic thinking will be cemented.

If states and firms add scientific and technological R&D collaboration in the strategic industry sectors they once protected so fiercely to the increasingly long list of transnational joint ventures, tremendous and longstanding psychological barriers will have to be overcome. Many policy-makers and policy advisors, especially in the US where concern about losing a technological edge has come to be a policy imperative, have argued that technology transfer should be restricted even if only for a short time, since in a dynamic environment a small lead can be turned into a large lead (Krasner 1990). Moreover, they are concerned that 'American industrial and technological decline has eroded the foundation of the post-war security system . . . [while] . . . industrial and technological initiative abroad is creating the basis of a wholly new system that could markedly reduce US influence' (Borrus and Zysman 1992: 7). From this more traditional perspective, sharing technology leads to a dangerous vulnerability: exposing the knowledge core enables others to gain competitive edge economically, politically and militarily. In addition, the level of compromise required for successful international collaborative projects reduces national ability to declare and pursue preferred foreign and economic policies.

Another interpretation is that the vulnerability associated with this deep level of mutual dependence at the core may generate enduring partnerships and decrease the likelihood that participants would undermine the potential benefits for the mere possibility of short-term gain in economic, political or military positioning. Studies of a number of successful transnational joint ventures and other strategic alliances reveal that they are founded upon mutual trust and respect, believed to generate a 'win-win' outcome for all participants, and involve long-term commitments. Partners have a clear and consensually agreed goal and strategy to achieve it. Each believes the other contributes something critical to goal achievement, and each has a sense of relatively equitable efficacy and influence with respect to critical decisions. Finally, cultural differences among partners are understood and embraced (Perlmutter and Heenan 1986: 83–4, 150–2; Gray 1989; Kohn 1992).

In sum, the synergy among technological, political and economic variables across a wide array of manufacturing and service sectors, as well as issue areas, has transformed the global political economy from a network of states and markets with distinct borders to a more chaotic web of connections and interactions, where boundaries are harder to distinguish (see Palan in this volume) and more difficult to recognise as fundamental to international relationships. Moreover, changes in technology, politics and economics have redefined what resources constitute assets in the pursuit of desired outcomes (see Talalay in this volume). Change is at once wonderful for those who may benefit and threatening to those who may not; it is particularly threatening to those who have thrived under the prevailing network of structures and processes. History is a long tale about societies, states and firms which have slipped into and out of hegemonic positions. It is a cliché and an axiom to say that those who can adapt to change are likely to survive it best. What remains uncertain is the precise nature and consequences of the changes occurring now, hence the tactics most likely to bring success in the new context.

NOTES

1 Airbus Industrie, using the *groupement* model introduced by the French in the early 1930s, can claim the credit for that process-change phenomenon.

2 Four characteristics can define a strategic industry: first, it produces goods or services directly related to national security; second, it earns higher returns with the resources it employs than would be earned elsewhere; third, it is prestigious; and fourth, it 'generates special benefits for the rest of the economy' (Tyson 1988: 112).

3 Several scholars have detailed the range of government intervention strategies (see *inter alia*, Miller and Sawers 1968; Mowery and Rosenberg 1982; Hayward 1983, 1986; Golich 1989; Chapman 1991). Even the economic regulation of US airlines, though considered a nuisance by many, actually served to ensure a flow of capital to pay for constant aircraft upgrades: airlines knew they could safely cover increased costs through increased fares, so capital costs were not a constraint.

4 A number of scholars have chronicled various aspects of this fantasy (see for example Lorell 1980; Hayward 1983; Chapman 1991; Golich 1991).

5 Commercial sales were hurt by negative publicity following two catastrophic crashes early in its flying career, though they eventually grew to a respectable number. The production run was consciously supported by government procurement of KC10s (the military equivalent of DC10s) in an effort to help MDD stay in business.

6 Unfortunately, it was a commercial disaster, at least in part because US officials refused to let the aircraft use its speed advantage while in US airspace. Many argue this restriction was put in place because the US did not have a competitive aircraft.

7 Some might argue these amenities have been annulled by the decreasing space between seats!

8 Fly-by-wire flight eliminates hundreds of pounds of wiring associated with hydraulics and other systems rendered unnecessary by the new technology.

9 Clearly some assets, for example arable land or mineral deposits, cannot be transferred as easily or without significantly greater transaction costs.

14 Technology, politics and the world civil aviation system

The case of the Global Navigation Satellite System (GNSS)

Keith Hayward

INTRODUCTION

As Skolnikoff observes (1993: 136), 'international dependencies are an inherent part of an interdependent world, a natural consequence of the integration made possible and stimulated by technological advances'. In his view, the growth of global technological systems for information and other services – mainly derived from the space-based capabilities that emerged in the late 1950s – represents one of the three generic changes in the character of dependency relations caused by technology. These space-based systems were built up by a mixture of public and private investment, with both sectors having a vested interest in the integration and continued development of associated services. Over time, reliance on these systems grew, 'with equitable access and assurance of continued availability representing essential elements of system performance'. Several of these global systems originated in national technology programmes – in several cases, from defence needs. However, their control and management is an international issue, with many states – especially those from the Third World – preferring these responsibilities to be located in international organisations. In practice, the industrial countries that first develop and deploy the systems 'prefer to reap the benefits and to continue their control, rather than submit to international management' (*ibid.*: 140).

Space-based technology, primarily from a geo-stationary orbit (GSO), whose significance Arthur C. Clarke first noted in 1948, offers a unique ability to observe, to scan and to communicate. Although the primacy of the telecommunication satellite is being challenged by the greater capacity and signal integrity offered by fibre-optics, the 'world-spanning' opportunities created by space-based systems, especially when people and their vehicles are on the move, is still a powerful technology. The exploitation of space was a political and strategic process driven first by the Cold War, but independent access to space has since become an important motive shaping technology policies in Europe, China, Japan and many other states with a security interest in space. The space industry and space-based services are also commercially important, giving rise to a wide range of national and transnational, public and private actors with an interest in space and its control. By definition, and since the late 1950s also by legal convention, the satellite is a technology that defies sovereignty. There are international agreements governing the distribution of GSO slots (recently challenged by a Chinese satellite) and certain prohibitions on the military use of space, but those countries with the requisite technology can spy, broadcast and communicate at will across boundaries. Space-based technologies and the powerful commercial forces they have spawned challenge the 'billiard-ball state' by making it less easy for national governments to control access to, and what goes on within, their territorial boundaries. In both cases, there is an archetypal confrontation between 'states and markets', where the political interests of the former and the better and more efficient functioning of the latter create a tension in the evolution of international political economy. The advent of space-based navigation and air-traffic control (ATC) has brought another such challenge to sovereignty.

The idea of a legal defined national airspace dates from 1919, and has underpinned much of subsequent air transport regulation (Strange 1988; Doganis 1991). In recent years, commercial pressure and ideological change have led to liberalisation in the airline industry; but aircraft entering national airspace are still subject to national control. This chapter explores the implications of the development of space-based ATC systems for national control over airspace and the extent to which they represent a further evolution in the dependency relations spawned by technological development. The international community is being offered a comprehensive technological solution to a global problem, the adoption of which is being driven by commercial pressures combined with a technological and operational *fait accompli* from the two states, the USA and Russia, that currently control the technology. As a result, the creation of a generally acceptable mechanism for international control is being shaped largely by those two states and their interests. The chapter begins with a brief survey of the public and private actors involved in ATC operations and a review of the problems for national and international ATC posed by the explosive growth in air transport. Finally, the chapter examines the emergence of space-based ATC systems as a technologically elegant and comprehensive solution to these problems. However, given that these are the result of military programmes developed by the USA and, to a lesser extent, Russia, the adoption of space-based ATC raises difficult questions of international control and guaranteed access to the system. It also illustrates ways in which technological advantages can become embedded in international relations as forms of structural power.

PUBLIC AND PRIVATE ACTORS IN ATC OPERATIONS

The basic function of the world civil aviation system is to transport people and high-value goods safely and economically from one point on the earth's surface to another. As a technology system, it comprises several interlocking and interdependent aspects: the airport and its immediate environment, the commercial airliner and *en route* control systems. All contain critical elements of safety and security, but local, regional and global air-traffic control systems (ATC) are clearly vital to maintain a safe and efficient operational environment. The development of modern ATC was greatly facilitated by the development of radar during World War Two and has been further enhanced by the information technology revolution which has transformed data handling and control processes. Under development are control systems that could link aircraft directly to ATC operations, the so-called 'spaghetti in the sky' concept, where airliners are freed from designated traffic corridors and are allocated individual flight paths.

Although operation of the world aviation system has demanded international coordination (for example in managing airline operations across the Atlantic and between European states), this rarely challenged the ability of nation-states to control aircraft operating over their defined airspace. The management of the ATC infrastructure is still largely an exercise in public administration, though in the case of Europe, a transnational body – Eurocontrol, is responsible for some aspects of European ATC operation. Most of the major international organisations affecting the operation of civil aviation – primarily the International Civil Aviation Organisation (ICAO) – are also IGOs. However, the combination of space-based technologies and information technology is set to revolutionise the operation of the world civil aviation system through the creation of a global navigation system. While this represents the latest in a series of state–market interactions and tensions that have characterised the evolution of the civil aviation system, it threatens national competence in controlling the operation of aircraft over national territory and raises questions of implicit dependence of the international system on a single, or at best two, nationally defined technological capabilities.

As the main users of ATC, the world's airlines have a vested interest in the operational efficiency and security of ATC systems.[1] Increasing competitive pressure, much of which has been generated by deregulation, has sharpened airline concern for cost-cutting, including efficiency gains though better management of flight operations. The airline industry is, therefore, increasingly sensitive to operational problems caused by ATC delays and airport congestion. Similarly, airlines have adopted stringent fuel-saving flight-management strategies. As a result, the airline customers are tending to favour equipment and technology-based systems that can ease these burdens, often through the orchestration of incremental improvements to existing products or to changes in the air transport infrastructure. The airline industry is, therefore, a strong supporter of more flexible, accurate and delay-reducing navigation and data-relay systems. On the other hand, the airline industry does not want to be burdened by duplicated or incompatible technologies caused by political failure to reach agreement on international standards.

The International Civil Aviation Organisation (ICAO) is the main focus for intergovernmental consultation on technical questions and, increasingly importantly, for environmental standard setting and as a possible location for international control over Global Satellite Navigation. The ICAO has also helped to ensure that Third World states are helped to achieve the necessary levels of technical competence in order to operate safely and to gain equal access to the air transport system. INMARSAT is the world body responsible for the operation of existing global maritime and aerial navigation satellite systems. The EU, confirmed by the Single European Act, has been increasingly responsible for the regulatory framework of EU airline operation and is also encouraging the creation of a more integrated approach to ATC. This includes coordinating national positions, liaison with established European ATC organisations such as Eurocontrol, and sponsoring research activity associated with new-generation ATC technologies.

THE ATC PROBLEM

According to 1996 estimates of airline traffic growth, the market for air travel is expected to double by 2005. Already, airspace in many parts of the world is so congested that travellers are subject to frustrating delays which cost the airline industry billions of dollars a year. As we have already noted, the airline industry is also increasingly sensitive to operating expenses, a substantial part of which is taken up by fuel and crew costs (see Golich in this volume). Any measures which can reduce both of these drains on revenue will be welcomed by the industry. A key element in resolving these problems and allowing airlines to operate more efficiently is to tackle airport and airway congestion, and enable airlines to route their aircraft more effectively, responding flexibly to weather conditions and to achieve an optimal flight path. Increasing use of on-board computer-driven systems helps to improve operational efficiencies, but in the final analysis the individual aircraft must conform to ATC constraints, separation requirements, restricted landing and take-off opportunities (slot times) and the vagaries of weather and individual national operational requirements.

The ATC/congestion problem is especially acute in North America and Western Europe. In the former, the question is largely one of saturation, especially around the major airport hubs (aircraft separation on approach tends to be less stringent than in Europe). For Europe, the main problem is the coordination of twenty-three states and their fifty-one separate ATC centres in a system where 'boundaries are defined by national rather than logical parameters' (*Flight*, 4 August 1993). As we will note below, the Europeans are slowly integrating this disparate collection of ATC responsibilities, but both they and the Americans need urgently to upgrade their ATC systems. East Europe needs a total modernisation of ATC, both near airports (approach ATC) and to manage the airways (*en route* ATC) – a particular problem for the Russian land mass, increasingly attractive to western airlines looking for optimal routes between Western Europe and Asia. Finally, with Asia set to record the fastest air-traffic growth of any region over the next two decades, there is a need for effective ATC and flight management covering very long, trans-oceanic routes.

The traditional solution to these problems, and one that has been employed over the last few years, has been to improve terrestrial systems, taking advantage of state-of-the-art radars and vastly more powerful information processing capabilities. Inter-regional coordination has also been improved by satellite-based communication relay systems. Finally, aircraft have been able to access conventional satellite navigation fixes through the INMARSAT organisation. However, thanks to large investment in military navigation and communications technology, there is a prospect for a much more integrated approach to ATC and airliner flight management based on systems such as the US Global Positioning Satellite and its Russian equivalent, GLOSNASS. These technologies would form the core of a Global Navigation Satellite System (GNSS).

The emergence of space-based ATC systems presents a new problem of technological access. To date, the costly technology required for highly accurate navigational positioning and the even more expensive commitments to installing a satellite constellation, have been borne by the military requirements of two superpowers. The technology itself is not so arcane as to be outside the realistic aspirations of any developed state with an established aerospace and electronics industry. Established manufacturers, especially those that have been involved in the development and production of GPS, have a significant competitive edge in the provision of additional or replacement vehicles, as their sunk costs have been written off under military contract and as they can derive some economies of scale through limited mass production. Similarly, data-relay satellites are already operated by the US and Russia and comparable vehicles are being developed by the European Space Agency. There are no problems with ground systems and the on-board interrogation units, all widely and commercially available. The Russian GLOSNASS and American GPS systems could be integrated into a single system, and there is no technical reason why a third or more additional systems could not be added to the world constellation. Access to space itself has become a fiercely competitive business, with European, American, Russian, Chinese and Japanese satellite launchers available on an open market.

The problem facing the world civil aviation system is whether to rely upon military systems which are still largely under the control of individual nations and subject therefore to unilateral withdrawal or degradation, or to develop an independent but costly world navigation system that may duplicate much of the existing system. Compromise solutions involving supplementary capabilities may be available, but problems of reconciling international control with security fears that a civil system could be exploited for military purposes will remain. The political economy aspects are further heightened by a clear conflict of interest between commercial actors such as airlines that want rapid and the most cost-effective improvements in ATC and flight control, and national governments that may fear the loss of control over airspace management and/or the security threats posed by access to highly accurate navigational data that they cannot veto or easily interdict.

THE GLOBAL NAVIGATION SATELLITE SYSTEM – TECHNOLOGICAL CHANGE AND POLITICAL INTERESTS IN THE WORLD CIVIL AVIATION SYSTEM

The NAVSTAR Global Positioning System (GPS) was declared operational by the US Department of Defense (DoD) in December 1993. The Russians have a similar, but geographically more limited system, GLOSNASS. The function of GPS and GLOSNASS is to provide highly accurate navigational data for military units, missiles and other mobile systems. GPS comprises a network of twenty-four geostationary satellites with several 'parked' back-up vehicles. It provides global coverage, and when calibrated by reference to ground-based systems, 'differential' GPS has an accuracy in three dimensions of one metre or less. GPS took over twenty years of development and was used operationally during the Gulf War with stunning success for target acquisition and guidance in an otherwise trackless environment. The GPS system can already be accessed by civilian users – albeit with a reduced degree of accuracy (around fifty metres) (US Congress 1994). Commercially available receivers are now widely used by yachtsmen, and in the Gulf War many American GIs were given low-accuracy receivers by family or friends. In the UK, the Birmingham ambulance service is experimenting with GPS as a control system and the Stoke-based PMT bus company uses GPS to monitor its services. The 'differential' system is already being used by the US Coastguard and by geological exploration companies.

The value of 'differential' GPS as a civil ATC system is readily apparent. The advantages of the GPS system lie in its unprecedented accuracies which could affect every aspect of flight control. It should lead to vastly improved levels of safety for both commercial and private flying. As part of a Global Navigational Satellite System (GNSS), GPS and similar constellations would help to revolutionise world ATC and much of airliner flight management. Full GNSS would be a mixture of space- and ground-based technologies. The navigation satellite constellation is at the core of the system, but to achieve the necessary accuracy, global coverage and continual access by aircraft, it also requires powerful data relay satellites and linked ground stations. Then space-based elements would have to have a measure of redundancy and orbitally 'parked' reserve vehicles. The system would also require a continual programme of upgrading and replacement. A full GNSS would have to be subject to international agreements, probably through ICAO, on standards and equipment compatibility. This would imply integration and inter-operability with the Russian GLOSNASS or any other satellite navigation network – such as one proposed by the French for the European Union (EU). Talks through the ICAO began early in 1994, and achieving a full international regime covering GNSS is expected no earlier than 2004.

However, technical preparations for the first stages of a GNSS are already in train. INMARSAT, the international maritime and aerial navigation organisation, will be launching five new geo-stationary satellites from 1995. These, the INMARSAT-3 series, will carry transponders able to interrogate GPS and to provide integrity monitoring, wide-area differential corrections and on-board atomic clocks to provide precise temporal fixes (*Interavia*, July 1994). However, as we will note, there are a number of major financial, security and control issues to be resolved before a full scope GNSS, linked to systems such as GPS, can be implemented.

More immediately, and subject in the first instance to national imple-mentation, GPS use would serve as an alternative to ground-based ATC, and in particular improve access to airports that do not presently possess instrument, all-weather landing capabilities. There could be large economies for both operators and ATC administrations. One-metre accuracy in *three* dimensions would allow the use of GPS to control aircraft during landing and take-off. Current research (on the so-called 'Integrity Beacon' GPS) already suggests that a positioning of between one and two centimetres may be possible during the landing phases. This would theoretically enable totally blind landings – or at least enable pilots to reach the airport perimeter and then to judge landing conditions visually – a capability well exceeding the current Category 3 automatic landing limit. More work needs to be done to identify the most reliable communication system for automatic dependent surveillance and to evaluate the full capabilities of a satellite-based ATC system. In the future, GPS might also be used for collision avoidance and to prevent 'controlled flight into terrain' (hitting mountains). The FAA expects to have demonstrated GPS capability for Category 3 landings by 1995, but GPS *en route* navigation and other basic applications for ATC are available now, or will be in the very short term. Continental Airlines is already using GPS systems and two US airports have been used to test its ATC capabilities. GPS guided instrument landings at Aspen in Colorado were allowed for the first time in 1993, avoiding 100 diversions in the first year of operation (US Congress 1994).

GPS's worldwide availability, and the prospect for a full GNSS, provides opportunities for both developed and underdeveloped countries to upgrade their ATC for a fraction of the cost of terrestrial equipment. Because GPS is carried by the aircraft, it largely, though not entirely, obviates the need for sophisticated and expensive *en route* control systems. This would be a boon for areas with limited provision (Asia Pacific and most of the Third World) and for areas such as North America and Western Europe suffering from airborne congestion, where the accuracy of GPS can increase the number of movements through airspace. GPS can offer precise velocity measurement which should be better than the inertial navigation systems currently in use by the airlines (US Congress 1994).

The extent to which GPS might remove the need for elaborate terrestrial ATC has still to be fully assessed. However, there are clear economic pressures favouring its introduction. Evidence to the US House of Representatives Science, Space and Technology Committee suggested that the savings to the US Federal Aviation Administration (FAA) by cancelling the advanced ground-based Microwave Landing System (MLS) could be up to $6.6 billion. *En route* savings for the US airline industry alone in terms of lower fuel costs due to improved timings and higher utilisation rates across the Atlantic and Pacific are put at $330 million annually (US Congress 1994). In May 1994, the FAA, supported by the US Air Transport Association, announced that it was abandoning its MLS programme in favour of GPS.

Any large-scale shift to satellite-based navigation systems will have considerable commercial implications for the supply of ATC equipment, especially for airport approach and landing. The market for world ATC upgrades is estimated at $14 billion per annum by the year 2002. Until the advent of GPS, the core of the new generation ATC was the so-called Microwave Landing System (MLS), backed by large-scale upgrades in computer and data handling facilities. The FAA's plans for a complete national MLS offered lucrative business for US manufacturers. The first-phase contract for the US MLS was worth $140 million, and the total cost of a national system would have exceeded $6 billion. The US home market, combined with the patronage of the FAA in an advisory role, would have offered significant opportunities for export business. Canadian and several European firms are also developing MLS for world markets. The use of GPS and related technologies could remove most of the market for MLS equipment, especially for the smaller airports where MLS installation would have been costly, or for airports in mountainous areas where conditions make current instrument landing systems less accurate (*Aviation Week*, 13 June 1994).

Other national and regional ATC administrations have not moved to embrace GPS as fast as the FAA. The Canadians, most directly affected by the US decision, are still unsure about their future plans, and the European Union states are strongly committed to MLS on commercial and political grounds. They also feel that MLS is a proven all-weather system, whereas several aspects of GPS remain untested. Although future meetings of ICAO might reach agreement on standardisation, it is not inconceivable that deadlock on this issue may require aircraft operating between the US and Europe to carry both GPS and MLS equipment. The claim by the US that GPS-equipped aircraft do not need MLS as well because GPS will permit landings up to Category 3 limits, was quickly dismissed on safety grounds by British ATC authorities (*Aviation Week*, 13 June 1994).

More important, however, are the questions of control and security. From one US perspective, the security implications of ATC quality GPS data are evident. The security issue is especially vital given the spread of missile technology worldwide. The DoD points out that access to this level of navigational information would give a crude cruise missile sufficient accuracy to hit the White House (*Aviation Week*, 13 June 1994). The US military is clearly worried about unrestricted access to such systems, and as a result the DoD has not yet authorised INMARSAT (the designated international satellite navigation carrier) to provide differential corrections via its next generation INMARSAT-3 satellites.

From a non-US perspective, the problems of control and guaranteed access to the technology are at the heart of opposition to complete reliance on the US (or even a combination of GPS and GLOSNASS). US airlines and the FAA recognise the sensitivity of this question. In evidence to the House of Representatives, a Continental Airlines executive observed that

> One of the dominating issues that must be confronted by the aviation community, if GPS or GNSS is to gain worldwide acceptance and use, is the operational control of the constellation. The Civil Aviation community throughout the world hesitates to place its total operational reliance and dependence on a system controlled by the military authorities. Few states are willing to support and use a system which they cannot control.
> (US Congress 1994)

As one possible answer to this problem, proponents of GPS in the US are pressing for the FAA to have two or three of its own supplementary navigation satellites. According to an FAA scientist, the payoffs would be 'enormous': 'the international community would view GPS navigation as supporting ICAO and other civil institutions, and would accept it much more readily if a portion of the system were under civil control'. Additional satellites would add to system integrity and increase the business opportunities for GPS equipment suppliers (US Congress 1994). An independent FAA capability would also avoid any continuity problems that might stem from relying on a military user.

US airlines would be prepared to place the FAA satellites under an international body, 'be it an ICAO or an INMARSAT type of body' (US Congress 1994). The FAA Administrator has written to the ICAO formally offering GPS to the world community with six years minimum notice for withdrawal of access. The problem might be convincing other US government organisations and political actors both to concede control and, perhaps more problematic, to convince Congress of the need to fund three more satellites. The 'FAA solution' might not satisfy non-American users. Under FAA auspices or not, GPS as currently configured would still be a US system and subject in the final analysis to US control. On the other hand, the creation of a supplementary or even a duplicated civil system would still present the US (or any threatened state for that matter) with even more tricky problems, as it would lose the unilateral ability to switch off the system or to substantially degrade its accuracy in time of crisis. So far, none of the interested international agencies has come up with a satisfactory solution to this dilemma.

The creation of a full GNSS under international control would in any case require international agreement on funding (the US DoD GPS system costs around $800 million a year to operate, and a full GNSS would cost as much as $10 billion just for installation costs). Agreement would also be needed on guarantees for integrity and accuracy (who would bear the cost of an airliner and its passengers in the event of a satellite or communications problem leading to an accident?). Reliance on the current US GPS would be much cheaper, but it would be vulnerable to interruption and degradation at the behest of the DoD – nor is the DoD willing to assume legal responsibility for the integrity of the system for civil operations (*Interavia*, July 1994). The users, mainly the major international carriers, want assurances about 100 per cent availability and how any charges will be levied and collected. According to one senior European ATC administrator, until these assurances are delivered, states are 'unlikely to dispose of their ground-based navigation aids. . . . Relying on a navigation facility which is controlled from outside your state is something entirely new' (*Flight*, 9 February 1994).

European attitudes towards the use of the GPS and GNSS concept in general are complicated by the long-running saga of regional coordination and national autonomy in ATC. Western Europe has one of the most congested airspaces in the world, complicated by the existence of separate ATC systems of varying quality, competence and technological advance. There is a partial European system, Eurocontrol, which coordinates *en route* movements over northern Europe, but most of the critical approach ATC is still in the hands of national bodies. The EU and other European civil aviation bodies are slowly evolving fully integrated regional approaches to the problem and several interim measures (including the EU-funded European Air Traffic Control Harmonisation and Integration Programme – or EATCHIP) have been introduced to reduce the notorious bottlenecks and delays in European air travel. However, the implementation of a single European air-traffic management system (EATMS) remains a distant goal, with European governments still reluctant to transfer national competencies (*Interavia*, July 1994).

In truth, the Europeans were surprised by the speed with which GPS emerged as an alternative to terrestrial ATC. Several governments and ATC authorities have yet to be convinced that satellite systems can be used effectively and economically in Europe, with its especially dense airspace. Part of the problem is that heavy industrial and financial commitments have been made to MLS and the upgrading of other ground ATC equipment. Several important European firms, such as Thomson and Siemens, are bidding for the work in western and eastern Europe. A shift to European space-based systems, although politically and technologically attractive to states such as France, would require a major and rapid shift of resources to match existing US and Russian capabilities. Yves Lambert, Director General of Eurocontrol, feels that the current plans for INMARSAT operations, combined with Europe's existing plans for ATC upgrading, will be sufficient in the short term until the technological and control issues can be fully resolved (*Interavia*, May 1994). Eurocontrol is working on a GNSS position paper. It will still assert regional/national autonomy over ATC infrastructure and argue that control over communications, navigation and surveillance should not pass out of European hands (*Flight*, 9 February 1994). More realistically, the key to a European embrace of GNSS will be the launch of a European satellite system capable of sustaining independent access to key navigational data.

The predicted growth in air transport, on top of the known limitations of world ATC, is creating pressure for change in the international system. The ICAO is well aware of the need for new solutions to the problem of global air-traffic management. Its own Future Air Navigation System (FANS) proposals already include satellite links between US and European controllers over the North Atlantic and other oceanic routes. There is mounting pressure for national (and regional) authorities to begin substantive talks on GNSS if the ICAO FANS timetable is to be met. Pacific operators in particular want action to improve oceanic control in their region. The first phase of FANS will be an important step in this direction, but they have interests in exploiting the opportunities afforded by GNSS. As one of the fastest growing air transport markets in the world, with some of the most important airlines (Asian and US), there is clear commercial interest in accessing the most advanced ATC and flight-management technology. However, all of the major carriers want to realise the kind of annual savings promised by more effective ATC and they will be unwilling to tolerate unjustifiable concerns over sovereignty and autonomy. They will want simple assurances about reliability and continuity, and an equitable way of paying transparent user costs. Although European governments are very much in favour of using the ICAO as the basis for discussions about GNSS implementation, US action in respect of national GPS-based ATC has already placed the Europeans on the defensive. Other countries may feel that the cost-saving aspects of GPS/GNSS might outweigh any political concerns about reliance on the US, or for that matter on Russia (*Flight*, 9 February 1994).

With the deadline for the next round of INMARSAT launches due towards the end of 1995, international agreement on the first stages of a GNSS is needed urgently. The EU and the US will be bidding for systems development covering large parts of the northern hemisphere. There will also be continuing negotiations on establishing a compatible architecture for a fully integrated GNSS. This may involve some sharing of technology between the US and Europe. The INMARSAT satellites could certainly be part of a comprehensive global navigation constellation. The INMARSAT organisation also sees itself as a potential location for control and authority over a civil GNSS. As its technical director observed, its satellites 'could be considered the foundation for a civil GNSS under international ownership and control to perform some functions in a new system' (*Flight*, 27 July 1994). However, INMARSAT would only be one element in a complete GNSS, and negotiations to set it up and to establish the terms of its operations will necessarily involve the ICAO and agreement amongst the major national actors in North America, Europe and Asia. The international airline industry will also be a far-from-passive observer in setting the terms of access and the bases of any pricing policy.

Part of the problem is trying to establish an international regime for global navigation before the exact nature of the system, its infrastructure and its technical limits have been fully clarified. The sudden arrival of a commercially usable satellite system in GPS has pushed many governments into a corner. More important, even when the US clarifies its position on the level of differentiation that it will guarantee for GPS ATC (even with GLOSNASS available to provide some alternative to total US domination), there will be long-term doubts about control and continuity in a crisis. In September 1994, the ICAO received assurances from the US and Russia about short-term access to the GPS/GLOSNASS array. The US confirmed that it would provide free access for ten years and that any decision to degrade the signal would be taken at presidential level. However, as one European ATC official observed, 'promises are not enough', adding that the international community needs time to work out a long-term solution to the implementation of a full-scope GNSS (*Flight*, 2 March 1994: 41).

More positively, some air transport executives feel that the sheer scale of commercial use will provide 'the greatest guarantee of its continuity' (*ibid.*). The logic of this argument suggests that even the US government might have to think more than twice about pulling the plug on a system the world may have come to rely upon to keep its air transport system going. As one Pentagon official remarked, 'we are going to have to have one hell of a crisis before we consider putting people out of business by altering or jamming the signal'. Still less is the DoD willing to run the risk of 'crashing commercial planes into the side of a mountain' (*Armed Services Journal*, August 1994: 18). In this respect, the power of US airlines and their lawyers might prove ultimately to be a more dependable defence of the integrity of the system than the power of nation-states. More cautious national governments, especially those in Europe, may still prefer old-fashioned international agreement backed by some independent access to the core technologies. However, the US, and to a lesser extent Russia, literally and figuratively possess the high ground. With an expensive system already in place, they may well be able largely to determine the shape and operation of any GNSS. In this respect, the DoD is already looking to find ways of limiting GPS signals in any particular zone and to establish counter-measures against unauthorised military use (*Armed Services Journal*, August 1994: 18).

FINAL OBSERVATIONS

One of the most fundamental changes in world civil aviation generally over the last decade has been the lessening of state control. Ideological and budget-driven adoption of deregulation and privatisation has seen a significant shift into private hands of the responsibility for control and governance in the civil aviation system. These trends have also extended to the countries of the former USSR and to China. In Europe, the need to coordinate ATC on a European level to solve congestion problems, as well as the unfolding of the single European market (SEM), have further weakened (or at least diluted) national political control over the civil aviation system. Equally, the advent of satellite ATC offers the travelling public significant gains in both safety and economy and as such it may constitute an increase in international public welfare. This is especially important for poorer states as it offers 'First World' ATC standards without the expense of ground stations and approach aids.

However, some of these advantages, especially to the airline operator, would be lost or undermined if they were forced by political circumstance or institutional inertia to compromise a global standard. In this respect, European reluctance to accept a technology dominated by either the US or Russia is at the heart of the matter. The Europeans have some valid technical reasons for preferring ground-based technology; they also have real problems in changing the direction of regional ATC plans that required several years to negotiate. However, they are concerned at the level of dependence implied by a rapid adoption of GPS or its international equivalent in time of crisis. The Japanese are already planning their own independent programme to supplement the GPS/GLOSNASS network, and European thinking envisages the development of similar complementary satellites in due course.

However, the European position is under pressure from the combined effect of, first, a 'system-in-being' on offer on a very generous short-term basis by the owner-operators; and second, the commercial interests of the airline industry. Whatever happens at an international level, the US is committed to GPS internally. Additionally, many other states feel that they have more to gain from a cheap solution to an expensive ATC problem than to lose by conceding some control over airspace to an ICAO-sanctioned US and Russian satellite-navigation condominium. The eventual outcome of this debate may not be as dramatic as developments in other complex technology systems, such as telecommunications. In the final analysis, an aircraft and its passengers must travel over territory (and as several cases attest, commercial aircraft are uniquely vulnerable to physical attack) and land somewhere. They are, therefore, always subject to direct physical controls. However, the scope for state control over much of the world civil aviation system is narrowing, and the fundamental cause is a potent combination of economic, corporate and technological forces. The advent of GNSS has presented this

dilemma in a particularly direct form, challenging as it does the first prin
of airspace autonomy and control as defined at the birth of the modern civi
aviation system in 1919.

NOTE

1 As does anyone who buys an airline ticket; consumer groups also take an active
   interest in the economic and safety issues raised by ATC.

ells, cars and world power

l Talalay

You get into your car and turn the key. The control panel lights up and tells you that all systems are go. You drive off. But there is no throaty roar, no massive vibration caused by the mechanical equivalent of 427 throbbing horses. There is not even the rattle and 'put-put' of a city runabout with its child seat and crisp-strewn floor. There is no internal combustion engine at all, no vibration and virtually no noise – just a gentle hum from under the bonnet.

'Ah,' says your passenger, a friend from out of town who hasn't visited you for some time, 'you've got an electric car. How "green" of you.'

'Of course, I don't drive one myself,' he continues, 'not practical. Takes hours to charge the batteries, doesn't it? Couldn't put up with that. How do you manage?'

You smile and pull into the next gas station.

As you accelerate off, quietly and with a full tank of fuel, your visitor scratches his head and stares at you, clearly puzzled. You say nothing. 'OK,' he sighs, 'I give up. What are you driving?'

You laugh. 'Nothing fancy. Just a cheap, pollution-free, energy efficient car, one that might radically shift the global balance of power – politically as well as economically. Fuel cell technology, you know. Been around for well over a hundred years.'

You drop him off at his hotel, promising that you'll fill in the details later. As you pull away, you look in your rearview mirror. He's still scratching his head.

It is difficult to exaggerate the importance of the automobile. It has, in the hundred-odd years of its existence, revolutionised urban development, changed sexual mores, driven economic growth, and fundamentally altered all our lifestyles. It has been and continues to be a major force in the global political economy.

Unfortunately, the motor vehicle also contributes substantially to two of the world's greatest problems: air pollution and fossil fuel exhaustion. Cars, buses and trucks produce a large portion of the greenhouse gases that lead to global warming. They also bear heavy responsibility for the foul, choking atmospheres of cities, a situation that will worsen with increasing urbanisation and a projected doubling of the global vehicle fleet within the next twenty to thirty years (WHO 1992: 7). At the same time, motor vehicles are one of the principal users of oil. They are by far the major component of non-aviation transport, a sector that on a conservative estimate accounts for over 30 per cent of world oil consumption (IEA 1993). With proven reserves of oil forecast on current usage to run out in under forty-five years (BP 1995: 2), the projected increase in cars will make a serious problem even worse. This growth, especially when combined with the coming industrialisation of China, India and other parts of the world, means that the energy crunch is here.

Given this situation, an automobile that produces no pollution and runs on renewable energy will have dramatic and far-reaching consequences – particularly if it at least matches current cars in price, performance, and convenience.

This is not an idle dream. Fuel cell technology promises just such a vehicle. Its potential consequences are dramatic, and not simply for its immediate benefits on pollution and energy exhaustion. It has the potential to revolutionise the automobile industry, to fundamentally change the politics and economics of energy, to restructure the environmental agenda, to alter the nature of Middle East politics, and to shift the international balance of power.

The objectives of this chapter are to outline briefly how fuel cell technology works, to indicate its benefits, to examine its technical and commercial feasibility, to look at what drivers exist to push it forward, and finally to suggest some of the likely consequences of fuel cell technology for the global political economy.

HOW FUEL CELLS WORK

Fuel cells produce electricity from an electro-chemical reaction. They do so without any combustion and without any moving parts. They are also virtually free of all emissions, their sole by-products being heat and water. However, unlike batteries, to which they bear a superficial similarity, fuel cells do not run out of electrical charge. They will work continuously as long as they are fed with hydrogen.

Though a number of different types of fuel cell exist, they all share similar operating principles. A fuel cell consists of two electrodes sandwiched around an electrolyte – a non-conducting and semi-permeable liquid or solid. Hydrogen gas continuously feeds the negative electrode (or anode). Here, in the presence of a platinum catalyst that serves to accelerate the reaction, the hydrogen atoms ionise, i.e. they lose an electron. These free electrons then flow through a circuit from the anode to the cathode (the positive electrode). This current forms the electrical output of the fuel cell and can drive a load such as an electric motor. The hydrogen ions created at the anode themselves migrate through the electrolyte also to the cathode. There, they recombine with the free electrons as well as with oxygen from the air to produce water – either as a liquid or as steam, depending upon the temperature at which the fuel cell is operating.[1] A single fuel cell produces an electric output of somewhat under one volt DC. Multiple cells can be connected to form a 'stack'. When linked, a number of such stacks can generate kilowatts and megawatts of power.

Fuel cell power units are scalable and modular, with an electrical efficiency that is essentially constant and independent of size. Consequently, they have a wide range of uses. Some types, especially the 'higher temperature' ones, are particularly suitable for stationary applications – for large-scale electricity generation where the very hot waste gases can drive a secondary turbine to produce overall efficiencies as high as 80 per cent, significantly in excess of any conventional technology;[2] and for combined heat and power (CHP) production, where a local unit provides electricity, space conditioning and hot water for a complex such as a factory, a department store or a hospital, or, scaled down further, for an individual house.[3] Lower-temperature fuel cells are more appropriate for transportation applications: for powering cars, trucks, buses, locomotives and even aeroplanes.

This chapter deals specifically with the use of fuel cells in motor vehicles.[4] Of the different varieties of fuel cell, the one most appropriate for these transportation applications is the proton exchange membrane (PEM). It offers long life and low maintenance, in large measure because it has a solid rather than a liquid electrolyte and thus avoids spills and leaks. Due to its low operating temperature of about eighty degrees centigrade, it has a quick start-up – essential for a practical car. As a result of its favourable power-to-weight ratio, it could fit into a standard automobile. Finally, and very importantly in terms of consumer acceptance, it would provide range and performance comparable to current conventional vehicles, and would allow for quick and easy refuelling (Siegel and San Martin 1993; Williams 1994).

The fuel for powering the vehicle would be hydrogen itself or alternatively methanol. Hydrogen could be stored either as a liquid, in which case special low-temperature tanks are necessary, or as a compressed gas, for which the technology also already exists in working form for natural gas vehicles. Methanol (CH_3OH), being a liquid under ambient pressure and temperature, would be easier to store. However, it would have to be 'reformed' to yield hydrogen, and that process does produce carbon dioxide emissions (see below for the implications of this). In either case, the logical choice in the short term for the feedstock is natural gas, of which the main constituent is methane (CH_4). Biogas – naturally occurring methane – provides a secondary possibility. In the longer term, biomass and solar energy could provide hydrogen without using fossil fuels as a feedstock. Safety, while likely to be a perceived issue, is not a real problem. Hydrogen is handled daily for commercial purposes, and pipelines and tankers have been transporting it safely for years (Wurster 1993: 33–4; Williams 1993: 34–5; Flavin 1995: 71). What is much more of a real problem is the lack of infrastructure – how to get hydrogen or methanol to consumers with the same convenience they currently enjoy with gasoline.[5]

Fuel cells are not a new technology. Sir William Grove demonstrated the first working example as long ago as 1839, and effort has been devoted to them on and off ever since. What finally made fuel cells a practical proposition was the US space programme, in which they served as power sources for both the Gemini and Apollo craft. More recently, the drive behind fuel cells has come from the growing concern about air pollution and fossil fuel exhaustion. On both of these issues, the fuel cell powered car promises substantial benefits.

BENEFITS OF FUEL CELL TECHNOLOGY

Air pollution and global warming

Despite substantial reductions due to more efficient engines, catalytic converters, and other measures, vehicle emissions are still a massive problem (see Table 15.1).

Table 15.1 Transport sources of emissions (as percentage of total)

	USA[*]	UK[1]
CO_2	33	24
CO	63	90
NO_x	38	57
VOCs	34	38
Particulates	20	48

Source:
[*] 1991 figures from OTT, 1993: 37
[1] 1992 figures from Royal Commission on Environmental Pollution, 1994: 23, 40

Unfortunately, further improvements in existing areas provide no guarantee that overall transport emissions will decrease. The US Office of Transportation Technology has warned that

> without technological breakthroughs, adverse energy and environmental impacts are forecast to increase at a rate that will offset gains in new vehicle efficiency and emissions control *because of projected increases in the vehicle fleet size and in miles travelled.*
>
> (OTT 1993: 36, my emphasis)

In Britain also, road traffic demand is predicted to increase, with the Royal Commission on Environmental Pollution (1992: 3) forecasting an increase from 1991 of 18–30 per cent by the year 2000 and 69–113 per cent by 2025. The problem clearly extends to the world as a whole where automobile numbers, as noted above, will likely double within thirty years – primarily in Eastern Europe and the developing countries, areas in which emission controls are unlikely to be as strict as in the United States. One Chinese government ministry, for example, predicts an increase in the size of the car fleet from 1.85 million in 1994 to 22 million by 2010 (Brown 1995: 48).

The problem of vehicle-generated emissions is serious and growing. It is important to note, however, that it has two distinctly different aspects. The first is the production of greenhouse gases such as carbon dioxide. Despite their potentially serious (if still unproved) effects, they do *not* provide the main impetus for dealing with motor-vehicle based pollution. That comes from local emissions such as carbon monoxide, various oxides of nitrogen, volatile organic compounds (VOCs), and particulates. These are what pollute the air in urban centres, make them increasingly unfit for habitation and provide an immediate and often serious health hazard. According to the World Health Organisation and the United Nations Environment Program (WHO 1992: 7) 'motor vehicles now constitute the main source of air pollutants in the majority of cities in industrialised countries.'

Two recent studies have evaluated the emissions produced by fuel cell electric vehicles (FCEVs) and by their two main alternatives, conventional internal combustion engine vehicles (ICEVs) and battery-powered electric vehicles (BPEVs). Both studies viewed pollution on a life-cycle basis: that is, they took into account the emissions produced by the manufacture and disposal of the vehicle, by its use, and also by the generation and distribution of its fuel. This last point may be easy to overlook, but it can prove essential to any analysis, because BPEVs will require massive amounts of added electricity generation – which will most likely increase emissions substantially. Consequently, each of the studies made certain assumptions about the likely sources of electricity. The British study, undertaken by the consulting firm PA (1992) on behalf of the Department of Trade and Industry, assumed that the electricity for BPEVs would come from the current UK fuel mix: 69 per cent coal, 21 per cent nuclear, 8 per cent oil and 2 per cent renewable. The US study, conducted by Professor Robert Williams (1993, 1994) and his colleagues at the Center for Energy and Environmental Studies of Princeton University's School of Engineering, assumed the mix of coal and nuclear forecast for the year 2000. Both studies further assumed that the source of hydrogen would be natural gas.

Each investigation concluded that on this life-cycle basis the fuel cell vehicle would be much superior to either alternative. With respect to greenhouse gases, it would be notably less polluting when run on hydrogen from natural gas, and dramatically so when the source of the hydrogen is either biomass or solar energy. According to Williams (1993: 71, 80), in comparison to the greenhouse gas emissions from conventional gasoline engines, battery-powered vehicles would give about a 40 per cent reduction, but fuel cell vehicles would reduce these emissions by over 50 per cent if running on hydrogen or methanol from natural gas and by over 90 per cent if these fuels derived from renewable sources. Even more importantly, the fuel cell vehicle also outscores both its rivals on local emissions. Once the requisite electricity generation is taken into account, battery-powered cars would generate higher emissions per mile of oxides of nitrogen as well as of sulphur dioxide and particulates than would conventional gasoline cars (Williams 1994: 24), and both would produce far more pollution than a fuel cell powered car, where the extremely small amount of emissions comes almost entirely from its production rather than its use or fuel generation. The PA report (Appendix D) projects that the fuel cell vehicle would outscore a conventional internal combustion vehicle by a factor of five and would do even better against the battery-powered vehicle. The evidence certainly suggests that fuel cells would produce far less air pollution than either batteries or internal combustion engines.[6]

Efficiency and renewable energy benefits

The second great benefit of fuel cells is their ability, in the short term, to use fossil fuels more efficiently, and, in the longer term, to use renewable energy. Because fuel cells are two to three times more efficient than internal combustion engines (Williams 1994: 22), they use less input for equal output and hence help to save scarce fossil fuels. Moreover, because they use natural gas for energy production, they conserve oil, preserving this 'heavy hydro-carbon' for petrochemical and polymer production (Blomen and Mugerwa 1993: 2).

In the longer term, fuel cell technology rids us of our dependence upon fossil fuels altogether. This is essential because, on the basis of current rates of consumption and proven reserves, natural gas supplies will run out in under seventy years (BP 1995: 18). This poses no problems for fuel cells as hydrogen is infinitely available from non-fossil sources. Biomass – consisting of urban refuse, agricultural and forestry waste products, and specially grown crops – provides one possibility (Williams 1993: 21). A side benefit to biomass utilisation would be the reduction of naturally occurring methane. As it is the primary greenhouse gas after carbon dioxide, this is not an insignificant point. The second main source would be solar energy – this can generate hydrogen in a totally non-polluting manner and in inexhaustible quantities (Dostrovsky 1991).

COMMERCIAL VIABILITY AND CURRENT DEVELOPMENT

At the moment, there appear to be only two contenders to replace the internal combustion engine – batteries and fuel cells. Until some totally different method of transportation ('beam me up, Scotty'!?) replaces the passenger vehicle as we know it, these are the main alternatives. Of the three options, fuel cells have a decided advantage in terms of pollution and renewable energy. But can they be commercially competitive?

The answer would appear to be yes. FCEVs could be cost-competitive with both ICEVs and BPEVs. Comparisons of all three options on a life-cycle basis (PA 1992; Williams 1993, 1994) suggest that while there might be as much as a 25 per cent difference per mile (or kilometre) between the most and least costly options, each of the three could be either the cheapest or the most expensive depending upon the assumptions made and the analytical model used. Assuming these figures are reasonably plausible, the cost differences will tend to become irrelevant when economies of scale, the benefits of the learning curve, and general technical improvements in mass production are taken into account.[7] Perhaps more tellingly, an unreleased study from General Motors, completed in November 1993, concluded that a fuel cell engine would cost roughly the same to manufacture as a conventional gasoline engine (*PRNewswire*, 14 April 1994).

Fuel cell vehicles are on the verge of commercialisation. Successful prototypes exist, and development programmes are well under way. Ballard Power Systems in Vancouver are probably the world leader in automotive fuel cell technology. In conjunction with the province of British Columbia, the federal government of Canada and the South Coast Air Quality Management District (SCAQMD, the agency responsible for air quality in the Los Angeles basin), Ballard have produced a hydrogen-powered fuel cell bus. This has undergone trials both in Vancouver and at Los Angeles airport, and three of the latest models will start service in 1996 with the Chicago Transit Authority (Prater 1995). Commercial production is scheduled to begin in 1998. Fleet vehicles, such as buses and taxis, are the logical initial choice for fuel cell vehicles. They avoid the problem of creating a fuel distribution infrastructure. Refilling buses at a central depot poses far fewer difficulties than creating a network for passenger cars. Nonetheless, Ballard are also collaborating with General Motors and the US Department of Energy to build a passenger car by 1996 and field-test it over the following two years. In addition, they are working with, among others, Daimler-Benz in Germany, Mazda, Nissan and Mitsubishi in Japan, Renault and Peugeot in France, as well as with Johnson Matthey in the UK on reducing the cost and improving the performance of the platinum catalyst. Fuel cell vehicles could be available for fleet applications by the end of the century and 'mass produced for general use before 2010' (Williams 1994: 28; see also PA 1992: 15; Ballard 1994; Daimler-Benz 1994).

DRIVERS BEHIND THE FUEL CELL VEHICLE

A number of drivers are pushing for the adoption of the fuel cell as the preferred technology for powering motor vehicles. To begin with, the size of the potential market is substantial. Worldwide sales of motor cars in 1994 were approximately thirty-three million (IMB 1995: 22). At a price of $10,000 – half the US average[8] – a mere 10 per cent market share for fuel cell cars would have resulted in revenues of $33 billion. Moreover, fuel cell technology may also become the dominant means of power generation – eventually replacing even the relatively clean and efficient combined-cycle gas turbine (see Hodrien and Fairbairn 1993; Makansi 1994) – thereby increasing the size of the overall market even further.[9] Clearly then, with a potential so large, commercial opportunity is in part leading companies to pursue this route. For some this is a new opportunity. For others, of course, it is a defensive measure to protect existing investments and markets.

Despite their environmental benefits and potential commercial implications, fuel cell vehicles will undoubtedly require some further external push to succeed – likely in the form of public policy. Both increased R&D funding[10] and a shift in tax policy, especially with respect to removing tax breaks given to conventional energy (Bryan 1993: 5), can help the fuel cell industry. Neither, however, will by itself lead to commercial exploitation. Overall transportation policy will also be important as will a national fuels strategy, particularly for electricity generation. If, as seems to be the case, nuclear energy continues to be unpopular and private finance remains opposed to it, then the battery option for powering cars becomes increasingly unacceptable and fuel cells may gain an edge. Other factors such as health and welfare legislation, utility deregulation, refuse disposal requirements, zoning by-laws and agricultural subsidy policies may all have some influence – for stationary as well as transport applications.

However, the area of public policy that will unquestionably play the most significant role is environmental legislation. It can force rather than merely encourage adoption of a new technology. The United States probably leads the world in this area. EPA emission requirements, the Clean Air Act, and the federal CAFE (corporate average fuel economy) programme have already reduced emission levels from vehicles (and from power stations). In Europe, EU and national policies are similarly driving towards clean technologies.

It is the state of California, driven particularly by air pollution in the Los Angeles basin, whence the most important measures and the major impetus for fuel cell commercialisation come. In addition to setting standards for low- and ultra-low emission vehicles, California has passed legislation mandating that new vehicle sales include percentages of zero emission vehicles (ZEVs). Table 15.2 gives the original 1990 requirements – these were to have come into effect in 1998 and then to be raised and extended in 2001 and again in 2003. According to James Lents (1993: 94) of SCAQMD, only BPEVs and pure hydrogen FCEVs can meet the ZEV definition.[11] Moreover, the California zero emission requirement was in the process of spreading to twelve states in the north-east (*Wall Street Journal*, 14 September 1994). The resulting standards would cover 40 per cent of the US market and lead to projected annual ZEV sales by 2003 of 640,000 vehicles (Ballard 1994: 22). This market

Table 15.2 California zero-emission vehicle requirements (as a percentage of total new car sales)

	1998	*2001*	*2003*
ZEVs	2%	5%	10%

would be worth $1 billion for the fuel cell stack and related components alone (*ibid.*) and, on the basis of the average cost in the US for a passenger car of $20,000 (*The Economist*, 10 February 1995: 88), close to $13 billion annually in total ZEV new car sales. By any measure, this is a market well worth fighting for – and against. Very recently, in fact, California has decided to back down from the initial deadline. In what the *Financial Times* (20 November 1995) described as 'a clear victory for the world's seven biggest motor groups, and California's big oil companies', the California Air Resources Board (CARB) will lower the level of ZEV sales required for 1998, though at least for the moment holding the percentages for 2001 and 2003. Instead of forcing a 2 per cent quota for the 1998 model year, the state authorities will enter into negotiations with the automakers on a more flexible approach but one where electric vehicles would begin to reach the market in 1996 (*International Herald Tribune*, 20 November 1995).[12] Knock-on effects are possible upon the ability of Massachusetts and New York to stick to their 2 per cent ZEV requirements for 1998 (*ibid.*).

The fate of the fuel cell vehicle rests upon a combination of commercial and public policy drivers. Behind these lurk environmental and fossil fuel exhaustion considerations. The major impetus, however, comes specifically from the state of California, with its regulatory legislation and huge market (thirteen million people and nine million cars in the Los Angeles area alone). California legislation is crucial in the hunt for alternative automotive technologies. Strengthening it would encourage if not ensure their development. Weakening it, as is currently happening, may mean that fuel cells will not succeed in becoming the primary power source for motor vehicles.[13] Either way, what happens in the next few years on the west coast of the United States will unquestionably exert the decisive influence on the world-wide future of the automobile.

IMPLICATIONS FOR THE INTERNATIONAL POLITICAL ECONOMY

The possible adoption of fuel cell technology as a power source for cars, buses and trucks has a number of major implications for the international political economy. These include the lifting of pollution and fossil fuel based constraints on growth and development, the restructuring of global environmental politics and a reduction in the probability of resource and environmental conflict, the shifting of international balances of payment and financial flows, and alterations in the Common Agricultural Policy of the European Union. Length limitations, however, preclude me from addressing these issues, interesting and important as they are. Instead, I will restrict myself to a brief look at the implications of the fuel cell car for the future of the automotive industry, for the power of the oil companies and the oil exporting countries, especially in the Middle East, and for the position of the United States as global superpower.

The automotive industry

Automotive manufacturing is one of the world's most important industries. Four of the top ten industrial companies in the 1994 *Fortune* global 500 (25 July 1994) were automotive manufacturers. In Europe, the added value of production of vehicles represents 9 per cent of GDP; the car industry employs 1.8 million people; and the industry accounts for 8.3 per cent of all manufacturing jobs.[14] Worldwide, the automotive industry (manufacturing, parts and components, and sales and service) is directly responsible for about 20 million jobs (Dicken 1992: 268). Massive change and dislocation in this industry could well create winners and losers on a corporate and on a national scale. The result could be trade wars (or at least severe restrictions) with untoward implications for the future of the World Trade Organization (WTO). It is clearly impossible to forecast exactly what will happen – given the uncertainty over the mandate for electric vehicles and the competition within that sector between batteries and fuel cells (not to mention all the various hybrid possibilities). Nevertheless, assuming that the electric vehicle becomes the auto technology of the future, then two broad predictions may be fairly confidently put forward. First, traditional suppliers of parts and components may find themselves under severe threat. A large number of these items, essential to a conventional car, will be irrelevant on an electric vehicle (whether battery- or fuel cell-powered). As two McKinsey analysts recently wrote:

> Traditional OEM suppliers will also have to contend with an influx of large, resourceful new competitors such as electric motor suppliers, which will have sufficient presence and 'critical mass' to serve automotive companies on a worldwide basis. In addition, new suppliers with entirely different skill sets will become important first-tier suppliers to the OEMs, replacing traditional players. Suppliers of fuel cells, for example, or advanced battery technologies will become critical first-tier partners.
>
> (Ealey and Gentile 1995: 113)

Moreover, the OEMs themselves will find one of their key activities threatened – engine manufacture. The end result is likely to be substantial dislocation and probably mergers and acquisitions not only among suppliers but even among the large OEM assembly companies themselves. Second, as long as California retains its position as the driving force behind EVs, a presence in that market will be crucial. This is essential not only in terms of sales but also to give manufacturers a technological head start. R&D and production facilities in California could lead to a 'fuel cell community' (as in the example of Silicon Valley) and thereby provide a significant advantage to those companies with manufacturing operations there, enabling them to get to the top of the learning curve well ahead of non-Californian competitors. In line with Michael Porter's thesis (1990) about competitive advantage from clustering and from the stimulus of environmental regulations, the US-based auto industry, regardless of actual ownership, should benefit from a technological shift from ICEVs to FCEVs (see also Sharp and Pavitt 1993) – unless of course other parts of the world very soon enact similar laws or California continues to weaken its legislation and abandons its environmental lead.

Oil and power

Both the oil companies and the oil exporting countries will find that fuel cells pose a challenge and a threat to them. This threat is not a short-term economic one. The tremendous projected increases in energy demand – almost 50 per cent from 1991 to 2010 according to the International Energy Agency (IEA 1994b: 31–2) – will ensure that revenues in the short term will not decrease. They will just increase more slowly than they might otherwise. In fact, the result will be to prolong the revenue streams of both countries and companies.

However, the *political* power of the oil exporters, particularly those in the Middle East, will be dramatically reduced. Because fuel cells will enable the United States to be self-sufficient in energy (see below), the ability of Middle East producers to influence global affairs will dramatically reduce and will be accompanied by a shift in power within the Arab world towards countries with a broader base to their economies. At the same time, the utility of the oil weapon against Israel will also reduce, although current events may be making this irrelevant.

For the oil companies, the situation is considerably different. Even without oil, they are in possession of a key asset – their distribution networks and skills. Without the convenience of being able to refuel their fuel cell cars as and when necessary, consumers will reject this technology. Only the oil companies have an existing infrastructure for achieving this. Thus while there will likely be winners and losers in the industry, those with downstream retail networks can view the fuel cell automobile as an opportunity rather than merely a threat.

The United States as global superpower

The adoption of fuel cells as the major transportation technology has very interesting implications for the United States. Its vast land mass allows for energy self-sufficiency through hydrogen production. The projected car and light truck fleet for the year 2010 in the US could be powered from biomass grown on about seventy million acres – 'the amount of cropland currently held out of agricultural production in the United States to support agricultural crop prices and to control erosion' (Williams 1994: 28). Moreover, given the large sun-drenched regions of the US, there is ample scope for producing hydrogen in even greater quantities. As the oil used to power cars and light trucks equals about 85 per cent of imports (Gibbons 1993: 10),

FCEVs alone could make the US almost self-sufficient. This would substantially ease US balance-of-payments problems and boost the dollar. It could also benefit the budget deficit in terms of reducing the need for agricultural subsidies and set-aside programmes.

Consider also the size of the market in the United States, its head start in technology and its commercial exploitation, and the American lead in environmental legislation. Combine this with the self-sufficiency argument. The result is a situation where US power increases not only in relational but also in structural terms (Strange 1988). Metaphorically, structural power refers to the ability to set the rules of the game, whereas relational power pertains to the ability to play it within those rules. The collapse of the Bretton Woods international monetary system in 1971 illustrates this distinction perfectly. Despite a (relationally) weak dollar, the US still had the structural power to force the end of fixed currencies and dollar–gold convertibility. Fuel cell technology could serve to augment United States power in both of these two senses. Being self-sufficient in energy would unquestionably increase American influence and freedom of action. In addition, the US would be in the position of being able to dictate the future shape of two of the world's largest and most globalised industries: energy and motor vehicles. On all counts, fuel cell technology is likely to raise the status of the United States as global superpower.

CONCLUSION

The automobile may eventually fade away as a result of some as-yet-unimagined technological development. For the time being, though, it is with us as a major method of transport, one of the world's largest industries, a prime source of pollution, and a wasteful user of scarce fossil fuels. Any technological development that can substantially reduce that level of pollution and extend the life of non-renewable energy resources is worthwhile pursuing.

Unlike all the other contributions to this volume, this one looks at a technology that does not exist commercially. You cannot buy a fuel cell car to drive on the streets. Consequently, the conclusions of this chapter are highly speculative. Fuel cell technology may or may not become the dominant automotive technology. If it does, it will have momentous global consequences, not only for the reasons given above but also because it will shift the world to a different technological trajectory. It will signal a jump from a hydro-carbon to a hydrogen economy. As with any such fundamental change, the consequences are likely to be both massive and surprising.

NOTES

1   The actual reactions are: $H_2 \longrightarrow 2H^+ + 2e^-$ (at the anode); $O_2 + 4H^+ + 4e^- \longrightarrow 2H_2O$ (at the cathode); and $H_2 + {}^1/_2O_2 \longrightarrow H_2O$ (overall). This description

applies to phosphoric acid and proton exchange membrane fuel cells (currently the two most important types). For alkali, molten carbonate, and solid oxide fuel cells, there are some differences in the direction of ion flow and in the exact nature of the reactions. However, the basic principles of operation remain the same. For more detail, see Hirschenhofer 1994.

2 Solid oxide fuel cells (SOFC) and molten carbonate fuel cells (MCFC) run at about 1,000 and 650 degrees centigrade respectively. Both are operating in demonstration projects, but neither is commercially available. The closest conventional alternative is the most advanced combined-cycle gas turbine which can approach 60 per cent efficiency.

3 Phosphoric acid fuel cells (PAFC) running at about 200 degrees centigrade are commercially available in 200 kW CHP units from an American company called ONSI, a subsidiary of International Fuel Cell Corporation which is itself a subsidiary of the much larger United Technologies Corporation (UTC). Ironically, UTC also owns Pratt and Whitney, one of the world's leading suppliers of gas turbines.

4 For a more extensive treatment of stationary and transportation applications and of the public policy and commercial forces driving them, see my paper on 'The coming energy revolution and the transformation of the international political economy' in *Competition and Change*, 1, 4, October 1996.

5 In theory, hydrogen could be produced from gasoline. However, while this has infrastructure advantages, it dilutes – to put it mildly – the emissions and renewable energy benefits of fuel cells.

6 Another problem with batteries is toxicity – not only with lead-acid but also with nickel-cadmium and nickel metal hydride batteries. For a discussion of this issue see Lave *et al.* 1995.

7 Both studies started with certain assumptions about future energy scenarios. The British study considered two alternatives. The first assumed high economic growth within the EU and a major policy change 'to encourage investment in energy technology in order to increase the efficiency of energy use' (PA 1992: A7). The second scenario added a 'carbon tax', making the 2010 pump price of petrol £4.45 per gallon in 1991 pounds (*ibid.*: E4). The US study made two sets of assumptions about the source and cost of fuels. For the medium term (2005–20), it assumed that hydrogen or methanol would come from either natural gas or biomass and that electricity would be generated from the average US mix. For the longer term, it assumed nuclear, wind, or solar hydrogen and nuclear generated electricity. Clearly, there is a certain amount of speculation involved in these estimates.

8 US Commerce Department statistics give the cost of the average American passenger car at over $20,000 (*The Economist*, 10 February 1995: 88).

9 A successful fuel cell car would guarantee the success of stationary applications. Most current CHP units use as their power source the automobile engine, incredibly cheap due to huge production runs. The world production of gasoline-fuelled internal combustion engines (not including motorcycle engines) in 1991 was over twenty-seven million (UN 1993). Fuel cell powered CHP units are already cleaner and more efficient. If they became cost-competitive as well, they could dominate the market. Pandit Patil, head of the Advanced Vehicles Technology programme at the USDOE, noted, in a talk at the 1994 Fuel Cell Seminar in San Diego, the likelihood that a successful fuel cell vehicle programme would lead to equally successful stationary applications.

10 Across the OECD as a whole in 1993, only 7.5 per cent of government R&D energy expenditure went to renewables whereas 61 per cent went to nuclear and 11.5 per cent to coal, oil and gas (IEA 1994a: 590–1).

11 California ZEV requirements pertain only to the running of the vehicle, not to its life-cycle emissions and not to the production of fuel.

12 This development does reflect, at least to some extent, the failure so far to develop a satisfactory battery technology.

13 On the other hand, there is also a possibility that weakening ZEV requirements but still maintaining low-emission requirements would actually benefit fuel cells because this would open the way for methanol cars – which are not ZEV vehicles but produce only carbon dioxide from the reformation process, a gas which while contributing to global warming is not a pollutant.

14 From *Reuter Textline*, 28 June 1995, reporting on an initiative by the European Commission on a task force for the 'The Car of the Future'.

Bibliography

Abernathy, W.J. and Utterback, J.M. (1978) 'Patterns of industrial innovation', *Technology Review*, 80, 7, June-July: 40–7.

Abramovitz, M. (1986) 'Catching up, forging ahead and falling behind', *Journal of Economic History*, 46, 2, June: 385–406.

ACOST (1990) *Developments in Biotechnology*, UK: Advisory Council for Science and Technology.

Acs, Z.J. and Audretsch, D.B. (1990) *Innovation and Small Firms*, Cambridge, MA: MIT Press.

—— (1991) *Has the Role of Small Firms Changed in the United States?*, Wissenschafts-zentrum Berlin für Sozialforschung (Research Unit Market Processes and Corporate Development, IIM) discussion paper FS IV: 91–13.

Aghion, J. and Howitt, P. (1993) 'A model of growth through creative destruction', in D. Foray and C. Freeman (eds) *Technology and the Wealth of Nations*, London, Pinter: 145–72.

Alcorta, L. (1994) 'The impact of new technologies on scale in manufacturing industries: issues and evidence', *World Development*, 22, 5, May: 755–69.

Alic, J. (1993) 'Technical knowledge and technology diffusion', *Technology Analysis and Strategic Management*, 5, 4: 369–83.

Allen, R.E. (1994) *Financial Crises and Recessions in the New Global Economy*, Cheltenham, Glos. and Brookfield, VT: Edward Elgar.

Alvesson, M. (1993) 'Organisations as rhetoric: knowledge-intensive firms and the struggle with ambiguity', *Journal of Management Studies*, special issue 'Knowledge Workers and Contemporary Organisations', 30, 6, November: 997–1015.

Amin, A. (ed.) (1994) *Post-Fordism: A Reader*, Oxford: Blackwell.

Amin, A. and Robins, K. (1990) 'The re-emergence of regional economies? The mythical geography of flexible accumulation', *Environment and Planning: Society and Space*, 8: 7–34.

Amin, A. and Tomaney, J. (1995a) 'The regional dilemma in a neo-liberal Europe', *European Urban and Regional Studies*, 2, 2: 171–88.

—— (1995b) 'The regional development potential of inward investment in the less favoured regions of the European Community', in A. Amin and J. Tomaney (eds) *Behind the Myth of the European Union: Prospects for Cohesion*, London: Routledge.

—— (eds) (1995c) *Behind the Myth of the European Union: Prospects for Cohesion*, London: Routledge.

Amin, A., Gills, B., Palan, R. and Taylor, P. (1994) 'Editorial: Forum for heterodox international political economy', *Review of International Political Economy*, 1, 1, Spring: 1–12.

Anchordoguy, M. (1989) *Computers Inc: Japan's Challenge to IBM*, Cambridge, MA: Harvard University Press.

Anderson, B. (1983) *Imagined Communities: Reflections on the Origins and Spread of Nationalism*, London: Verso.

Andrews, David M. (1994) 'Capital mobility and state autonomy: toward a structural theory of international monetary relations', *International Studies Quarterly*, 38, 2, June: 193–218.

Anon (1986) 'Belgian retailers refuse to pay', *RBI EFTPOS*, March: 6, London: Lafferty Publications.

—— (1987a) 'Retailers develop own EFTPOS', *RBI EFTPOS*, February: 1, London: Lafferty Publications.

—— (1987b) 'Banks threaten increased charges', *RBI EFTPOS*, June: 11, London: Lafferty Publications.

Antonelli, C. (1993) 'The dynamics of technological interrelatedness: the case of information and communication technologies', in D. Foray and C. Freeman (eds) *Technology and the Wealth of Nations*, London, Pinter: 194–207.

Archibugi, D. and Michie, J. (1993) 'The globalisation of technology: myths and realities', *Research Papers in Management Studies*, Cambridge: Judge Institute of Management Studies.

—— (1995) 'Technology and Innovation: an introduction', *Cambridge Journal of Economics*, special issue, 'Technology and Innovation', 19, 1, February: 1–4.

Aristotle (1981) *The Politics*, trans. T.A. Sinclair, Harmondsworth: Penguin.

Armstrong, P. (1993) 'Professional knowledge and social mobility: post-war changes in the knowledge-base of management accounting', *Work, Employment and Society*, 7, 1, March: 1–21.

Arthur, W.B. (1993) 'Pandora's marketplace. Economists are challenging some key assumptions. Their field may never be the same again', *New Scientist*, supplement, 6 February: 6–8.

Ashley, R.K. (1980) *The Political Economy of War and Peace: The Sino-Soviet Triangle and the Modern Security Problematique*, London: Pinter.

—— (1981) 'Three modes of economism', *International Studies Quarterly*, 25, 2, June: 204–36.

—— (1984) 'The poverty of neorealism', *International Organization*, 38, 2, Spring: 225–86.

—— (1989) 'Living on borderlines: man, poststructuralism and war', in J. Der Derian and M. Shapiro (eds) *International/Intertextual Relations: Postmodern Readings of World Politics*, New York: Macmillan: 259–321.

Atkinson, J. (1985) 'Flexibility, uncertainty and manpower management', *IMS Report 89*, Sussex: IMS.

Attali, J. (1982) *Histoire du Temps*, Paris: Fayard.

Auster, R.D. and Silver, M. (1979) *The State as A Firm: Economic Forces in Political Development*, Boston, MA: Martin Nijhoff.

AWST (1994) 'Boeing rolls out 777 to tentative market', *Aviation Week and Space Technology*, 40, 15, 11 April: 36–58.

Bacher, T. (1984) 'The economics of the commercial aircraft industry', paper presented at a conference on 'The Role of South-East Asia in World Airline and Aerospace Development' sponsored by the *Financial Times* in Singapore, 24–25 September.

Badaracco, J. (1991) *The Knowledge Link*, Boston, MA: Harvard Business School Press.

Balandier, G. (1988) *Les Disordres: Eloge du Mouvement*, Paris: Fayard.

Baldwin, R. and Krugman, P. (1988) 'Market access and international competition', in E. Feenstra (ed.) *Empirical Methods in International Economics*, Cambridge, MA: MIT Press: 171–201.

Ballard (1994) *Ballard Power Systems Inc. Annual Report for 1993*, Vancover.
Barrow, J.D. and Tipler, F.J. (1986) *The Anthropic Cosmological Principle*, Oxford: Oxford University Press.
Battiau, M. (1985) *Le Textile: Vers une Nouvelle Donnée Mondiale*, Paris: CEDES.
Bauman, Z. (1992) *Intimations of Postmodernity*, London: Routledge.
BBC (1994) Television series, 'White Heat'.
Beaty, J. and Gwynne, S.C. (1993) *The Outlaw Bank: A Wild Ride into the Secret Heart of BCCI*, New York: Random House.
Beck, U. (1992) *Risk Society: Towards a New Modernity*, London: Sage.
Becker, G.S. (1957) *The Economics of Discrimination*, Chicago, IL: University of Chicago Press.
——(1962) 'Investment in human capital', *Journal of Political Economy*, 70, 5, part 2: 9–19.
——(1964) *Human Capital*, New York: Columbia University Press.
Bell, D. (1973) *The Coming of Post-Industrial Society*, New York: Basic Books.
Benedict, R. (1935) *Patterns of Culture*, London: Routledge and Kegan Paul.
Benke, William (1987). Personal correspondence with Manager of International Business, Boeing Commercial Airplane Company (4 December 1987).
Benseler, F. (1980) 'On the history of systems thinking in sociology', in F. Benseler *et al.* (eds) *Autopoiesis, Communication and Society*, Frankfurt and New York: Campus Verlag.
Berger, S. (1981) 'The traditional sector in France and Italy,' in S. Berger and M.S. Piore (eds) *Dualism and Discontinuity in Industrial Societies*, Cambridge: Cambridge University Press: 88–131.
Berrier, R.J. (1978) 'The politics of industrial survival: the French textile industry', unpublished PhD thesis, MIT.
Bijker, W., Hughes, T.P. and Pinch, T.J. (1987) *The Social Construction of Technological Systems*, Cambridge, MA: MIT Press.
Blackler, F., Reed, M. and Whitaker, A. (1993) 'Editorial introduction: knowledge workers and contemporary organisations', *Journal of Management Studies*, 30, 6, November: 851–62.
Blomen, L.J.M.J. and Mugerwa, M.N. (eds) (1993) *Fuel Cell Systems*, New York and London: Plenum Press.
Bohm, D. (1983) *Wholeness and the Implicate Order*, London: Ark.
Borrus, M. and Zysman, J. (1992) 'Industrial competitiveness and American national security', in W. Sandholtz, M. Borrus, J. Zysman, K. Conca, J. Stowsky, S. Vogel and S. Weber (eds) *The Highest Stakes: The Economic Foundations of the Next Security System*, New York: Oxford University Press: 7–52.
Bosworth, D.L. (1990) 'Professional skill shortages', *International Journal of Manpower*, 11, 2/3: 6–17.
Botero, G. (1956) *The Reason of State*, London: Routledge and Kegan Paul.
Bougnoux, D. (ed.) (1993) *Sciences de l'Information et de la Communication*, Paris: Larousse.
Boussemart, B. and Rabier, J.-C. (1983) *Le Dossier Agache-Willot: un Capitalisme à Contre-Courant*, Paris: Presses de la FNSP.
BP (1995) *BP Statistical Review of World Energy*, London: British Petroleum, June.
Bravermann, H. (1974) *Labor and Monopoly Capital*, New York: Monthly Review Press.
Brooks, H. (1980) 'Technology, evolution, and purpose' in 'Modern Technology: Problem or Opportunity?', *Daedalus*, 109, 1, Winter: 65–81.
Brown, L. (1995) 'Averting a global food crisis', *Technology Review*, 98, 8, November-December: 44–53.
Bryan, R., Senator from Nevada (1993) Written statement submitted for the record to the US Senate Hearing, *Environmental Aspects of Current Hydrogen and Renewable*

Energy Programs, before the Subcommittee on Toxic Substances, Research and Development of the Committee on Environment and Public Works of the United States Senate. 103rd Congress, first session, 22 March 1993, Washington: US Government Printing Office: 4–6.

Bryce, C.F.A. and Bennett, D. (eds) (1990) *Manpower and Training Needs for European Biotechnology*, Report by the UK Interest Group on Biotechnology Education, London: The Biochemical Society.

Bryce, C.F.A., Bennett, D. and Griffin, M. (eds) (1989) *Manpower and Training Needs for UK Biotechnology*, Report by the UK Interest Group on Biotechnology Education, London: The Biochemical Society.

Bryce, J. (1968) [1864] *The Holy Roman Empire*, London: Macmillan.

Bull, H. (1977) *The Anarchical Society: A Study of Order in World Politics*, London: Macmillan.

Buzan, B. (1991) *People, States and Fear*, 2nd edition, London: Harvester-Wheatsheaf.

Byrne, J.A. (1993a) 'The virtual corporation', *Business Week*, 3292, 8 February: 36–41.

—— (1993b) 'The horizontal corporation', *Business Week*, 3337, 20 December: 44–49.

Cantwell, J. (1989) *Technological Innovation and Multinational Corporations*, Oxford: Blackwell.

Carchedi, G. (1983) *Problems in Class Analysis: Production, Knowledge and the Function of Capital*, London: Routledge and Kegan Paul.

Carlsson, B. (ed.) (1991) *Industrial Dynamics: Technological, Organizational and Structural Changes in Industries and Firms*, Leyden: Kluwer.

Carlsson, B. and Jacobsson, S. (1993) 'Technological systems and economic performance: the diffusion of factory automation in Sweden', in D. Foray and C. Freeman (eds) *Technology and the Wealth of Nations*, London, Pinter: 77–92.

Carnoy, M., Castells, M., Cohen, S. and Cardoso, F.H. (1993) *The New Global Economy in the Information Age*, University Park, PA: The Pennsylvania University State Press.

Castells, M. (1989) *The Informational City*, Oxford: Basil Blackwell.

—— (1993) 'The informational economy and the new international division of labour' in M. Carnoy, M. Castells, S. Cohen and F.H. Cardoso, *The New Global Economy in the Information Age*, University Park, PA: The Pennsylvania University State Press: 15–45.

—— (1994) 'European cities, the informational society and the global economy', *New Left Review*, 204, March-April: 18–32.

Castells, M. and Hall, P. (1994) *Technopoles of the World*, London: Routledge.

Cawson, A., Morgan, K., Webber, D., Holmes, P. and Stevens, A. (1990) *Hostile Brothers: Competition and Closure in the European Electronics Industry*, Oxford: Clarendon Press.

CEC (1990) (Commission of the European Communities) *Making Payments in the Internal Market: Improving Banking Services for Individuals and Organisations*, Background report ISEC/B29/1990, London: CEC.

—— (1993) *Growth, Competitiveness and Ways Forward into the 21st Century*, Com (93) 700, Final, 5 December, Brussels: CEC.

CEPII (1978) (Centre d'Etudes Prospectives et d'Informations Internationales) *Les Economies Industrialisées Face à la Concurrence du Tiers-Monde: le Cas de la Filière Textile*, Paris: CEPII.

CEREQ (1979) (Centre d'Etudes et de Recherches sur les Qualifications) *L'evolution des Emplois et de la Main d'Oeuvre dans l'Industrie Textile*, Paris: Les Dossiers du CEREQ no. 20, La Documentation Française.

Cerny, P.G. (1990) *The Changing Architecture of Politics: Structure, Agency, and the Future of the State*, London and Newbury Park, CA: Sage Publications.

—— (1994a) 'The dynamics of financial globalization: technology, market structure, and policy response', *Policy Sciences*, 27, 4: 319–42.

—— (1994b) 'The infrastructure of the infrastructure? Toward "embedded financial orthodoxy" in the international political economy', in R.P. Palan and B. Gills (eds) *Transcending the State-Global Divide: A Neostructuralist Agenda in International Relations*, Boulder, Co: Lynne Rienner: 223–49.

—— (1994c) 'Money and power: the American financial system from free banking to global competition', in G. Thompson (ed.) *Markets*, volume 2 of R. Maidment, *et al.* (eds) *The United States in the Twentieth Century*, London: Hodder and Stoughton: 175–213.

—— (1995) 'Globalization and the changing logic of collective action', *International Organization*, 49, 4, Autumn: 595–625.

—— (ed.) (1993) *Finance and World Politics: Markets, Regimes, and States in the Post-Hegemonic Era*, Cheltenham, Glos. and Brookfield, VT: Edward Elgar.

CES (1982) (Conseil Economique et Social) 'Le devenir des industries du textile et de l'habillement,' *Journal Officiel*, Avis et Rapports du CES, 25 February.

Chadwick, J. (1958) *The Decipherment of Linear B*, Cambridge: Cambridge University Press.

Chalmers, A.F. (1982) *What is This Thing Called Science?*, 2nd edition, Milton Keynes: Open University Press.

Chapman, H. (1991) *State Capitalism and Working-Class Radicalism in the French Aircraft Industry*, Berkeley, CA: University of California Press.

Charles, D., Hayward, S. and Thomas, D. (1995) 'Science Parks and regional technology strategies: European experiences', *Industry and Higher Education*, 'Special Focus: The Role of Science Parks in University-Industry Co-operation', 9, 6, December: 332–9.

Chiaromonte, F. and Dosi, G. (1993) 'The micro foundations of competitiveness and their macroeconomic implications', in D. Foray and C. Freeman (eds) *Technology and the Wealth of Nations*, London, Pinter: 107–34.

Chorafas, D.N. (1992) *The New Technology of Financial Management*, New York: John Wiley and Sons.

Cohen, W. and Levinthal, D. (1989) 'Innovation and learning: the two faces of R&D', *Economic Journal*, 99, 397, September: 569–96.

Cohendet, P., Ledoux, M.J., and Zuscovitch, E. (1988) *Les Materiaux Nouveaux*, Paris: Economica.

Cook, P.L. (1985) 'The offshore supplies industry', in M. Sharp (ed.) *Europe and the New Technologies*, London: Pinter: 213–62.

Coombs, R., Saviotti, P., and Walsh, V. (1987) *Economics and Technological Change*, London: Macmillan.

Cox, R.W. (1981) 'Social forces, states and world orders: beyond international relations theory', *Millennium*, 10, 2, Summer: 126–55.

—— (1987) *Production, Power and World Order: Social Forces in the Making of History*, New York: Columbia University Press.

—— (1992) 'Towards a post-hegemonic conceptualisation of world order: reflections on the relevancy of Ibn Khaldun', in J.N. Rosenau and E.-O. Czempiel (eds) *Governance without Government: Order and Change in World Politics*, Cambridge: Cambridge University Press: 132–59.

—— (1994) 'Global restructuring: making sense of the changing international political economy', in R. Stubbs and G.R.D. Underhill (eds) *Political Economy and the Changing Global Order*, London: Macmillan: 45–59.

Cox, R.W. and Jacobson, H.K. (eds) (1974) *The Anatomy of Influence*, New Haven and London: Yale University Press.

Crawford, R.D. and Sihler, W.W. (1991) *The Troubled Money Business: The Death of an Old Order and the Rise of a New Order*, New York: Harper Business.

Cross, N. (1989) *Engineering Design Methods*, London: Wiley.
Crozier, M. and Friedberg, E. (1977) *L'Acteur et le Système: les Contraintes de l'Action Collective*, Paris: Editions du Seuil.
Curran, L. and Lovering, J. (1994) *As the State Contracts: Emerging Tensions in the Scientific Labour Market in Britain*, mimeo EASST Conference, Budapest.
Cusumano, M.A. and Elenkov, D. (1994) 'Linking international technology transfer with strategy and management: a literature commentary', *Research Policy*, 23, 2, March: 195–215.
Dahl, R. (1976) *Modern Political Analysis*, 3rd edition, Englewood Cliffs, NJ: Prentice-Hall.
Daimler-Benz (1994) 'Fuel cells hit the road', *Daimler-Benz HighTech Report*, 3/1994.
Daly, P. (1985) *The Biotechnology Business: A Strategic Analysis*, London: Pinter.
Daniels, P. (1993) 'Research and development, human capital and trade performance in technology intensive manufactures: a cross-country analysis', *Research Policy*, 22, 3, June: 207–41.
Davidow, W.H. and Malone, M.S. (1993) *The Virtual Corporation: Structuring and Revitalizing the Corporation for the 21st Century*, New York: HarperCollins.
Davies, R.E.G. (1964) *A History of the World's Airlines*, London: Oxford University Press.
Davis, K. (1959) 'The myth of functional analysis as a special method in sociology and anthropology', *American Sociological Review*, 24, 6, December: 757–72.
De Nettancourt, D. and Magnien, E. (1993) 'What drives European biotechnological research?', in E.J. Blakely and K.W. Willoughby (eds) *Biotechnology Review no. 1: The Management and Economic Potential of Biotechnology*: 47–58.
De Woot, P. (1990) *High Tech Europe: Strategic Issues for Global Competitiveness*, Oxford: Blackwell.
Debray, R. (1981) *Critique of Political Reason*, London: New Left Books.
Der Derian, J. and Shapiro, M. (eds) (1989) *International/Intertextual Relations: Postmodern Readings of World Politics*, New York: Macmillan.
Derry, M. (1992) 'Cyberculture', *South Atlantic Quarterly*, 91, Summer: 501–23.
Dicken, P. (1992) *Global Shift*, 2nd edition, London: Paul Chapman.
Doganis, R. (1991) *Flying Off Course: the Economics of International Airlines*, London: Routledge.
Dosi, G. (1984) *Technical Change and Industrial Transformation*, London, Macmillan.
—— (1988a) 'Sources, procedures and microeconomic effects of innovation', *Journal of Economic Literature*, 26, 3, September: 1120–71.
—— (1988b) 'The nature of the innovation process' in G. Dosi, C. Freeman, R. Nelson, G. Silverberg and L. Soete (eds) *Technical Change and Economic Theory*, London: Pinter: 221–38.
Dosi, G., Pavitt, K. and Soete, L. (1990) *The Economics of Technical Change and International Trade*, London: Harvester-Wheatsheaf.
Dosi, G., Freeman, C., Nelson, R., Silverberg, G. and Soete, L. (eds) (1988) *Technical Change and Economic Theory*, London: Pinter.
Dostrovsky, I. (1991) 'Chemical fuels from the sun', *Scientific American*, 265, 6, December: 50–66.
Doval Adan, A. (1992) *La Penetracion de Tecnologia Estranjera en Galicia*, Ourense: Deputacion Provincial de Ourense.
Drucker, P. (1983) 'Quality education: the new growth era', *Wall Street Journal*, 19 July.
—— (1993) *Post-Capitalist Society*, Oxford: Butterworth-Heinemann.
Dubois, P. (1981) 'Mort d'une industrie? L'emploi dans l'habillement,' *Revue Française des Affaires Sociales*, 35–1, April-June: 139–59.
Dunning, J.H. (1988) *Multinationals, Technology and Competitiveness*, London: Unwin Hyman.

——(1993) *The Globalization of Business*, London: Routledge.
——(1994) 'Multinational enterprises and the globalisation of innovatory capacity', *Research Policy*, 23, 1, January: 67–88.
Dunning, J.H. and Robson, P. (1988) *Multinationals and the European Community*, Oxford: Blackwell.
Durkheim, E. (1976) *The Elementary Forms of Religious Life*, London: Allen & Unwin.
Ealey, L. and Gentile, T. (1995) 'The potential impact of electric vehicles on the automotive business system', *International Motor Business*, 2nd quarter, London: The Economist Intelligence Unit: 102–15.
Earle, E.M. (ed.) (1951) *Modern France: Problems of the Third and Fourth Republics*, Princeton, NJ: Princeton University Press.
Easton, D. (1953) *The Political System*, Chicago, IL: University of Chicago Press.
EC (1981) *Communication de la Commission au Conseil sur la Situation et les Perspectives de l'Industrie du Textile et de l'Habillement dans la Communauté*, COM (81) 388 Final, Brussels, 27 July.
Eccles, R.G. (1985) *The Transfer Pricing Problem: a Theory for Practice*, Lexington, MA: Lexington Books.
Economie-Géographie (1992) 'l'Industrie Textile', no. 192, February: 1–16.
Edwards, F.R. and Patrick, H.T. (eds) (1992) *Regulating Financial Markets: Issues and Policies*, London: Kluwer.
Edwards, R.C., Reich, M. and Gordon, D.M. (eds.) (1973) *Labour Market Segmentation*, Lexington, MA: Lexington Books.
Ernst and Young (1995) *European Biotech '95 Gathering Momentum: the Industry Annual Report*, The Netherlands: Ernst and Young.
Eurobarometer (1991) *Opinions of Europeans towards Biotechnology*, Brussels: CEC.
Ezling, C. M., Bilderbeek, R. and Otto, S. R. (1991) *Biotechnology Companies in The Netherlands: Human Resources in R&D and Production*, summary of a report to the Dutch Ministry of Economic Affairs, Leyden: TNO Centre for Technology and Policy Studies.
Farrands, C. (1979) 'Textile diplomacy: the making and implementation of European textile policy 1974–8', *Journal of Common Market Studies*, XVIII, 1, September: 22–39.
——(1990) *New Materials in Manufacturing Industry*, London: The Economist Intelligence Unit (special report no. 2026).
——(1995) 'Knowledge, power and the governance of intellectual property regimes in the global political economy', in E. Kofman and G. Youngs (eds) *Globalisation: Theory and Practice*, London: Pinter: 175–87
Farrands, C. and Talalay, M. (1994) 'Technology, globalisation and the international political economy', paper presented to the International Studies Association Convention, Washington, DC, March/April.
Faulkner, D. and Johnson, G. (1992) *The Challenge of Strategic Management*, London: Kogan Page.
Featherstone, M. (ed.) (1990) *Global Culture: Nationalism, Globalization and Modernity*, London: Sage.
Ferguson, M. (1980) *The Aquarian Conspiracy: Personal and Social Transformation in our Times*, London: HarperCollins.
Financial Times Biotechnology Survey (1994) 'Location a high priority', 9 May.
Flamm, K. (1990) 'Semiconductors', in G.C. Hufbauer (ed.) *Europe 1992: An American Perspective*, Washington, DC: Brookings: 225–92.
——(1992) 'Strategic aspects of international competition in semiconductors', paper presented at CERETIM Conference, University of Rennes, St. Malo, France, June.
Flavin, C. (1995) 'Harnessing the sun and wind', in L.R. Brown (ed.) *State of the World 1995*, London: Earthscan Publications for the Worldwatch Institute: 58–75.

Fleck, J. (1991) *Configurations: Crystallising Contingency*, working paper series 91/15, University of Edinburgh, Department of Business Studies.

Fletcher, D. (1994) 'Small firms' strategic alliances and value added networks: a critical review', *Piccola Impresa* (Genoa) 2: 27–60.

Foray, D. (1993) 'General Introduction', in D. Foray and C. Freeman (eds) *Technology and the Wealth of Nations*, London: Pinter: 1–22.

Foray, D. and Freeman, C. (eds) (1993) *Technology and the Wealth of Nations*, London: Pinter.

Fortes, M. (1936) 'Culture contact as a dynamic process: an investigation in the Northern Territories of the Gold Coast', *Africa*, IX, I, January: 24–55.

Foucault, M. (1972) *Histoire de la Folie à l'Age Classique*, Paris: Gallimard.

France (1981) (Assemblée Nationale) *Rapport Fait au Nom de la Commission d'Enquête Parlementaire Chargée d'Examiner les Problèmes de l'Industrie Textile et les Moyens à Mettre en Oeuvre pour les Resoudre*, 3 vols, 6e Législature, no. 2254, 18 March.

—— (1982a) 'Décret no. 82–34 du 16 Avril 1982 (cotisations de sécurité sociale/textile et de l'habillement)', *Journal Officiel*, Edition Lois et Décrets, no. 90, 17 April: 1151–2.

—— (1982b) 'Ordonnance no. 204 du 1er mars 1982 (cotisations de sécurité sociale/textile et de l'habillement)', *Journal Officiel*, Edition Lois et Décrets, no. 51, 1–2 March: 719–20.

Franklin, U. (1990) *The Real World of Technology*, Toronto: The Massey Lectures, Canadian Broadcasting Corporation.

Freeman, C. (1982) *The Economics of Industrial Innovation*, 2nd edition, London: Pinter.

—— (1987a) 'The challenge of new technologies', in OECD, *Interdependence and Co-operation in Tomorrow's World*, Paris: OECD: 123–56.

—— (1987b) *Technology Policy and Economic Performance*, London: Pinter.

—— (ed.) (1984) *Long Waves in the World Economy*, London : Pinter.

—— (ed.) (1990) *The Economics of Innovation*, Aldershot: Edward Elgar.

Freeman, C. and Oldham, G. (1991) 'Introduction: beyond the single market', in C. Freeman, M. Sharp and W. Walker (eds) *Technology and the Future of Europe: Global Competition and the Environment in the 1990s*, London: Pinter.

Freeman, C. and Perez, C. (1988) 'Structural crises of adjustment, business cycles and investment behaviour', in G. Dosi, C. Freeman, R. Nelson, G. Silverberg and L. Soete (eds) *Technical Change and Economic Theory*, London: Pinter: 38–66.

Freeman, C. and Soete, L. (1994) *Work for All or Mass Unemployment*, London: Pinter.

Freeman, C., Sharp, M. and Walker, W. (eds) (1991) *Technology and the Future of Europe: Global Competition and the Environment in the 1990s*, London: Pinter.

Friedberg, E. (1976) *L'Etat et l'Industrie en France: Rapport d'Enquête*, Paris: CNRS.

Frieden, J.A. and Lake, D.A. (1991a) 'The contemporary international political economy', in J.A. Frieden and D.A. Lake (eds) *International Political Economy*, London: Unwin Hyman: 1–15.

—— (eds) (1991b) *International Political Economy*, London: Unwin Hyman.

Friedman, D. (1988) *The Misunderstood Miracle: Industrial Development and Political Change in Japan*, Ithaca, NY and London: Cornell University Press.

Friedman, J. (1990) 'Being in the world: globalization and localization', in M. Featherstone (ed.) *Global Culture: Nationalism, Globalization and Modernity*, London: Sage: 311–28.

Fröbel, F., Heinrichs, J. and Kreye, O. (1980) *The New International Division of Labour*, Cambridge: Cambridge University Press.

Fukao, M. and Hanazaki, M. (1987) 'Internationalization of financial markets and the allocation of capital', *OECD Economic Studies*, 8: 36–92.

Fukuyama, F. (1992) *The End of History and the Last Man*, London: Penguin.

Fuqua, D. (1989) 'The FSX: looking backward, look forward', *Aerospace Industries Association Newsletter*, 2, 4, October: 3.

Gettell, R. (1924) *History of Political Thought*, London: Allen & Unwin.

Gibbons, J. (1993) Director, Office of Science and Technology Policy, The White House; testimony and written statement to the US Senate Hearing, *Environmental Aspects of Current Hydrogen and Renewable Energy Programs*, hearing before the Subcommittee on Toxic Substances, Research and Development of the Committee on Environment and Public Works of the United States Senate. 103rd Congress, first session, 22 March 1993, Washington: US Government Printing Office: 9–18 and 58–65.

Gill, S. (1993) 'Epistemology, ontology, and the "Italian school" ', in S. Gill (ed.) *Gramsci, Historical Materialism and International Relations*, Cambridge: Cambridge University Press.

Gill, S. and Law, D. (1988) *The Global Political Economy*, New York and London: Harvester.

Gilpin, R. (1987) *The Political Economy of International Economic Relations*, Princeton, NJ: Princeton University Press.

Ginzberg, E. and Vojta, G. (1985) *Beyond Human Scale: the Large Corporation at Risk*, New York: Basic Books.

Giry-Deloison, P. and Masson, P. (1988) 'Vers un marché financier mondial: les rouages de la globalisation', *Revue Banque*, 485: 725–9.

Gloger, A. (1993) 'Mehr Hierarchie im Unternehmen stört oft den Informationsfluß: von der vertikalen zur horizontalen Organisation', *Blick durch die Wirtschaft*, 7, September.

Golaszewski, R.S. (1993) 'Airline strategic alliances: definition and a case for caution', *Transport Adviser*, 3, 1, January: 1–4.

Golich, V.L. (1989) *The Political Economy of International Air Safety: Design for Disaster?*, New York: St. Martin's Press.

——(1991) 'Resisting integration: aerospace national champions' in P.M.R. Stirk and D. Willis (eds) *Shaping Postwar Europe: European Unity and Disunity 1945–57*, London: Pinter: 124–40.

——(1992) 'From competition to collaboration: the challenge of commercial-class aircraft manufacturing', *International Organization*, 46, 4, Autumn: 899–934.

Goodman, R. (1979) *The Last Entrepreneurs*, New York: Basic Books.

Gorz, A. (1991) *Capitalisme, Socialisme, Ecologie*, Paris: Editions Galilée.

Gray, B. (1989) *Collaborating: Finding Common Ground for Multiparty Problems*, San Francisco, CA: Jossey-Bass Publishers.

Griffin, M., Hayward, S. and Curtis, J. (eds) (1993a) *Manpower and Training Needs for Biotechnology in North and South Europe in the 90s*, report of a meeting held in Orense, Spain, 18–19 September; London: BEMET.

Griffin, M., Curtis, J., Hayward, S. and Walshe, A. (eds) (1993b) *Directory of Higher Education Courses in European Biotechnology*, BEMET, UK Interest Group, London.

Gustatz, M. (1983) 'Les dangers de l'auto' in P. Dumouchel and J.P. Dupy (eds) *L'Auto Organisation: De la Physique au Politique*, Paris: Seuil.

Guzzini, S. (1993) 'Structural power: the limits of neorealist analysis', *International Organization*, 47, 3, Summer: 443–78.

Haas, P. (ed.) (1992) 'Knowledge, power, and international policy coordination', special edition of *International Organisation*, 46, 1, Winter.

Hagedoorn, J. and Schakenraad, J. (1990a) 'Leading companies and the structure of strategic alliances in core technologies', MERIT Working Paper, Maastricht, The Netherlands.

——(1990b) 'Inter-firm partnerships and co-operative strategies in core technologies', in C. Freeman and L. Soete (eds) *New Explorations in the Economics of Technical Change*, London: Pinter: 3–37.

Hall, G. (1972) 'The logical typing of the symbolic, the imaginary, and the real', appendix to Chapter IX in Anthony Wilden, *System and Structure: Essays in Communication and Exchange*, London: Tavistock Publishing.

Hall, J.A. (1986) *Powers and Liberties: the Causes and Consequences of the Rise of the West*, London: Pelican.

——(1993) 'Ideas and the social sciences', in J. Goldstein and R.O. Keohane (eds) *Ideas and Foreign Policy*, Ithaca and London: Cornell University Press: 31–54.

Harrison, B. (1991) 'Industrial districts: old wine in new bottles?', *Regional Studies*, vol. 26: 469–83.

Harvey, D. (1990) *The Condition of Postmodernity: an Enquiry into the Origins of Social Change*, Oxford: Blackwell.

Hayward, K. (1983) *Government and British Civil Aerospace: a Case Study in Post-War Technology Policy*, Manchester: Manchester University Press.

——(1986) *International Collaboration in Civil Aerospace*, New York: St. Martin's Press.

Hayward, S. (forthcoming) *Political Economy of Biotechnology Labour Markets*, PhD thesis, the Nottingham Trent University.

Hayward, S. and Griffin, M. (1994a) *Europe at Work: Labour and Training in the Biotechnology Small Firm Sector*, BEMET, The UK Interest Group, London.

——(1994b) 'De la formation a l'emploi' (Labour market trends in the small firm sector) *Biofutur*, hors serie no. 2: 72–6.

——(1994c) 'Europe at BioWork: challenges and prospects', *Bio/technology*, 12, July: 667–70.

Heenan, D.A. (1991) 'The end of centralized power', *The Journal of Business Strategy*, 46, March-April.

Heidegger, M. (1962) *Being And Time*, Oxford: Blackwell.

Heinz, M. (1991) 'Electronic cash: the German banks', final approach to EFTPOS, paper presented to European Payments Conference, 19–21 November, Sheraton Hotel, Edinburgh.

Henderson, J. (1989) *The Globalisation of High Technology Production*, London: Routledge.

Hicks, D. and Hirooka, M. (1991) 'Science in Japanese companies: a preliminary analysis', Tokyo: National Institute of Science and Technology Policy (NISTEP).

Hilpert, U. (ed.) (1991) *State Policies and Techno-Industrial Innovation*, London: Routledge.

Hine, J. and Howells, J. (1993) 'The UK banking context for EFTPOS development' in J. Howells and J. Hines (eds) *Innovative Banking: Competition and the Configuration of a New Network Technology*, London: Routledge.

Hirschenhofer, J.H., Stauffer, D.B. and Engleman, R.R. (1994) *Fuel Cells: A Handbook (Revision 3)*, Morgantown, WVa: US Department of Energy, Office of Fossil Energy, January.

Hobbes, T. (1951) *Leviathan*, C.B. Macpherson (ed.) Harmondsworth: Penguin.

Hochmuth, M.S. (1974) 'Aerospace', in R. Vernon (ed.) *Big Business and the State: Changing Relations in Western Europe*, Cambridge, MA: Harvard University Press: 145–69.

Hodder, J.E. (1991) 'Is the cost of capital lower in Japan?', *Journal of the Japanese and International Economies*, 5, 1, March: 86–100.

Hodrien, R.C. and Fairbairn, G. (1993) 'Power into the 21st century', a paper presented to the 59th meeting of the Institution of Gas Engineers, London, November 1993, published by the institution as *Communication 1545*.

Hoggett, P. (1991) 'A new management in the public sector?', *Policy and Politics*, 19, 4, October: 243–56.

Howells, Jeremy and Wood, M. (1993) *The Globalisation of Production and Technology*, London: Belhaven Press.

Howells, John (1990) 'The globalisation of research and development: a new era of change?', *Science and Public Policy*, 17, 4, October: 273–85.

—— (1992) 'The management of expertise' paper delivered to conference 'Exploring Expertise', University of Edinburgh, November.

—— (1993a) 'Competition, cooperation and the design of an EFTPOS network', in J. Howells and J. Hine (eds) *Innovative Banking: Competition and the Configuration of a New Network Technology*, London: Routledge.

—— (eds) (1993b) *Innovative Banking: Competition and the Management of a New Networks Technology*, London: Routledge.

Howells, J., Alexander, N. and Hine, J. (1993) 'The design of EFTPOS and the bank–retailer relationship' in J. Howells and J. Hine (eds) *Innovative Banking: Competition and the Configuration of a New Network Technology*, London: Routledge.

Hu, Y.S. (1992) 'Global or stateless corporations are national firms with international operations', *California Management Review*, 34, 2, Winter: 107–26.

Huff, A.S. (ed.) (1990) *Mapping Strategic Thought*, Chichester: Wiley.

Hughes, T. (1983) *Networks of Power: Electrification in Western Society, 1880–1930*, Baltimore, MD and London: Johns Hopkins University Press.

Humbert, M. (1994) 'Strategic industrial policies in a global industrial system', *Review of International Political Economy*, 1, 3, Autumn: 445–63.

Hutton, W. (1995) *The State We're In*, London: Jonathan Cape.

IDA (1995) *Ireland: Leading Location for Call Centres and Teleservicing*, Dublin: Industrial Development Agency.

IEA (1993) (International Energy Agency) *Oil and Gas Information 1992*, Paris: OECD/IEA.

—— (1994a) *Energy Policies of IEA Countries, 1993 Review*, Paris: OECD/IEA.

—— (1994b) *World Energy Outlook, 1994 Edition*, Paris: OECD/IEA.

IMB (1995) *International Motor Business*, 3rd quarter 1995, London: *The Economist* Intelligence Unit.

IMS (1983) (Institute of Manpower Studies) *The Biotechnology Brain Drain*, Swindon, UK: SERC.

—— (1987) *Monitoring the Biotechnology Labour Market*, UK: SERC.

Ingram, J.C. and Dunn, R.M. (1993) *International Economics*, 3rd edition, New York: John Wiley.

INSEE (Institut National de la Statistique et des Etudes Economiques) unpublished data set covering the years 1970–82. For an explanation of the accounting principles employed in the data set, see INSEE (1981) *Entreprises Non-Financières en Termes de Comptabilité d'Entreprises*, Paris: Les Collections de l'INSEE, no. E78, September.

IRDAC (1992) (Industrial Research and Development Advisory Committee of the Commission of the European Communities) *Skills Shortages in Europe*, Brussels: CEC.

—— (1994) *Quality and Relevance*, Brussels: CEC.

Jackson, M. (1993) *Dangerous: the Short Films*, MJJ Productions, SMV Enterprises.

Jameson, F. (1991) *Postmodernism, or The Cultural Logic of Late Capitalism*, London: Verso.

Jarillo, J.C. (1988) 'On strategic networks', *Strategic Management Journal*, 9, 1, January-February: 31–41.

Jessop, B. (1992) 'Fordism and post-Fordism: critique and reformulation' in M. Storper and A.J. Scott (eds) *Pathways to Industrialisation and Regional Development*, London: Routledge.

Johannisson, B. (1987) 'Beyond process and structure: social exchange networks', *International Studies of Management and Organisation*, 17, 1, Spring: 3–23.

Johnston, R. and Gummett, P. (eds) (1979) *Directing Technology*, London: Croom Helm.

Jones, R.J.B. (1995) *Globalisation and Interdependence in the International Political Economy*, London: Pinter.

Journal of Management Studies (1993) special issue on 'Knowledge workers and contemporary organisations', 30, 6, November.

Jovanovic, B. and MacDonald, G. M. (1994) 'Competitive diffusion', *Journal of Political Economy*, 102, 1, February: 24–52.

Julius, D. (1990) *Global Companies and Public Policies: the Growing Challenge of Foreign Direct Investment*, London: Royal Institute of International Affairs.

Kahn, A.E. (1988) 'Surprises of deregulation', *American Economic Review*, 78, 2, May: 316–22.

Kasper, D.M. (1988) *Deregulation and Globalization: Liberalizing International Trade in Air Services*, Cambridge, MA: Ballinger Publishing Co.

Kato, M. (1993) 'Nuclear globalism: traversing rockets, satellites, and nuclear war via the strategic gaze', *Alternatives*, 18: 339–60.

Keesing, D.B. and Wolf, M. (1981) 'Questions on international trade in textiles and clothing,' *The World Economy*, 4, 1, March: 79–101.

Kelly, K., Oneal, M., DeGeorge, G. and Vogel, T. (1991) 'All the trouble isn't in the sky', *Business Week*, March 11: 84–5.

Kennedy, P. (1993) *Preparing for the Twenty-First Century*, London: HarperCollins.

Keohane, R.O. and Nye, J.S. (1970) *Transnational Relations and World Politics*, London: Harvard University Press.

——(eds) (1977) *Power and Interdependence*, Boston, MA: Little, Brown.

Kiechel III, W. (1994) 'A manager's career in the new economy', *Fortune*, April 4: 50–4.

Kim, L.S. and Dahlman, C.J. (1992) 'Technology policy for industrialization: an integrative framework and Korea's experience', *Research Policy*, 21, 5, October: 437–52.

Kitschelt, H. (1991) 'Industrial governance structures, innovation strategies, and the case of Japan: sectoral or cross-national comparative analysis?', *International Organization*, 45, 4, Autumn: 453–93.

Klein, E. (1966) *A Comprehensive Etymological Dictionary of the English Language*, Amsterdam: Elsevier.

Kogut, B. and Zander, U. (1993) 'Knowledge of the firm and the evolutionary theory of the multinational corporation', *Journal of International Business Studies*, 24, 4, Fourth Quarter: 625–45.

Kohn, A.O. (1992) 'A case study of a successful GE/SNECMA joint venture', unpublished paper presented at the International Symposium on Joint Ventures and Strategic Alliances, Pennsylvania State University, 6–8 April.

Krasner, S.D. (1985) *Structural Conflict: The Third World Against Global Liberalism*, Berkeley, CA and London: University of California Press.

——(1990) personal correspondence, 6 August 1990.

Kratochwil, F. and Ruggie, J.G. (1986) 'International organization: a state of the art on an art of the state', *International Organization*, 40, 4, Autumn: 753–75.

Krugman, P.R. (1990) *Rethinking International Trade*, Cambridge, MA: MIT Press.

——(1994) *Peddling Prosperity: Economic Sense in the Age of Diminished Expectations*, New York: Norton.

——(ed.) (1986) *Strategic Trade Policy and the New International Economics*, Cambridge, MA: MIT Press.

Kuhn, T. (1962) *The Structure of Scientific Revolutions*, 2nd edition, Chicago, IL and London: University of Chicago Press.

Lakatos, I. (1974) 'Falsification and the methodology of scientific research programmes', in I. Lakatos and A. Musgrave (eds) *Criticism and the Growth of Knowledge*, Cambridge: Cambridge University Press: 91–196.

La Mettrie, J.O. de (1748) *L'Homme Machine*, Princeton, NJ: Princeton University Press, 1960 (English translation of 1748 original).

Lambert, J. (1969) *Le Patron*, Brussels: Bloud and Gay.

Landes, D.S. (1951) 'French business and the businessman: a social and cultural analysis,' in E.M. Earle (ed.) *Modern France: Problems of the Third and Fourth Republics*, Princeton, NJ: Princeton University Press: 334–53.

Landry, R. (1987) 'The challenges of the analysis of systems of collective action', *Journal of Applied Systems Analysis*, 14, April: 17–31.

Larson, J. and Rogers, E. (1985) *Silicon Valley Fever: Growth of High Technology Culture*, London: Allen & Unwin.

Lave, L.B., Hendrickson, C.T., and McMichael, F.C. (1995) 'Environmental implications of electric cars', *Science*, 268, 19 May: 993–5.

Lazonick, W. (1993) 'Industry clusters versus global webs: organisational changes in the American economy', *Industrial and Corporate Change*, 2, 1: 1–24.

Leborgne, D. and Lipietz, A. (1992) 'Conceptual fallacies and open questions on post-Fordism', in M. Storper and A.J. Scott (eds) *Pathways to Industrialisation and Regional Development*, London: Routledge.

Lents, J. (1993) Executive Officer, Southern California Air Quality Management District, testimony and written statement to US Senate Hearing (1993) *Environmental Aspects of Current Hydrogen and Renewable Energy Programs*, hearing before the Subcommittee on Toxic Substances, Research and Development of the Committee on Environment and Public Works of the United States Senate. 103rd Congress, first session, 22 March 1993, Washington: US Government Printing Office: 21–3 and 90–102.

Levinson, P. (1986) 'Information technologies as vehicles of evolution', in C. Mitcham and A. Huning (eds) *Philosophy and Technology II: Information Technology and Computers in Theory and Practice*, Dordrecht, The Netherlands: D. Reidel Publishing Company: 29–47.

Levitt T. (1983) 'The globalisation of markets', *Harvard Business Review*, 61, May-June: 92–102.

Litman, J. (1991) 'Copyright legislation and technological change', *Oregon Law Review*, 68, 2: 423–509.

Lopez, V.C. and Yager, L. (1987) 'An aerospace profile and the industry's role in the economy: the importance of R&D', *Facts and Perspectives*, Washington, DC: Aerospace Industries Association of America, April.

Lorange, P. and Roos, J. (1992) *Strategic Alliances: Formation, Implementation and Evolution*, Oxford: Blackwell.

Lorell, M.A. (1980) *Multinational Development of Large Aircraft: the European Experience R-2596-DR&E*, Santa Monica, CA: Rand Corporation.

Loubiere, P. and Riché, P. (1992) 'Les puces grimpent sur la carte bancaire', *Liberation*, 7–8 April: 10.

Lundvall, B.A. (1992) *National Systems of Innovation*, London: Pinter.

MacKenzie, D. and Wajcman, J. (1985) *The Social Shaping of Technology*, Milton Keynes: Open University Press.

McLellan, D. (1980) *Marx's Grundrisse*, London: Macmillan.

McNabb, R. and Ryan, P. (1990) 'Segmented labour markets', in D. Sapsford and Z. Tzannatos (eds) *Current Issues in Labour Economics*, London: Macmillan: 151–76.

McNabb, R. and Whitefield, K. (1993) 'Key issues in the economics of training', *International Journal of Manpower*, 14, 2/3: 4–16.

——(1994) 'Market failure, institutional structure and skill formation', *International Journal of Manpower*, 15, 5: 5–15.

Makansi, J. (1994) 'Are fuel cells heir apparent to the gas turbine?', *Power*, 138, 6, June: 82–90.

Mansfield, E. (1985) 'How rapidly does new technology leak out?', *Journal of Industrial Economics*, XXXIV, 2, December: 217–23.

Mansfield, E., Rapoport, J., Romeo, A., Villani, E., Wagner, S. and Husic, F. (1977) *The Production and Application of New Technology*, New York: Norton.

Marshall, A. (1919) *Industry and Trade*, London: Macmillan.

Massey, D. (1994) 'Scientists, transcendence and the work/home boundary', occasional paper no. 10, South-east programme funded by ESRC programme on *High Status Growth? Aspects of Home and Work Around High Technology Sectors*, Milton Keynes: Open University Press.

Massey, D., Quintas, P. and Wield, D. (1992) *High Tech Fantasies: Science Parks, Society, Science and Space*, London, Routledge.

Meessen, K.M. (1987) 'Intellectual property rights in international trade', *Journal of World Trade Law*, 21, 1, February: 67–74.

Meunier, P. (1981) 'L'evolution des echanges et de la pénétration etrangère dans le secteur du textile et de l'habillement,' in *Chroniques de l'Actualité de la SEDEIS*, vol. 24/12, 15 June: 394–401.

Midgley, D., Morrison, P. and Roberts, J. (1992) 'The effect of network structure in industrial diffusion processes', *Research Policy*, 21, 6, December: 533–52.

Miller, R. and Sawers, D. (1968) *The Technical Development of Modern Aviation*, London: Routledge and Kegan Paul.

Miller, S.K. (1993) 'Clinton vows to take lead over conservation', *New Scientist*, 138, 13 February: 8.

Milner, H.V. and Yoffie, D.B. (1989) 'Between free trade and protectionism: strategic trade policy and a theory of corporate trade demands', *International Organization*, 43, 2, Spring: 239–72.

Mitchell, A. (1991) 'Major stores threaten to boycott Barclays Bank', *Marketing*, 14 May: 1.

Mokyr, J. (1990) *The Lever of Riches: Technological Creativity and Economic Growth*, Oxford: Oxford University Press.

Molina, A.H. (1989) *The Transputer Constituency: Building Up UK/European Capabilities in Information Technology*, Edinburgh: Programme on Information and Communication Technologies.

Morgenthau, H.J. (1967) *Politics Among Nations: The Struggle for Power and Peace*, 4th edition, New York: Alfred Knopf.

Moss Kantor, E. (1994) 'Cities in the global economy', address to inaugural meeting, Atlantic Rim Network, Boston, MA, November.

Mowery, D. (1988) *International Collaborative Ventures in US Manufacturing*, Cambridge, MA: Ballinger.

Mowery, D.C. and Rosenberg, N. (1982) 'The commercial aircraft industry', in R. Nelson (ed.) *Government and Technical Progress: A Cross-Industry Analysis*, New York: Pergamon Press: 101–61.

Mumford, L. (1964) *The Pentagon of Power: the Myth of the Machine*, London: Secker and Warburg.

Murphy, C. and Tooze, R. (1991a) 'Getting beyond the "common sense" of the IPE orthodoxy', in C. Murphy and R. Tooze (eds) *The New International Political Economy*, Boulder, Co: Lynne Rienner: 11–31.

——(eds) (1991b) *The New International Political Economy*, Boulder, Co: Lynne Rienner.

Murray, R. (ed.) (1981) *Multinationals Beyond the Market: Intra-Firm Trade and the Control of Transfer Pricing*, Brighton: Harvester.

Mytelka, L.K. (ed.) (1991) *Strategic Partnerships and the World Economy*, London: Pinter.

National Academy of Engineering (1985) *The Competitive Status of the US Civil Aviation Manufacturing Industry: a Study of the Influences of Technology in Determining International Industrial Competitive Advantage, 88N70308*, Washington, DC: National Academy Press.

Nelson, R. (1992) *National Systems Supporting Technical Advance in Industry*, Oxford: Oxford University Press.

Newhouse, J. (1982) *The Sporty Game*, New York: Alfred Knopf.

Nivola, P.S. (1993) *Regulating Unfair Trade*, Washington, DC: The Brookings Institution.

Northedge, F.S. (1976) *The International Political System*, London: Faber and Faber.

O'Barr, W.M. and Conley, J.M., with economic analysis by Brancato, C.K. (1992) *Fortune and Folly: the Wealth and Power of Institutional Investing*, Homewood, IL: Business One Irwin.

O'Brien, R. (1992) *Global Financial Integration: the End of Geography*, London: Pinter, for the Royal Institute of International Affairs.

O'Lone, R. (1991) 'Airframe makers foresee continuing strong market', *Aviation Week and Space Technology*, 34, 11, 18 March: 77–82.

O'Reilly, B. (1994) 'The new face of small business', *Fortune*, 2 May: 54–8.

OECD (1977) *Towards Full Employment and Price Stability*, the McCracken Report, Paris: OECD.

——(1982) *Biotechnology: International Trends and Perspectives*, Paris: OECD.

——(1983) *Textile and Clothing Industries: Structural Problems and Policies in OECD Countries*, Paris: OECD.

——(1989) *Biotechnology: Economic and Wider Impacts*, Paris: OECD.

——(1992) *Technology and the Economy: the Key Relationships*, Paris: OECD.

Ofuatey-Kodjoe, W. (1991) 'African international political economy: an assessment of the current literature', in C. Murphy and R. Tooze (eds) *The New International Political Economy*, Boulder, Co: Lynne Rienner: 171–89.

Ohmae, K. (1990) *The Borderless World: Power and Strategy in the Interlinked Economy*, London: Fontana.

Olson, M. (1971) *The Logic of Collective Action*, Cambridge, MA: Harvard University Press.

Oman, C. (1994) *Globalisation and Regionalisation: the Challenge for Developing Countries*, Paris: OECD.

Orrù, M. (1994) 'Three Faces of Capitalism', paper presented at the Sixth Annual International Conference on Socio-Economics, the Society for the Advancement of Socio-Economics, Paris, 15–17 July.

Orsenigo, L. (1989) *The Emergence of Biotechnology*, London: Pinter.

Ostry, S. (1991) 'Beyond the border: the new international policy arena', in OECD, *Strategic Industries in a Global Economy: Policy Issues for the 1990s*, Paris: OECD.

OTT (1993) *National Program Plan: Fuel Cells in Transportation*, Washington: Office of Transportation Technology of the US Department of the Environment, February 1993. Reprinted in US House of Representatives Hearing (1993) *Fuel Cells: Clean Technology for the Future*, hearing before the Subcommittee on Energy of the Committee on Science, Space and Technology of the US House of Representatives. 103rd Congress, first Session, 20 July 1993, Washington: US Government Printing Office: 29–63.

PA (1992) *Environmental Aspects of Battery and Fuel Cell Technologies*, London: PA for the Department of Trade and Industry.

Palan, R. and Blair, B. (1993) 'On the idealist origins of the realist theory of international relations', *Review of International Studies*, 19, 4, October: 385–99.

Parente, S.L. and Prescott, E.C. (1994) 'Barriers to technological adoption and development', *Journal of Political Economy*, 102, 2, April: 298–321.

Parsons, T. (1937) *The Structure of Social Action*, New York: The Free Press.

Patel, P. and Pavitt, K. (1991a) 'Large firms in the production of the world's technology: an important case of "non-globalisation" ', *Journal of International Business Studies*, 22, 1, first quarter: 1–21.

—— (1991b) 'Europe's technological performance', in C. Freeman, M. Sharp and W. Walker (eds) *Technology and the Future of Europe: Global Competition and the Environment in the 1990s*, London: Pinter: 37–58.

—— (1992) 'The innovative performance of the world's largest firms: some new evidence', in P. Patel and K. Pavitt (eds) *The Economics of Innovation and New Technology*, London: Pinter: 91–102.

Pavitt, K. (1984) 'Sectoral patterns of technical change: towards a taxonomy and a theory', *Research Policy*, 13, 6, December: 343–73.

—— (1991) 'What makes basic research economically useful?', *Research Policy*, 20, 2, April: 87–107.

Pearson, R. (1987a) 'Biotechnology: where to next?', *Nature*, 328, 2 July: 96.

—— (1987b) 'Biotechnology manpower in the UK', *Nature*, 109, 14 June: 84.

—— (1989) 'When will biotechnology mature?', *Nature*, 341, 7 September: 86.

Perez, C. (1983) 'Structural change and assimilation of new technologies in the economic and social systems', *Futures*, 15, 5, October: 357–75.

Perlmutter, H.V. and Heenan, D.A. (1986) 'Cooperate to compete globally', *Harvard Business Review*, 64, 2, March-April: 136–52.

Perrow, C. (1984) *Normal Catastrophes*, New York: Basic Books.

—— (1986) *Complex Organizations: a Critical Essay*, 3rd edition, New York: Random House.

Piaget, J. (1965) *Insights and Illusions of Philosophy*, trans. W. Mays, London: Routledge and Kegan Paul.

Pierrard, P. (1978) *Histoire du Nord*, Paris: Hachette.

Pinelli, T.E., Kennedy, J.M., Barclay, R.O. and Bishop, A.P. (1997, forthcoming) *Knowledge Diffusion in the US Aircraft Industry: Perspectives, Findings, and Strategies for Improvement*, Norwood, NJ: Ablex Press.

Piore, M. and Sabel, C. (1984) *The Second Industrial Divide: Possibilities for Prosperity*, New York: Basic Books.

Pisano, G.P. (1991) 'The governance of innovation: vertical integration and collaborative arrangements in the biotechnology industry', *Research Policy*, 20, 3, June: 237–49.

Plan (1971) (Commissariat Général du Plan) *VIè Plan de Développement Economique et Social*, Paris: Imprimerie des Journaux Officiels.

Polanyi, K. (1944) *The Great Transformation: the Political and Economic Origins of Our Time*, New York: Rinehart.

Pollert, A. (1988) 'Dismantling flexibility', *Capital and Class*, 34: 42–75.

Porter, M. (1990) *The Competitive Advantage of Nations*, London and New York: Macmillan.

Poulantzas, N. (1979) *State, Power, Socialism*, London: Verso.

Prakke, F. (1993) 'Dinosaurussen en ondernemingen', *Ingenieurskrant*, 18–19, 2, September: 5.

Prater, K. (1995) of Ballard Power Systems Inc., presentation to the Fourth Grove Fuel Cell Symposium, London, 19–22 September.

Prigogine, I. and Stengers, I. (1984) *Order out of Chaos: Man's New Dialogue with Nature*, New York: Bantam Books.

Pringle, P. and Spigelman, J. (1981) *The Nuclear Barons*, London: Sphere Books.

Radcliffe-Brown, A.R. (1952) *Structure and Function in Primitive Society*, London: Cohen and West.

Raphael, D.E. (1993) 'Global aviation alliances', paper presented at the Eighth International Workshop on Future Aviation Activities, sponsored by the Trans-

240   *Bibliography*

portation Research Board of the National Academy of Sciences, Washington, DC, 13 September.

Ravetz, J. (1979) 'DNA research as "high-intensity science" ', *Trends in Biochemical Sciences*, May: N97–8.

Realising Our Potential (1993) *Strategy for Science, Engineering and Technology*, UK government white paper, London: HMSO.

Reddy, N.M. and Zhao, L. (1990) 'International technology transfer: a review', *Research Policy*, 19, 4, August: 285–307.

Reich, R. (1991) *The Work of Nations*, London and New York: Simon and Schuster.

—— (1992) *The Work of Nations*, revised paperback edition, New York: Vintage Books.

Rheingold, H. (1994) *The Virtual Community: Homesteading on the Electronic Frontier*, New York: Harper Perennial.

Roobeek, A. (1993) *Strategisch Management van Onderop*, een action research projekt over democratisering van de strategsiche besluitvorming in de Nederlandse industrie, final report to the Industriebond FNV (Dutch Trade Union) Amsterdam, March 1993.

Rosecrance, R. (1986) *The Rise of the Trading State*, New York: Basic Books.

Rosenau, J.N. (1990) *Turbulence in World Politics*, London: Harvester-Wheatsheaf.

Rosenberg, N. (1976) *Perspectives on Technology*, Cambridge: Cambridge University Press.

—— (1982) *Inside the Black Box: Technology and Economics*, Cambridge: Cambridge University Press.

Roy, R. (1978) 'Social control of technology', in *Control of Technology*, Unit 1, Milton Keynes: Open University Press.

Royal Commission on Environmental Pollution (1992) Transport and the Environment Study, *Joint Memorandum by the Departments of the Environment and Transport*, November, London: HMSO.

—— (1994) *Eighteenth Report: Transport and the Environment*, London: HMSO.

Ruigrok, W. and Van Tulder, R. (1993) 'The ideology of interdependence: the link between restructuring, internationalisation and international trade', unpublished PhD dissertation, University of Amsterdam, 1993.

—— (1995) *The Logic of International Restructuring*, London and New York: Routledge.

Rushkoff, D. (1994) *Cyberia: Life in the Trenches of Hyperspace*, London: Flamingo.

Russell, A. (1995) 'Merging technological paradigms and the knowledge structure in international political economy', *Science and Public Policy*, 22, 2, April, 106–16.

Russell, B. (1946) *History of Western Philosophy*, London: Allen & Unwin.

Ryan, A. (1970) *The Philosophy of the Social Sciences*, London: Macmillan.

—— (ed.) (1973) *The Philosophy of Social Explanation*, Oxford: Oxford University Press.

Sabel, C. (1982) *Work and Politics: the Division of Labour in Industry*, Cambridge: Cambridge University Press.

Sabel, C. and Zeitlin, J. (1985) 'Historical alternatives to mass production: politics, markets and technology in the nineteenth century industrialisation', *Past and Present*, 108: 133–76.

SAGB (1990) (Senior Advisory Group On Biotechnology) *Economic Benefits and European Competitiveness*, Brussels: Commission of the European Communities.

Sahal, D. (ed.) (1982) *The Transfer and Utilization of Technical Knowledge*, Lexington, MA: Lexington Books.

Sampson, A. (1989) *The Midas Touch: Money, People and Power from West to East*, London: BBC Books.

Sandholtz, W. (1992) *High-Tech Europe: the Politics of International Cooperation*, Berkeley, CA: University of California Press.

Sandholtz, W., Burnes, M., Zusman, J., Conca, K., Stowsky, J., Vogel, S. and Weber, S. (eds) (1992) *The Highest Stakes: The Economic Foundations of the Next Security System*, New York: Oxford University Press.

Sapienza, A. (1989) 'R&D collaboration as a global competitive tactic: biotechnology and the ethical pharmaceutical industry', *R&D Management*, 19, 4: 285–95.

Sawyer, J.E. (1951) 'Strains in the social structure of modern France,' in E.M. Earle (ed.) *Modern France: Problems of the Third and Fourth Republics*, Princeton, NJ: Princeton University Press: 293–312.

Saxenian, A. (1994) 'Lessons from Silicon Valley', *Technology Review*, 97, 5, July: 42–51.

Schaufele, R.D. (1988) personal interview with Vice-President and General Manager of Commercial Advanced Products for Douglas Aircraft Company, 8 July.

Scholte, J.A. (1993) *International Relations of Social Change*, Buckingham: Open University Press.

Schultz, T.W. (1963) *The Economic Value of Education*, New York: Columbia University Press.

Schwartz, H. (1994) *States Versus Markets*, New York: St. Martin's Press.

Sellers, P. (1988) 'Why bigger is badder at Sears', *Fortune*, 5 December: 55–60.

Sénat (1981) (France) *Rapport au Nom de la Commission d'Enquête Parlementaire Chargée d'Examiner les Difficultés de l'Industrie du Textile et de l'Habillement*, 2è session ordinaire de 1980–1, no. 282, 6 June.

Senker, J. and Faulkner, W. (1991) 'Industrial use of public sector research in advanced technologies' (mimeo working paper) Brighton, UK: Science Policy Research Unit, University of Sussex.

——— (1992) 'Industrial use of public sector research in advanced technologies', *R&D Management*, 22, 2, April: 157–75.

Servan-Schreiber, J.-J. (1968) *The American Challenge*, New York: Atheneum.

Seyoum, B. (1993) 'Property rights versus public welfare in the protection of trade secrets in developing countries', *International Trade Journal*, VII, 3, Spring: 341–60.

Sharp, M. (1985) *The New Biotechnology*, Sussex European Paper no. 15, University of Sussex.

——— (1989a) 'Collaboration and the pharmaceutical industry: is it the way forward?', paper prepared for *Conference on Advancing Biomedical Science in the Twenty-First Century: Competition and Collaboration*, Harvard, May 1989. Also issued as DRC Discussion Paper no. 71, SPRU, University of Sussex.

——— (1989b) 'European countries in science based competition: the case of biotechnology', DRC Discussion Paper no. 72, Science Policy Research Unit, University of Sussex.

——— (1991a) 'The single market and European technology policies' in C. Freeman, M. Sharp and W. Walker (eds) *Technology and the Future of Europe: Global Competition and the Environment in the 1990s*, London: Pinter: 59–76.

——— (1991b) 'Pharmaceuticals and biotechnology' in C. Freeman, M. Sharp and W. Walker (eds) *Technology and the Future of Europe: Global Competition and the Environment in the 1990s*, London: Pinter.

——— (ed.) (1985) *Europe and the New Technologies: Six Case Studies of Adjustment and Innovation*, London: Pinter.

Sharp, M. and Pavitt, K. (1993) 'Technology policy in the 1990s: old trends and new realities', *Journal of Common Market Studies*, 31, 2, June: 129–51.

Sharp, M. and Shearman, C. (1987) *European Technological Collaboration*, Chatham House Paper 36, London: Routledge and Kegan Paul for the Royal Institute of International Affairs.

Sharp, M., Thomas, S. and Martin, P. (1993) 'Technology transfer and innovation

policy:', STEEP Discussion Paper No. 6, Science Policy Research Unit (SPRU), University of Sussex, Brighton BN1 9MP, UK
—— (1994) 'Transferts de technologie et politique de l'innovation: le cas des biotechnologies' in F. Sachwald (ed.) *Les Defis de la Mondialisation: Innovation et concurrence*, Paris: IFRI: 115–212.
Shearman, C. (1986) 'European Collaboration in computing and telecommunications: a policy approach', in K. Dyson and P. Humphreys (eds) *The Politics of the Communications Revolution in Western Europe*, London: Cass.
Shearman, C. and Burrell, G. (1987) 'The structures of industrial development', *Journal of Management Studies*, 24, 4, July: 325–45.
—— (1988) 'New technology based firms and new industries: some employment implications', *New Technology, Work and Employment*, 3, 2, Autumn: 87–99.
Siegel, J.S. and San Martin, R.L. (1993) 'The US Department of Energy's Fuel Cell Technology Program', joint statement of Jack S. Siegel, Acting Assistant Secretary for Fossil Energy, US Department of Energy, and Robert L. San Martin, Acting Assistant Secretary for Energy Efficiency and Renewable Energy, US Department of Energy, to the Subcommittee on Energy, Committee on Science, Space and Technology, US House of Representatives, 20 July 1993, in US House of Representatives Hearing, *Fuel Cells: Clean Technology for the Future*, hearing before the Subcommittee on Energy of the Committee on Science, Space and Technology of the US House of Representatives. 103rd Congress, first Session, 20 July 1993, Washington: US Government Printing Office: 3–8 and 9–28.
Skolnikoff, E. (1993) *The Elusive Transformation: Science, Technology and the Evolution of International Politics*, Princeton, NJ: Princeton University Press.
Smith, A.D. (1990) 'Towards a global culture?', in M. Featherstone (ed.) *Global Culture: Nationalism, Globalization and Modernity*, London: Sage: 171–91.
Solberg, C. (1979) *Conquest of the Skies: a History of Commercial Aviation in America*, Boston, MA: Little, Brown.
Sorokin, P.A. (1941) *Social and Cultural Dynamics, vol. 4: Basic Problems, Principles and Methods*, New York: American Book Company.
Sparen, P.O. (1991) 'PIN in checkout: a retail and bank joint project', paper presented to European Payments Conference, 19–21 November, Sheraton Hotel, Edinburgh.
Spencer, H. (1884) *The Man Versus the State*, 1981 reprint, Indianapolis, IN: Liberty Classics.
Spero, J. (1993) *The Politics of International Economic Relations*, 4th edition, London: Routledge.
Spinks, A. (1980) *Biotechnology: Report of the Joint Working Party of ACARD, the ABRC and the Royal Society*, London: HMSO.
Spoerer, S. (1982) 'L'industrie textile: ou sont les véritables concurrences?', *Faim-Développement*, no. 82–3, March: 7–10.
Stiles, K. and Akaha, T. (1991) 'Preface', in K. Stiles and T. Akaha (eds) *International Political Economy: a Reader*, New York: HarperCollins.
Stone, C., Zissu A. and Lederman J. (eds) (1993) *The Global Asset Backed Securities Market: Structuring, Managing, and Allocating Risk*, Chicago, IL and Cambridge: Probus.
Stone, P. (1989) 'Block exemption for knowhow licences', *European Trends*, 2: 58–61.
Stoneman, P. (1983) *The Economic Analysis of Technological Change*, Oxford: Oxford University Press.
Stopford, J. and Strange, S. with Henley, J.S. (1991) *Rival States, Rival Firms: Competition for World Market Shares*, Cambridge: Cambridge University Press.
Storey, D.J., Keasey, K., Watson, R. and Wynarczyk, P. (1987) *The Performance of Small Firms*, London: Croom Helm.

Storper, M. and Harrison, B. (1991) 'Flexibility, hierarchy and regional development: the changing structure of industrial production systems and their forms of governance in the 1990s', *Research Policy*, 20, 5, October: 407–22.

Storper, M. and Scott, A.J. (eds) (1992) *Pathways to Industrialisation and Regional Development*, London: Routledge.

Strange, S. (1988) *States and Markets*, London: Pinter.

—— (1990) 'Finance, information, and power', *Review of International Studies*, 16, 3, July: 259–74.

—— (1991) 'An eclectic approach', in C. Murphy and R. Tooze (eds) *The New International Political Economy*, Boulder, Co: Lynne Rienner: 33–49.

—— (1994a) *States and Markets*, 2nd edition, London: Pinter.

—— (1994b) 'Foreword' in R.P. Palan and B. Gills (eds) *Transcending the State-Global Divide: a Neostructuralist Agenda in International Relations*, London: Lynne Rienner.

—— (1994c) 'Rethinking structural change in the international political economy: states, firms and diplomacy', in R. Stubbs and G.R.D. Underhill (eds) *Political Economy and the Changing Global Order*, London: Macmillan: 103–115.

Streeck, W. (1989) 'Skills and the limits of neo-liberalism: the enterprise of the future as a place of learning', *Work, Employment and Society*, 3, March: 89–104.

Stubbs, R. and Underhill, G.R.D. (eds) (1994) *Political Economy and the Changing Global Order*, London: Macmillan.

Talalay, M. (1996) 'The coming energy revolution and the transformation of the international political economy: fuel cell technology, public policy and global power shifts', *Competition and Change*, 1, 4, October.

Talalay, M. and Farrands, C. (1993) 'Technology, change and the global political economy', paper presented to the BISA Annual Conference, University of Warwick, December.

Taneja, N.K. (1980) *US International Aviation Policy*, Lexington, MA: D.C. Heath.

—— (1994) 'Significant trends', presentation for the Transportation Research Board Annual Meeting, Washington, DC, January 10.

Teague, P. (1995) 'Europe of the regions and the future of national systems of industrial relations', in A. Amin and J. Tomaney (eds) *Behind the Myth of the European Union: Prospects for Cohesion*, London: Routledge: 149–74.

Teece, D. (1987) 'Profiting from technological innovation: implications for integration, collaboration, licensing and public policy', in D. Teece (ed.) *The Competitive Challenge*, Cambridge, MA: Ballinger.

—— (1991) 'Support policies for strategic industries: impact on home economies', in OECD, *Strategic Industries in a Global Economy: Policy Issues for the 1990s*, Paris: OECD.

Tenbruck, F.H. (1990) 'The dream of a secular ecumene: the meaning and limits of policies of development', in M. Featherstone (ed.) *Global Culture: Nationalism, Globalization and Modernity*, London: Sage: 193–206.

Texier, M. (1979) 'L'industrie Française de l'habillement', *Bulletin du Crédit National*, 2e trimestre: 41–52.

Thomas, R. (1978) *The British Philosophy of Administration*, London: Longman.

Thomas, S. (1993) *Global Perspective 2010: the case of biotechnology*, a report for the FAST Programme, Brussels: CEC.

Thomas, S. and Sharp, M. (1993) 'Biotechnology in Europe, present and future trends: implications for manpower training', in Griffin, M., Hayward, S. and Curtis, J., *Report from a Conference on Manpower and Training Needs in Europe in the 90s*, London: BEMET The Biochemical Society.

Tomaney, J., Hayward, S., Cornford, A., Pike, A. and Thomas, D. (1995) 'Survey of redundant Tyneside ship-yard workers', Report for BBC Radio 5 Live, London.

Tomlinson, J. (1991) *Cultural Imperialism*, London: Pinter.

Treitschke, H. von (1916) *Politics*, London: Constable.

Troberg, P. (1991) 'Making payments in the EC internal market', paper presented to European Payments Conference, 19–21 November, Sheraton Hotel, Edinburgh.

Tyson, L.D. (1988) 'Competitiveness: an analysis of the problem and a perspective on future policy', in M.K. Starr (ed.) *Global Competitiveness: Getting the US Back on Track*, New York: Norton: 95–120.

—— (1992) *Who's Bashing Whom? Trade Conflict in High-Technology Industries*, Washington, DC: Institute for International Economics.

UIH (1978) (Union des Industries de l'Habillement) *Livre Blanc de l'Habillement*, Paris: UIH mimeo.

UIT (1974) (Union des Industries Textiles) 'Lettre adressée par le Président de l'UIT aux personnalités du secteur public et du CNPF', Paris: UIT mimeo, 7 May.

—— (1975) *Memorandum sur l'Avenir de l'Industrie Textile Française*, Paris: UIT mimeo, October: 185–206.

—— (1982) *L'industrie Textile Française*, Paris: UIT, annual.

UN (1993) *1991 International Trade Statistics Yearbook*, New York: United Nations.

UNCTAD (1993) *Small and Medium-Sized Transnational Corporations: Role, Impact and Policy Implications*, UNCTAD Programme on Transnational Corporations, ST/CTC/160, New York: United Nations.

UNCTC (1990) *World Investment Report: the Triad in Foreign Direct Investment*, New York: United Nations.

Underhill, G.R.D. (1990) 'Industrial crisis and international regimes: France, the EEC, and international trade in textiles, 1974–84', *Millennium: Journal of International Studies*, 19, 2, Summer: 185–206.

—— (1991) 'Markets beyond politics? The state and the internationalization of financial markets', in P.G. Cerny (ed.) *The Politics of Transnational Regulation: Deregulation or Reregulation?*, special issue of the *European Journal of Political Research*, 19, 2 and 3, March-April: 197–225.

—— (1995) 'Keeping governments out of politics: transnational securities markets, regulatory co-operation, and political legitimacy', *Review of International Studies*, 21, 3, July: 251–78.

—— (1997) *Industrial Crisis and the Open Economy: Politics, Global Trade, and the Textile Industry in the Advanced Economies*, London: Macmillan.

UNEP (1993) (United Nations Environment Programme) *Environmental Data Report, 1993–4*, Oxford: Blackwell.

US Congress (1994) *The Global Positioning System: What can't it do?*, hearing before the House Committee on Science, Space, and Technology, March 24, 1994. no. 102, Washington: US Government Printing Office.

US House of Representatives Hearing (1993) *Fuel Cells: Clean Technology for the Future*, hearing before the Subcommittee on Energy of the Committee on Science, Space and Technology of the US House of Representatives. 103rd Congress, first Session, 20 July 1993, Washington, DC: US Government Printing Office.

US Senate Hearing (1993) *Environmental Aspects of Current Hydrogen and Renewable Energy Programs*, hearing before the Subcommittee on Toxic Substances, Research and Development of the Committee on Environment and Public Works of the United States Senate. 103rd Congress, first session, 22 March 1993, Washington, DC: US Government Printing Office.

Van Griethuysen, A.J. (ed.) (1987) *New Applications of Materials*, The Hague: STT.

Van Tulder, R. and Junne, G. (1987) *European Multinationals in Core Technologies*, New York: John Wiley.

Vasquez, J.A. (1983) *The Power of Power Politics*, New Brunswick, NJ: Rutgers University Press.

Vattimo, G. (1992) *The Transparent Society*, Cambridge: Polity.

Vernon, R. (1971) *Sovereignty at Bay*, New York: Basic Books.

Villeneuve, C. (1977) 'Textile: La débandade', *Le Nouvel Economiste*, no. 91, 25 July.

von Hippel, E. (1991) 'Cooperation between rivals: informal know-how trading', in B. Carlsson (ed.) *Industrial Dynamics: Technological, Organizational and Structural Changes in Industries and Firms*, Leyden: Kluwer: 157–75.

Wagner, P. (1979) 'Textile: la technique va tout changer', *L'Usine Nouvelle*, 39, 27 September: 100–8.

Walshe, A., Hayward, S. and Griffin, M. (1992) *Positive Actions: Sectoral Survey of COMETT Training Projects in the Biotechnology Sector*, survey undertaken by the BEMET UETP in framework of the COMETT Positive Actions Exercise, COMETT Technical Assistance Office, Brussels, CEC.

Walters, R.S. and Blake, D.H. (1992) *The Politics of Global Economic Relations*, Englewood Cliffs, New Jersey: Prentice Hall.

Waltz, K.N. (1979) *Theory of International Politics*, Reading, MA: Addison-Wesley.

Warnock, M. (1985) *The Warnock Report: Report of the Committee of Inquiry into Human Fertilisation and Embryology*, Oxford: Blackwell.

Webb, M.C. (1991) 'International economic structures, government interests, and international coordination of macroeconomic adjustment policies', *International Organization*, 45, 3, Summer: 309–42.

White Jr., L. (1962) *Medieval Technology and Social Change*, Oxford: Oxford University Press.

Whittock, M.J. (1986) *The Origins of England*, London: Croom Helm.

WHO (1992) World Health Organization / United Nations Environment Programme, *Urban Air Pollution in Megacities of the World*, Oxford: Blackwell.

Williams, M. (1994) *International Economic Organisations and the Third World*, London: Harvester-Wheatsheaf.

Williams, R. (1990 [1958]) *Culture and Society*, London: Hogarth Press.

Williams, R.H. (1993) Princeton University School of Engineering, Center for Energy and Environmental Studies, testimony and written statement to US Senate Hearing, *Environmental Aspects of Current Hydrogen and Renewable Energy Programs*, hearing before the Subcommittee on Toxic Substances, Research and Development of the Committee on Environment and Public Works of the United States Senate. 103rd Congress, first session, 22 March 1993, Washington, DC: US Government Printing Office: 18–35 and 66–89.

—— (1994) 'The clean machine', *Technology Review*, 97, 3, April: 20–30.

Williamson, O.E. (1975) *Markets and Hierarchies: Analysis and Anti-Trust Implications*, New York: Free Press.

Winter, W., Byshyn, W. and Clark, H. (1969) *Airplanes of the World, 1490–1969*, New York: Simon and Schuster.

Witteveen, A. (ed.) (1994) *Top Twintig Trends in Strategisch Management*, Amsterdam and Brussels: Management Press.

Wood, S. (ed.) (1989) *The Transformation of Work*, London: Unwin Hyman.

Woodman R.C. (1991) 'A retailer's view', paper presented to European Payments Conference, 19–21 November, Sheraton Hotel, Edinburgh.

Womack, J.P., Jones, D.T. and Roos, D. (1990) *The Machine that Changed the World*, New York: Macmillan.

Wurster, R. (1993) Diplom Ingenieur, Ludwig-Bölkow-Systemtechnik Gmbh, Munich, Germany, testimony and written statement to US Senate Hearing, *Environmental Aspects of Current Hydrogen and Renewable Energy Programs*, hearing before the Subcommittee on Toxic Substances, Research and Development of the Committee on Environment and Public Works of the United States Senate. 103rd Congress, first session, 22 March 1993, Washington: US Government Printing Office: 23–6 and 103–37.

Wynarczyk, P., Watson, R., Storey, D.J., Short, H. and Keasey, K. (1993) *Managerial Labour Markets in the Small Firm Sector*, London: Routledge.

Youngs, G. (1996) 'Dangers of discourse: the case of globalization', in E. Kofman and G. Youngs (eds) *Globalisation: Theory and Practice*, London: Pinter: 58–71.

Zysman, J. (1977) *Political Strategies for Industrial Order: State, Market and Industry in France*, Berkeley, CA: University of California Press.

Index

256 *Index*